FOCUS
Institutions and Markets

WRITING TEAM

Don R. Leet

Sandra J. Odorzynski

Mary Suiter

Phillip J. VanFossen

Michael Watts, Chair

WITH AN INTRODUCTORY ESSAY BY

George Horwich

NCEE

National Council on Economic Education

AUTHORS

George Horwich
Professor Emeritus of Economics
Purdue University

Don R. Leet
Professor of Economics
Director, Center for Economic Education
California State University, Fresno

Sandra J. Odorzynski
Professor of Economics
Director, Center for Economic Education
St. Norbert College

Mary Suiter
Associate Director, Center for Entrepreneurship
  and Economic Education
University of Missouri-St. Louis

Phillip J. VanFossen
Associate Professor of Social Studies Education
Director, James F. Ackerman Center for Democratic Citizenship,
Associate Director, Center for Economic Education
Purdue University

Michael Watts
Professor of Economics
Director, Center for Economic Education
Purdue University

FUNDING

The National Council on Economic Education gratefully acknowledges the funding of this publication by the U.S. Department of Education, Office of Safe and Drug-Free Schools under PR Grant # R304A020010. Any opinions, findings, conclusions, or recommendations expressed in the publication are those of the authors and do not necessarily reflect the view of the U.S. Department of Education.

ISBN 1-56183-616-8

CONTENTS

FOREWORD

Focus: Institutions and Markets is the latest volume in a series of National Council on Economic Education (NCEE) publications dedicated to increasing the economic literacy of all students. The *Focus* publications, a centerpiece of NCEE's comprehensive **Economics**America program, build on over five decades of success in delivering effective economic education to America's students.

The *Focus* series is innovative, using economics to enhance learning in subjects such as history, geography, civics, and personal finance, as well as economics. Activities are interactive, reflecting the belief that students learn best through active, highly personalized experiences with economics. Applications of economic understanding to real-world situations and contexts dominate the lessons. In addition, the lessons are explicitly correlated with NCEE's *Voluntary National Content Standards in Economics* and *A Framework for Teaching Basic Economic Concepts*.

Over the past decade the importance of institutions in the development or gradual evolution of markets and market economies was once again made clear by the experience of the transition economies in eastern and central Europe and the former Soviet Union. It soon became clear that many of the problems facing these countries had surfaced before – in developing nations where educational and technological resources are far less advanced than in the transition economies and even in the U.S. and other Western market economies during extended periods in their history. Clearly, then, the economic and broader social effects of institutions are important to understand no matter where or when someone is living. This volume is designed for use by teachers in a wide range of secondary social studies classes. As in all NCEE volumes, there is a premium on active and cooperative learning, the occasional use of direct instruction where that is most appropriate, and extensive use of current data from the U.S. and other countries.

The development of this publication was undertaken as part of the Cooperative Civic Education and Economic Education Exchange Program (CCEEEEP) funded by the U.S. Department of Education, Office of Safe and Drug-Free Schools (PR Grant # R304A020010), in coordination with the U.S. Department of State. NCEE extends its deep appreciation to Dr. Ram Singh (Institute of Education Sciences) and Ms. Rita Foy Moss (Office of Safe and Drug-Free Schools) for their support as CCEEEEP Program Officers. We are grateful that the U.S. Congress had the foresight to recognize the need for economic education in emerging market economies and the vision to see how an international exchange program such as this could benefit U.S. teachers and students.

NCEE thanks the authors, Michael Watts, Professor of Economics and Director of the Center for Economic Education at Purdue University, who took the lead on this project; Don R. Leet, Director of the Center for Economic Education at California State University, Fresno, Sandra J. Odorzynski, Director of the Center for Economic Education at St. Norbert College; Mary Suiter, Associate Director of the Center for Entrepreneurship and Economic Education at the University of Missouri, St. Louis; and Phillip J. VanFossen, Associate Director of the Center for Economic Education at Purdue University. NCEE also thanks George Horwich, Professor Emeritus of Economics at Purdue University, for his enlightening introductory essay on markets and institutions.

Robert F. Duvall, Ph.D.
President and CEO
National Council on Economic Education

ACKNOWLEDGMENTS

The members of the writing team are grateful for the support from Patty Elder, Barbara DeVita, and other staff members at the National Council on Economic Education (NCEE), who conceived of and commissioned this publication and then supported its development in many other ways.

Generous financial support to the NCEE from the U.S. Department of Education, Office of Safe and Drug-Free Schools, for this publication and a wide range of activities involving economic educators from the United States and over 20 transition economies, is also greatly appreciated.

George Horwich's introductory essay was immensely helpful as we wrote and edited the lessons. We believe it will also be a valuable resource for secondary teachers, and many of the classroom teacher reviewers/field-testers independently said that it was a great help to them.

Our special thanks to Suzanne Becker for her typically careful, helpful, and thoughtful copy editing, and to April Fidler for her work in preparing camera-ready copy for publication and handling uncounted administrative issues and tasks on the project, large and small.

Finally, the publication was substantially improved by the following classroom teachers who field-tested selected lessons in their classes:

Joe Barron, Fresno High School,
    Fresno, CA
Keith Coleman, East De Pere High School,
    De Pere, WI
Joe Fleischman, Whitefish Bay High School,
    Whitefish Bay, WI
Eva Johnston, Marquette High School,
    Chesterfield, MO
Joy Joyce, Willowbrook High School,
    Villa Park, IL
Leslie Labrucherie, Madera High School,
    Madera, CA

Kris Oliveira, Clovis West High School,
    Fresno, CA
Bob Schultz, Freedom High School,
    Freedom, WI
Carla Vinoski, Washington Middle School,
    Green Bay, WI
Raymond Walker, Grosse Ile High School,
    Grosse Ile, MI

PREFACE

This volume of lessons for secondary social studies (particularly economics, civics, government, and history) and business education courses was inspired by the World Bank *2002 World Development Report: Building Institutions for Markets*. This is the second time the National Council on Economic Education (NCEE) has developed a set of lessons building on the content of the annual *World Development Reports* – the earlier work was based on the 1996 World Bank *World Development Report: From Plan to Market*. The roles of markets, government, and other institutions in market economies are also explored in some of the lessons designed for use in secondary classes included in the NCEE's *Focus: Economic Systems* (2001) and *Focus: High School Economics* (2nd ed., 2002). But this is the first NCEE publication in which each lesson addresses the role of institutions and their effects in a market economy.

We confess that the writing team and George Horwich, who wrote the introductory essay for the volume, approached the project enthusiastically but with some trepidation, in part because until recent decades institutional economics had a controversial and somewhat checkered history in the discipline. Also because, while the importance of institutions is now widely accepted and frequently incorporated into mainstream economic models, empirical investigations, and experiments, it is a challenging and difficult task to reflect those approaches in lessons for secondary students who might not even be taking a course in economics. Even after a planning meeting at which the basic topics for lessons were selected from an incredibly wide range of possible topics, it was not clear how the lessons were going to be structured to reflect the institutional theme of the volume.

What finally emerged were lessons that typically include a few key theoretical propositions (usually indicated in the standard(s) and benchmarks listed near the beginning of each lesson), extended discussion and information about one or more key institutions, and often data dealing with either the issues facing those institutions or the policies used by the institutions to address those issues. In consequence, and somewhat unexpectedly, we found that most of the lessons in this volume ran somewhat longer than the typical lessons in other volumes of secondary lessons published by the NCEE. Many of the lessons will require a minimum of two or three standard class periods to teach – that's the bad news. The good news is that the ideas covered in the lessons are almost never "new additions" to the standard curriculum. In other words, the lessons do not ask teachers to change *what* they teach, but they do offer some new approaches in terms of *how* to teach the topics, meaning not only somewhat more attention to institutions but also new activities and data to use.

We received more and unexpected good news, after all of the lessons had been submitted and most of them revised at least once, with the publication of the December 2, 2002 *IMF Survey*. In an article on the key role of institutions, and how the International Monetary Fund is increasingly "getting involved" in institutional issues, we were very pleased to see the table that is reprinted on the next page. The institutions listed there, and the evaluation of "How sure are economists that they have the right answer?" to a wide range of institutional issues, matches very well to the institutions that are covered in the lessons of this volume, and generally with how those institutions are presented. That is just one more indication of how important these topics are now recognized to be, and the increasing professional consensus on policies involving some – but certainly not all – of these institutions. We do not stress the relationship between these institutions and balance of payment issues, which of course is the key concern of the IMF. Nevertheless, the list and institutional evaluations of issues were very reassuring even coming *ex post*.

Undoubtedly, we would have featured the following table more often and with more prominence in this volume if it had been available to us earlier.

Finally, because most of these institutions are tangible parts of the world that students can see or hear about in the media, and because students already have some experience with some of the institutions, a focus on institutions helps to ground the abstract theoretical ideas that are essential to developing a general understanding of economic forces in any society. That has always been the strength of institutional economics – the difficult part is to present that while keeping sight of the conceptual ideas and framework used in economics. We hope we have been successful in developing lessons that will help secondary teachers accomplish that, and that future volumes published by the NCEE, the World Bank, and others, whether for teachers, economists, policymakers, or other audiences, are even more successful in doing so.

A Table and Evaluations of Institutional Issues from the International Monetary Fund (IMF)

How relevant is the issue to balance of payments problems?	How sure are economists that they have the right answer?			
	Not very	Somewhat	Fairly	Very
Not very	religion	capital punishment; drug policy	democratic elections; labor rights	human rights; environment
Somewhat	social capital	intellectual property rights rules; executive compensation	legal systems; competition policy; land tenure	poverty; education; military spending
Fairly	closing banks; disposing of nonperforming loans; best accounting rules; bankruptcy procedures	corporate governance; financial systems (capital adequacy; or relationship banking versus securities markets)	property rights; trade policy	corruption; fiscal transparency
Very	restoring confidence in a crisis	exchange rate regime; capital control; private sector involvement	budget deficits	monetary policy

Source: *IMF Survey 31* (22), December 2, 2002, p. 373.

INTRODUCTORY ESSAY
INSTITUTIONS FOR BUILDING A MARKET ECONOMY

George Horwich
Purdue University

CONTENTS

Over the past few decades, one centrally planned economy after another has sought to transform itself into a more or less free-market system. The People's Republic of China began to liberalize its economy in the late 1970s. Then, in 1991, the collapse of the Soviet Union brought the transition to market economies to Russia and eastern and central Europe. The paths taken by these economies have not been smooth; indeed, for some they have been perilously unstable, resulting in lower standards of living than prevailed under planning. Others, however, have been far more successful in moving to a market system, achieving higher levels of income and economic growth. This essay provides an overview of why some of these countries have been more successful than others, and identifies the institutions, practices, and incentives necessary for market-based economic development.

INSTITUTIONS AND MARKETS DEFINED

The word institution refers broadly to any formal or informal set of rules, beliefs, or behaviors that play a role in carrying out organized activity. Markets, which are mechanisms for coordinating and carrying out the production, distribution, and consumption of goods and services using scarce resources, are themselves institutions. There are additional institutional requirements, however, involving both the private and government sectors, which help to establish a market economy and make it work more efficiently and humanely. These will be discussed below; but first I describe more fully what a market is and how a market system determines what, how, and for whom goods and services are produced.

Markets

Most resources in a market economy are privately owned, most production is organized and carried out voluntarily by private individuals, and most output is directed by choices made by individual consumers. The market process typically is one of monetary exchanges for goods and services at prices determined jointly by buyers and sellers. More precisely, we can think of a market as the interaction of demand and supply. Perhaps the most basic and powerful idea in economics is that consumers (demanders) are willing to buy increasing quantities of a good as the price of the good decreases. Producers (suppliers) will supply more of a good only at higher prices because the cost of each additional unit generally rises with increasing output, especially when producers are working with one or more fixed inputs, such as land, buildings, or machinery.

On a basic supply and demand graph (see Figure 1) this relationship between the price and quantity of a good or service that is demanded or supplied is shown with the demand curve (D) downward sloping and the supply curve (S) upward sloping. That means there will be an intersection of demand and supply at an equilibrium price. Only at that price will the quantity supplied just equal the quantity demanded. At any other price, if there are no

laws or regulations preventing price from rising or falling, the difference between quantities demanded and supplied – also called shortages or surpluses – tends to drive the price and quantity to the equilibrium level.

In a functioning market economy, markets emerge spontaneously and evolve over time. Those who decide to become producers will discover, through trial and error, what products consumers want most and are willing to pay for. Spurred by competition and the profit motive, producers will also seek the least-cost ways of producing those products. Over time, new technologies lower costs of production, expand markets geographically, and stimulate the creation of new products.

All of these changes affect demand and supply, causing prices of goods to rise or fall automatically, which in turn cause consumers and producers, wherever they may be, to respond to the new mix of prices. For example, increased demand for a product – a rightward shift of the demand curve – will raise the market price above cost, creating a temporarily higher level of profits. In response, producers increase their demand for productive resources or inputs, and use them to increase the quantity of the product supplied. This supply increment, a movement along the supply curve, moderates the price rise. The amount of the good produced and sold will continue to increase until, in a competitive market, profit rates have fallen to their previous level.

Markets and Efficiency

In a sense, most economic activity other than that of a solitary Robinson Crusoe or a rigidly controlled military operation involves some role for markets. Even in planned economies in which the government owns and allocates all productive resources, detailed plans for production methods and employment levels are prepared for only a limited number of "basic" goods. The vast majority of enterprises under central planning try to meet state production quotas by trading with each other for resources and materials; but they must do this

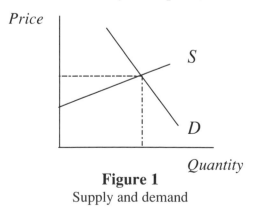

Figure 1
Supply and demand

without the guidance and information provided by meaningful prices.

In a command economy prices are set administratively and do not reflect relative scarcities of products or resources.[1] Such prices offer no guidance on where or how to use resources to satisfy consumer preferences, or on how to take account of relative resource scarcities to minimize costs of production. In the former Soviet Union any monetary payments between firms that were not authorized by the planning authority were regarded as illegal bribes, so most trading between firms was nonmonetary or barter – the exchange of goods for goods or services, including personal favors. In this crude approximation to a market, finding and trading goods and resources was costly and time consuming – in a word, inefficient – for both buyers and sellers.

Product markets maximize economic efficiency – including output per unit of input – when firms can freely enter markets that offer the highest return (adjusted for risk) and leave markets that do not. In that setting, markets are open and competitive – there are no artificial barriers or inducements to enter or remain in the market, and firms that cannot match the efficiency of their rivals are free to fail and go out of business.

Markets for the resources used to produce goods and services are similarly efficient in the absence of artificial barriers and inducements. Workers are free to invest in themselves by acquiring additional education and skills, and to accept or reject available employment in any location, limited only by legal and voluntary contractual obligations. Capital resources – factories, buildings, machines, and inventories – will also move into their most profitable uses as long as the costs of transferring them from one owner or one use to another are not prohibitive.

As markets spontaneously form and begin to operate automatically, institutional features and practices are developed that further enhance their performance. Mergers, spinoffs, buyouts, and hostile takeovers of firms are market-based attempts to increase the efficiency and profitability of businesses. Marketing devices, such as advertising, improve the flow of information to consumers and, in competitive markets, encourage producers to price their products at or near the costs of production (which include a level of profit just high enough to compensate producers for the risks they face). The use of brand names creates an immediate institutional way to identify product quality. The freedom to return goods purchased at many retail establishments protects consumers against poor choices and faulty merchandise. Better business bureaus and industry producer associations establish and enforce standards of conduct and product quality among their members.

The Role of Government: Public Goods

Markets also require a less spontaneous infrastructure that generally only government can supply. That includes a legal system – legislatures to pass laws; agencies, including the courts, to implement and enforce the laws; police and prisons to monitor and punish violators; regulations aimed at keeping markets open and competitive; and policies to stabilize the overall (macro) economy. The government must also ensure the production of goods that markets do not supply, or do not supply in adequate amounts, as determined ultimately through the political process. These are so-called public goods, which have the characteristic that they are consumed jointly, and one person's consumption does not reduce the quantity of the good available to anyone else.

Examples of pure public goods are national defense and a reduction in environmental pollution. Once national security or, say, acceptably clean air is supplied, all those in the region benefit from them and there is no way to limit their consumption to those who have paid for them. Although the private sector can produce public goods, adequate market demand fails to materialize because it is in each prospective buyer's interest to wait for someone else to purchase them. Government's role is thus to produce, or to direct tax revenues or user fees to the private-sector production of, the appropriate level of public goods that all may consume.

A *partial* public good is a good or service which, even though supplied and purchased by private individuals, offers benefits (positive "externalities") to some, but not necessarily all, nonpurchasers. An example would be landscaping for a private home, which creates aesthetic enjoyment and higher property values not only for the homeowner, but for an entire neighborhood. Social programs, such as income transfers, food stamps, or health care for the needy can also be thought of as partial public goods because they benefit not only the program's recipients, but all citizens who believe that the programs will reduce crime rates and contribute to a just and more humane society.

To maintain economic efficiency, it is important that government initiatives and policies be compatible with private markets and their supporting institutions. That means that the natural tendency of markets to employ new technology and respond to changing consumer tastes should not be inhibited, and due account should be taken of the often unavoidable tendency of government itself to perform inefficiently. This can be difficult to accomplish, because special interest groups and sometimes even widespread political pressures can lead to the adoption of programs that reduce economic efficiency and welfare. Government-imposed price ceilings, for example, whether on product prices, interest rates, or housing rents, are almost always counterproductive. They effectively prevent supply and demand forces from operating, causing the market to take on pathologies usually seen in command economies, including pervasive supply shortages and searching, begging, bribing, and queuing by demanders who have no way to express their desires through market price signals.

ENABLING INSTITUTIONS

In the remainder of this essay I will discuss the key institutions and practices necessary for an effective market economy, including the role of government. The most important institutions are: (1) a system for defining and enforcing property rights; (2) socially efficient forms of business enterprises; (3) arrangements for ensuring competition and the smooth functioning of product, labor, and capital markets; (4) a system for supplying public goods, both through government programs and nonprofit organizations, in such areas as infrastructure (including physical capital and provisions for public health and safety), education, and a social safety net for low income families; and (5) a monetary and financial system, including fiscal and monetary policies for macroeconomic stabilization and mechanisms to promote international trade and economic development.

Property Rights and the Rule of Law

The first essential institution of a market economy is a rule of law and, in particular, a system of defining, recording, and enforcing private property rights. That allows property owners, including owners of productive resources, to use their assets and the income from them freely (subject to the legal norms and values of the community) and to sell or transfer property to others. Without strong, legally established private property rights, the market exchange of goods and services will be sharply curtailed. Businesses will be reluctant to invest in new capital or employ existing capital, especially in long-term, high-risk ventures. Private economic transactions – buying and selling goods and resource services, and the flow of saving into investment – will tend to be locally based among people who know or are related to each other. Specialization, the division of labor, and total output and income will be severely limited as people try to be economically self-sufficient and risk trading with others as little as possible.

Inadequate property rights may result from the government's failure to issue licenses to businesses and to provide other protections of commercial law. In fact, many developing countries impose long bureaucratic delays on enterprises seeking licenses to do business. Peru has been among the most notorious, with the result that it now has an unlicensed or "informal" economy that is much larger than its formal (licensed) economy.[2]

The developed world, especially western Europe and Japan, is not completely free of these bureaucratic tendencies. But advanced market economies are more likely to restrict the freedom of a firm to reduce its labor force and exit an industry to avoid losses or pursue more profitable opportunities elsewhere. In some cases governments choose to keep firms in their current markets by providing cash subsidies or loans at below-market rates of interest. Generally, artificial limitations on entry into, and exit from, particular markets prevent capital from being employed in its most productive uses and earning a higher rate of return. The long-term result is less investment and lower levels of national output and growth.

Special Problems of the Transition Economies

Problems resulting from the past and present government ownership of productive resources still plague China and the former communist states of eastern and central Europe. Under central planning these nations built huge factory complexes without reference to market-determined prices. As a result, the transition to market economies in these nations began with a capital stock designed to produce goods that people often did not want, using production methods that ignored the prices of resources – land, labor, and capital.

Each of these national economies has since sought to overcome its inefficiencies in different ways. China gradually freed most prices and opened its economy to private investment. It retains the myth that all resources are owned by the state, but grants investors an absolute claim to the *income* generated by investments, whether funded privately, publicly, or some mixture of the two. Investors are free to use or sell the claim as they wish. Some state-owned enterprises (SOEs) remain, but as the economy has grown they have shrunk from producing most of the nation's industrial output to less

than one-fourth. China has even tried to introduce capitalist-style managerial principles to these enterprises, such as tying managers' compensation to various measures of performance, but has met with scant success in making them profitable.

China's overall success springs from its gradualist approach in moving to a market economy, with an emphasis on creating as few "losers" in the transition process as possible.[3] Agriculture, the nation's largest employment sector, was reformed first, and in stages. Initially the state-owned farms ("communes") permitted individual farmers to cultivate small parcels of land belonging to the commune. After meeting government output quotas and selling that output at fixed prices, farmers on these plots were free to produce as much of anything they wished at whatever prices the market would bring. Consumers were thus able to maintain their pre-reform level of food consumption at fixed prices, while paying more only for additional output and products that became more affordable as the economy grew and productivity and wages increased. Over time the price ceilings and production quotas were gradually removed from most crops. Eventually the communes renewed leases to individual plots for long-term periods, effectively privatizing ownership of the land.

At the same time, township and village enterprises (TVEs) producing manufactured goods were built up in largely rural areas. These enterprises created jobs for the huge numbers of surplus farm workers – as many as 100 million – who were no longer needed on the increasingly efficient and privately run farms. Private investors, both separately and jointly with local governments, financed and now own the TVEs. That meant the government gained from profitable enterprises, which encouraged it to keep taxes on them at a minimum and provide public infrastructure – roads, security, sanitation, schools, etc. – that would make these firms more profitable and competitive.

Urban industries, meanwhile, were "marketized" by allowing foreigners, alone or jointly with Chinese nationals, to invest in enterprises in designated coastal cities, such as Shanghai. These investors were free to hire and fire workers as they wished and to sell output under the same two-tier level of prices permitted in the agricultural sector. Over time the industrial price ceilings and mandatory product allocations were removed, the "free" industrial zones were extended to most of the country, and the freedom to invest in these firms was extended to everyone in China.

The European transition economies took a less gradualist approach to market reforms by freeing prices and privatizing most productive assets almost immediately. That worked well in some nations, such as Poland; but in Russia the former communist managers of the SOEs acquired most of the ownership shares, leaving a small portion for the workers and the general public.[4] Effectively, the managers retained control of the same enterprises they had managed as central planners, without acquiring market-oriented skills in such areas as pricing, marketing, and managerial accounting. The transfer from public to private ownership in Russia also occurred before a viable legal system that could protect private property rights was in place. Instead of the orderly world of efficient resource allocation envisioned by the competitive model, a Mafia-dominated system of property "protection" arose. Unsure of the long-term value of their claims in such an uncertain environment, owners tended to depreciate their assets physically even more rapidly than the economic obsolescence of the capital stock (due to the collapse of the command economy) might have justified. The lack of law enforcement meant that government itself was unable to enforce tax collection and almost went bankrupt in 1998.

A relative handful of individuals became astronomically rich by receiving monopoly franchises for state-controlled media operations and electronic services, or for Russia's considerable oil and mineral wealth. The misuse of productive assets in Russia in the 1990s was in many ways a continuation of the response to the breakdown of government authority in the last several decades of the Soviet era. Throughout that earlier period, private individuals increasingly appropriated (and physically abused) collectively owned assets for their own illegal use.

The Russian economy and political environment finally began to stabilize in 1999, and significant growth has occurred since then. Many of the other former Soviet republics have done less well, but the countries of Poland, Hungary, East Germany, and the Czech and Slovak Republics, which were controlled by the Soviet Union for a considerably shorter period of time, have done much better. All of these nations had some history of democratic government with an established rule of law under market economies, and thus have been politically more stable in the post-Soviet era. None of these nations was ever as totally centrally planned as the former Soviet Union, and in some cases their market liberalization had begun even before 1991. Privatization in these countries was carried out on a broader popular scale than in Russia, often with more sales to, and investment by, companies and individuals from other nations.

BUSINESS ENTERPRISES

Business enterprises other than sole proprietorships are created when a number of individuals believe they can produce a product at a lower cost by forming a single economic entity. The optimal size of a competitive firm is the output level at which costs per unit of output are lowest. Technology and market conditions determine the degree to which various stages of production are integrated within the firm. Thus, an automobile manufacturer will produce its own steel and sell the finished car directly to consumers if the resulting costs are less than buying steel from outside producers and selling cars through independent dealers. In centrally planned economies, there tended to be a very few highly integrated firms of enormous size in each industry, because the lack of efficient markets for inputs and marketing networks made it necessary for firms to consolidate as many functions under one roof as possible. Central planners also found it easier to deal with a few huge firms than with dozens or hundreds of smaller, decentralized firms. For all these reasons, firms and individual plants in the former Soviet Union and communist China were typically many times larger than their capitalist counterparts, with firms often employing hundreds of thousands of workers.

The Varieties of Business Enterprise

A key institution in market economies is the limited-liability company or corporation. Ownership in corporations consists of shares of stock which, under corporate law, represent the maximum loss that a shareholder can experience if the company fails. Other personal assets of shareholders, such as homes, automobiles, and pensions, are not at risk. This makes corporations exceedingly popular enterprises for undertaking large-scale investments that have a potentially huge but uncertain payoff. With access to masses of investors, corporations have spearheaded the growth of most of the developed world's major industries, including automobile, aircraft, and electronic-products manufacturing; rail and airline travel; oil exploration, drilling, and refining; retailing; banking; computers; and telecommunications and information transmission technology.

Enterprises for the services provided by lawyers, doctors, accountants, consultants, other kinds of professionals, and small retailers have typically been sole proprietorships or partnerships. Limited liability tends to be less important to such firms because most of their wealth lies in the owners' human capital; and they use (or own) *relatively* little plant and equipment and thus do not have to raise vast sums of money to finance them. Un-incorporated businesses are generally subject to lower taxes and fewer regulations, which increases their appeal to entrepreneurs who want maximum control over operations and more freedom to enter and leave markets.

Business Failure

One of America's most enduring economic strengths is its willingness to allow unprofitable businesses to fail. This is part of the capitalist process that Joseph Schumpeter called "creative destruction," a force for constant renewal, efficiency, and competitiveness.[5] Any change in consumer preferences, resource availability, and technology immediately affects producers, sparing only the hardiest and most adaptable firms. This is especially important in the United States, where at least a third of long-term economic growth is caused by technological innovation and people change jobs and move far more frequently than people in any other industrialized economy.[6]

The U.S. government does occasionally grant loans at below-market interest rates to highly visible failing corporations, such as Lockheed Aircraft and Chrysler, or to numerous small businesses through the Small Business Administration. These "bailouts" are extremely controversial because if companies are truly competitive they can usually secure funding from the private capital market, and if they aren't competitive the bailout isn't likely to work. That means the companies funded by government either may not need it or they eventually collapse despite government support (for example, the Penn Central Railroad in 1970). Or troubled companies may eventually merge with more viable ones (for example, Chrysler's merger with the German company Daimler in 1996). In Chrysler's case, the government loan allowed the company to postpone extensive reforms – plant closings and spin-offs – that private lenders felt should not have been delayed.

One alternative to public bailouts is bankruptcy, which is actually a longstanding American tradition. U.S. bankruptcy law is not as harsh as in other countries, allowing insolvent firms various options to restructure and continue to do business while looking for ways to become profitable again. But as long as they operate, bankrupt firms remain accountable to their creditors and the courts.

Buyouts are another method of corporate reform, in which outside investors buy up enough outstanding shares of stock to gain control of a company whenever they believe they can manage or restructure those assets more efficiently. Unlike buyouts, which are frequently hostile takeovers, mergers are voluntary agreements between companies that attempt to achieve economies of scale or other cost saving as technology and markets change. Mergers can be horizontal, between competitors selling the same product; or vertical, between a firm and its suppliers of raw materials or semi-finished products; or can entail the creation of a conglomerate, where firms produce products that are essentially unrelated but at a lower cost in a single firm that combines various management or financing functions. Reverse mergers also occur when firms spin off subsidiaries that are no longer profitable, or which can become more profitable operating independently or as part of another firm.

MAINTAINING COMPETITION

Antitrust and the Sherman Act

To promote economic efficiency and protect consumers, governments help to maintain open and competitive markets. The U.S. government has been more active in this regard than governments in any other developed nation, beginning with the passage of the Sherman Antitrust Act in 1890. This act makes it illegal for firms to engage in any collusion in restraint of trade or commerce, including price-fixing, setting production quotas, or individually or collusively blocking the entry or operation of other firms. Later antitrust legislation outlawed discriminatory pricing, in which firms with monopoly power charge different classes of consumers different prices for the same product, even though there are no differences in the costs of supplying the product to the different groups.

In practice, enforcement of U.S. antitrust legislation rests with the Department of Justice and the courts, where it has proven to be a complex and controversial undertaking. Defining the relevant product market and identifying anti-competitive behavior requires a thorough command of both economics and statistics. For antitrust policy, the relevant product market is one for which there are no close substitutes. That sometimes means that perceived dominance by a firm may simply be

an artifact of an overly narrow definition of the industry or market. For example, the production of "high-gloss vinyl floor covering " might appear to be monopolized because only one or two firms manufacture it. But the true market in which this product competes includes all varieties of floor covering, which are made and sold by many producers and which most consumers treat as close substitutes. The existence of so many close substitutes means that no manufacturer of any one variety of floor covering can charge a price very much above that of any similar quality of floor covering without losing most of its customers. In short, the market for the many different types of floor covering, including the one or two producers of high-gloss vinyl covering, is effectively competitive.

Even after the relevant market is correctly identified, dominance by just one or two firms in a market is not necessarily the result of illegal restraint of trade. Market dominance may also be the outcome of highly innovative product development and cost and price-cutting behavior by the leading firm or firms. Judges and the Antitrust Division of the Department of Justice have not always recognized this. One example of dubious antitrust enforcement occurred shortly after World War II when the Great Atlantic and Pacific (A&P) grocery chain was prosecuted and fined by Justice for driving small independent grocers out of business.[7] In a literal sense, A&P did drive many competitors out of business, but not for any behavior that should have been regarded as anti-social or illegal. A&P and other national grocery chains were responding to the rapid increase in automobile ownership and the dispersal of populations to suburban areas. That allowed grocery stores to offer parking space for consumers and achieve operating efficiencies and lower costs (and prices) in much larger stores. The 19th and early 20th century pattern of urban consumers living within walking distance of their jobs and most of the retail outlets that served them was rapidly disappearing. Nevertheless, as late as 1966 the Von's grocery chain in Los Angeles was prohibited from merging with Shopping Bag Food Stores on the grounds that it would accelerate the decline of "mom and pop" grocery stores.[8]

In the mainframe computer industry, International Business Machines (IBM) for many years had a history of producing a superior product at constantly falling prices, but was prosecuted because of its huge market share (60 to 80 percent) and various practices that seemed designed to maintain that share artificially. IBM successfully resisted the Department of Justice attempts to break it up, but as usually happens to such super competitors, the industry matured and rival firms eventually were able to challenge IBM on its own terms – producing equally or even more innovative products. Today IBM is still a viable competitor, but with an altered and more diverse product line and a much smaller market share in each of its markets.[9]

More recently, the government's antitrust suit against Microsoft originally sought to break up one of the industry's most innovative firms because of its dominance of the Internet market, achieved primarily by tying its Internet explorer software to its popular operating and office-applications software, and selling that software at constantly declining prices. The court ruled that Microsoft was guilty of several illegal practices against competitors, but in the view of many economists these neither accounted for Microsoft's overall success nor justified the breakup of the firm. In fact, the initial decision to break up the firm, made under the Clinton administration, was later reversed by the Bush administration.

Despite these and other pitfalls in enforcement, historically the Antitrust Division has acted effectively to end collusive price-fixing, as in its successful case against General Electric and other electrical equipment suppliers in the 1960s. In general, the mere existence of the Division serves as an important deterrent to monopoly behavior, whether it is price fixing or attempts by groups of firms to form cartels that fix both prices and production levels.

In the early 1970s the Division liberalized the criteria identifying anti-competitive behavior. Under these guidelines large market shares, independent of other considerations, were no longer considered sufficient to establish that firms had monopoly power. Evidence of competition was extended to include not only firms already in an industry, but also "potential" entrants – firms poised to enter the industry if profit levels or other conditions justified it. And enforcers were to look at markets and competition globally, whether that took place within or across national boundaries.

Natural Monopoly

Natural monopoly occurs when a single company serving a market experiences declining average costs of production over the entire range of potential market demand. That means the least-cost way of producing that product is to have just one firm – a natural monopoly – produce it. For example, it would be prohibitively expensive to have, say, two electric power companies serving a city with two sets of power lines running to every home and building, each utilized at half capacity. That could only result in higher average costs, and higher prices to cover those costs. On the other hand, allowing one private company to operate and supply the market at lower average costs does not guarantee that electric consumers would enjoy a correspondingly lower price. A single supplier, by definition, is a monopolist. Despite having lower costs, an unregulated monopolist would tend to produce less electricity in order to drive prices above the competitive level.

A similar tendency to natural monopoly occurs in other public utilities, such as local telephone service, natural gas distribution, municipal water supply, and sanitation systems, where it does not pay to have multiple sets of telephone wires or networks of pipes for gas, water, or sewerage. One solution to this problem is to have government itself operate the utility. But for reasons discussed below, government agencies tend not to be as innovative and efficient as competitive enterprises. As a result, although water and sanitation systems seem to operate adequately as government-owned monopolies, the preferred solution for electric power, telephone, and gas distribution is usually to allow a single company to supply the market, but regulate it so that it produces at or near the competitive price and output.

In practice, however, regulation has proved to be a very difficult undertaking. In addition to the formidable statistical task facing regulators in determining the competitive price and output, utilities have tended to overinvest in plant and equipment to justify higher prices and profits.[10] Regulators have also tended to treat these industries generously, viewing them as clients to whom they could later turn for lucrative jobs.

Fortunately, over time, technological advances have eroded the natural monopoly character of many regulated industries. It is now possible, for example, to transmit electricity vast distances over very efficient power lines, so that the relevant market for a power producer stretches at least a thousand miles in all directions. That means a city in Indiana may buy its power from a plant in West Virginia or some other state. Similarly, the technology of long distance telephone transmission now includes satellites and microwave towers, allowing consumers to choose from many different providers of long-distance telephone companies, including cellular systems.

But the bureaucratic inertia of regulation is very slow to change. It was approximately 25 years after their development that regulators permitted satellite and microwave technologies to enter the long-distance telephone market and end what had become the government-protected monopoly of the American Telephone and Telegraph Company. It is doubtful that a completely unregulated natural monopoly would, on average, have charged higher prices over a longer period of time or resisted the competition and the new technology as long and as effectively as AT&T was able to do under the benign control of its regulators.[11]

One creative solution to the failures of public utility regulation is to open natural monopoly pricing and producing decisions to competitive forces. In each natural monopoly, government could sell or lease a franchise to a single producer who wins a competitive bid to supply the market. Each bidder would propose a price at which it would meet market demand. The winning bid would be the lowest proposed price that covers costs and, to the best statistical determination, yields little or no monopoly profit.[12] As technology and the market change over time, the bidding could be reopened to all interested suppliers, or the bidding could be renewed periodically as a matter of course.

International Trade and Investment

Foreign trade and investment is a powerful force for competitive behavior. A 1992 study by the McKinsey Global Institute showed that all countries covered in the study, which included the United States, Britain, France, Germany, and Japan, were most productive in goods that are exposed to foreign competition.[13] For the United States, a competitive force even more powerful than foreign trade is foreign direct investment – in other words, foreign-owned factories and subsidiaries operating in the United States, which are a major source of learning for domestic companies.[14] Another significant finding from the study is that while the United States does not spend as much per-capita as other advanced countries on investment, it gets more return on each dollar of investment.[15] The authors of the study attributed this to lower levels of regulation in the United States, the greater freedom to hire and fire workers as conditions change, the greater ease with which businesses can enter and leave an industry, and more intense foreign competition in the United States.

Foreign investment is also of strategic importance for developing countries. It played a major role in U.S. economic development in the 19th century, in the enormous growth of China since 1979, and in the new market economies of eastern and central Europe (except Russia and most of the former Soviet republics, which have not yet attracted much outside capital).

LABOR MARKETS

A mobile, well-informed labor force with only minimal constraints on workers' movements out of declining markets and into expanding ones is a key factor in building and maintaining a successful market economy. There are no significant limits on the ability of American companies to lay off workers in response to changes in technology, consumer tastes, or competition from other firms. This is in marked contrast to the rest of the world, where firms face numerous government and union-contract restrictions on the rate at which they can cut back their workforce, the length of the work week, etc. Whereas many people view such restraints on layoffs as equitable, they take their toll on workers when firms are making decisions about hiring, because firms are naturally slower to hire workers they cannot easily lay off. As a result of these and other restrictive labor market practices, unemployment rates in most western European countries are persistently above or very close to double digits, even during periods of strong economic growth.

In Japan, despite an economy that has stagnated for the past decade, mass layoffs in declining industries are virtually unheard of and firm bankruptcy also occurs infrequently. The tradition of lifetime employment, although declining and practiced in less than one-third of Japanese companies, leads to repeated and costly shuffling of employees among a firm's various departments. This is done in an attempt to keep the workers employed long after changes in product and resource markets have reduced their value to the company.

More than any other factor, removal of numerous government-mandated labor market regulations pertaining to the firing and work time of workers in New Zealand led to increased output and employment, and brought the country out of a long economic slump in the 1990s.[16] China's explosive growth began in the 1980s only after it granted foreign investors complete discretion to hire and fire labor, ending China's longtime policy of *zero* unemployment.

Downsizing in the 1990s

Dramatic downsizing in U.S. industry occurred in the 1990s. This seems to have happened because managerial and production efficiency sharply increased when computers and other information technology were introduced. Whatever the reason, the downsizing occurred rapidly and smoothly in the United States, partly because of the American public's widespread acceptance of market outcomes, especially in periods of rising income. Government-supported unemployment compensation, which is available for six to 12 months following job loss, further muted resistance to the downsizing, as did the ease with which most workers found new jobs – despite mass layoffs, national unemployment rates fell steadily from 1992 to 2001.

Unions

Unions are institutions that give workers in some occupations and industries a voice and a sense of representation in the workplace they are unlikely to achieve as individuals. In this sense, and under a legal framework that clearly defines key procedures and rules for collective bargaining, unions can enhance both the democratic process and, in some cases, even the effective operation of large enterprises. There is little evidence, however, that unionization has materially influenced the *average* level of either wages or measurable working conditions, such as the length of the workweek, for all workers. The unionized percentage of employed workers in the United States was minuscule throughout the 19th century, and no more than 33 percent at its height in the mid 1950s, from which it has declined steadily to about 13 percent today. Since the 1950s unionization has increased only among public employees, and private-sector service industries that now dominate U.S. employment growth have not been receptive to organized labor. Meanwhile, the continuing rise of wages over the past two centuries has been primarily influenced by population growth (including immigration), the rate of technological change, and other market forces, rather than the degree of unionization.[17]

CAPITAL MARKETS

A country's capital market is the collection of firms and financial institutions that transmit the flow of funds into investment and other uses of credit. This includes banks of all varieties – commercial and savings banks, savings and loan associations – insurance companies, investment houses, mutual investment funds, the postal savings system (in some countries), and other government credit agencies. These organizations play a critical role in channeling the funds of savers and wealth holders to investing firms, government agencies, and individuals. At the same time, they help keep product markets competitive by directing investment to markets in which firms are earning unusually high profits because of a lack of competition.

Capital markets also perform a valuable function of monitoring the performance of firms to which they transmit large amounts of funds. Such oversight is not worthwhile to a financial institution holding just a small number of a company's shares, but large investors tend to establish expertise and a large stake in a few companies and monitor them closely, perhaps even sitting on their boards. This kind of corporate governance was an important concern to authorities in some of the transition economies of central and eastern Europe, who argued that with the privatization of state enterprises the government should explicitly designate and fund a few major shareholders for each new company.[18]

Capital markets are effectively the central nervous system of a market economy, processing the flow of funds to firms, helping to determine whether they will expand, decline, or remain at their present size. The absence of an open and competitive capital market continues to slow the rate of economic growth in Russia, China, and even some affluent countries, such as Israel and Japan. As much as a third of Japan's investment is financed through its government postal savings system, which often allocates funds based more on political than economic grounds (for example, building expensive bullet trains to lightly populated, but politically influential regions).

SUPPLYING PUBLIC GOODS

The Problem and the Solution

As explained earlier, public goods are consumed jointly – wholly or in part. Although private individuals can produce these goods, consumers do not fully express their demand for public goods in the market because everyone benefits from their production as soon as anyone makes a purchase. The economic role of government is therefore to ensure that public goods are produced up to the point that the additional benefits of one more unit equal the additional cost of producing it. Government does not have to make these products itself – indeed, cost considerations may point to the private sector as the more efficient producer. But government must provide the necessary funding to pay for this production through tax revenues or other sources. For some public goods, such as the reduction of environmental pollution, government's role may be to mandate various kinds of pollution-reducing behavior by the private sector (and by government itself). It should do so, however, in a socially least-cost and, where possible, "market-compatible" way.

Pollution Reduction and the Market

Government can employ pollution reduction schemes that are market-compatible by not imposing a uniform pollution limit and not mandating specific pollution control technologies on all firms. Instead, government should encourage firms that can reduce pollution more cheaply to do more of the pollution reduction, using any technology or means they wish. Put differently, for a given target level of pollution reduction, the least-cost way to achieve it is to have more abatement take place where the costs of abatement are lower, and less where the costs are higher. This can be accomplished by levying a tax on pollution emissions, because firms that can reduce pollution more cheaply will avoid paying the tax by reducing their emissions, whereas firms with plants that are older and less technologically advanced will find it cheaper to pay the tax and continue polluting instead of sharply cutting production or even closing the plant. This approach minimizes the decline in total industry output and employment for any desired level of pollution reduction. And under the emissions tax, firms always have an incentive to reduce pollution and the tax they are paying by seeking and installing more effective and less costly anti-pollution technologies.

The sale of marketable "permits to pollute" is another way to lower the total costs of compliance. For example, under this policy power plants decide whether to buy permits and continue polluting to the degree authorized by the permits, or instead to incur the expense of cutting back on pollution so that they can spend less on permits. The government sets the number of pollution permits in a given region at a level that achieves the desired overall pollution reduction, then sells or auctions off the permits.

Government as the Producer of Public Goods

As a general rule, the government should try to avoid being the producer of public goods, and wherever possible rely on private, competitive suppliers, as it usually does in constructing highways, bridges, and public buildings. There are four main reasons for this general rule. First, government is typically a monopoly supplier of the goods or services it provides. Its "customers" have no choice of turning to other suppliers. Without competitors who, if they are successful, can and must be imitated, government agencies have neither the knowledge nor a strong incentive to discover and produce at the lowest possible cost. Second, consumers are often required to pay for the government service, such as first-class mail delivery and licenses to own and operate businesses or automobiles, at prices set administratively rather than by market forces. Without market signals to guide many if not most of its production decisions, government agencies do not receive the daily information about consumer preferences that most private firms have constant access to through changing

prices. Instead, government's information comes from elections, debates, op-ed pieces, and hearings on special topics that are conducted only periodically – in the case of U.S. elections, every two, four, or six years. Third, many of those who participate regularly in government hearings or contribute to political campaigns represent special-interest groups, so that government policymakers may be unduly reliant on, and influenced by, information originating with these groups. Fourth, compensation for most government employees falls under civil-service protection and is tied only loosely to performance. Because neither government agencies nor their employees can earn profits for successful risk-taking or cost cutting, the typical agency head has little incentive to experiment with new technologies or to reduce the number of employees.

The record of the U.S. Postal Service is instructive. It has had an official monopoly in the delivery of first-class mail since the beginning of the republic. The monopoly has not always been consistently or rigidly enforced, however, and the Service has repeatedly been outperformed by innovative, sometimes illegal, private competitors, including the Pony Express, the Wells Fargo Bank stage lines, Lysander Spooner's American Letter Mail Company, and the modern creators of facsimile transmission and electronic mail. In response to public pressure, the Service has tolerated the competition for limited periods, though in the case of electronic mail it tried unsuccessfully to remove it from the private sector and absorb it into its own system.[19]

Military services are an exception to these general rules, however, because in battle loyalty and following orders to meet a planned objective are an absolute necessity, which even the most skilled mercenaries can not provide as reliably. The government's ability to secure loyalty by instilling patriotism and maintaining disciplinary control of its own military personnel exceeds any leverage it could hope to have over mercenaries, no matter how much it paid them. On the other hand, for its ordinance (hardware) and much of its technical advice, the

U.S. Department of Defense relies almost exclusively on private-sector manufacturers and consultants, who must submit competitive bids for contracts.

For the nonmilitary bureaucracy, New Zealand has pioneered in introducing market-like incentives. Government agencies are considered "enterprises," with missions and goals stated as explicitly as possible. Agency heads are reviewed periodically, and can be removed by vote of the reviewing committee. The head of the central bank, for example, is called to a hearing if the country's inflation rate exceeds a specified rate (say, 3 percent). When there is no satisfactory explanation (for example, inflation can, of course, be caused by nonmonetary forces, such as a supply-side shock), the head is removed.[20]

Nonprofit Organizations

A supplementary source of public goods is the private nonprofit sector, which includes charitable, educational, and public interest organizations. Although their output (such as education and health care) is often supplied both as private goods in for-profit markets and by government as partial public goods, nonprofit institutions are established to broaden the beneficiaries of such programs through voluntary giving. These programs offer an outlet to donors who want to support particular causes and groups and, generally, to have more control over charitable or public interest spending than they have through government programs. The disadvantage of nonprofits is that, like many government initiatives, they have no easily determined bottom line showing a profit or loss. That means assessment of their accomplishments by donors is often imprecise and subjective at best. Yet these organizations provide many valuable services in market economies, including some that neither markets nor government agencies undertake.

Public Infrastructure: Physical Capital

Effective means of transportation and communication are critical for economic development. A major factor inhibiting market

and economic development from the fall of Rome to the Renaissance was the inability to transport large numbers of people and goods over long distances. Navigable waterways and roads are thus among the first and most important components of physical infrastructure needed to establish effective market economies. Because it is usually too costly, if not impossible, for private owners to build roads, bridges, and canals, and to monitor and limit their use to paying customers, most major transportation infrastructure is effectively a public good. That means it becomes the financial responsibility of the state to provide and maintain.[21]

In the 19th century U.S. railroads developed as private enterprises, following generous donations of land and rights-of-way by the federal government. Because their average costs declined over a wide range of passenger use, the federal Interstate Commerce Commission (ICC) regulated them as natural monopolies. The ICC continued to set rates and routes long after alternative competing forms of transportation had sprung up, including trucks, automobiles, and airplanes. Even if railroads continued to enjoy declining costs, the increasing competition from motor vehicles and aircraft would have prevented any serious monopoly pricing on their part in an unregulated market. Railroads continued to be regulated, however, even as their business declined drastically in both the freight and passenger markets after World War II. Attempts to revive passenger use through large federal subsidies to Amtrak, which is operated as a government agency, have been largely unsuccessful.

In the 1930s the ICC also imposed rate and route regulation on trucks and airlines engaged in interstate traffic, even though there was no evidence that these industries were natural monopolies or enjoyed any significant monopoly power. It is difficult to avoid the conclusion that the Commission regulated trucking and airlines mainly to protect the railroads from the competition that the new forms of transportation would have provided if they had not been tightly controlled. The ICC set trucking rates and a Byzantine pattern of routes, which loaded trucks could enter only at specified "Gateways." At all other entries, trucks had to be empty. This anti-competitive and obviously inefficient regulatory practice lasted over 40 years, ending only in the early 1980s when an unusual political coalition, ranging from liberal Democratic to conservative Republican senators and congressional representatives, responded to complaints by economists, businesses that relied on trucking to deliver their goods, and an angry public. None of these groups wanted fleets of empty trucks consuming tons of gasoline during an energy crisis. Interstate regulation of the airlines ended at about the same time, when it was observed that unregulated airlines flying entirely within the intrastate Texas and California markets charged passengers half as much as they charged for identical-distance, but regulated, interstate service.

Infrastructure: Health and Safety

Many public goods bear directly on public health. Inoculation against communicable diseases, for example, benefits people who are not inoculated as well as those who are. Clearly inoculation is a public good that should not be left entirely to private decision-making. Sanitation systems are another good for which unrestricted private provision is not likely to ensure public health and meet desirable environmental standards.

Safety features in products, the workplace, and transportation, however, are not necessarily public goods. Many of these features benefit purchasers, but not nonpurchasers, and thus are demanded by consumers and regularly provided by private producers in the marketplace. In fact, most safety features in machinery, construction, transportation, and consumer products originated through a trial-and-error market process in which individual buyers weighed the cost of each new feasible increment of safety against its expected benefit. If they decided the balance was favorable, they purchased it. Over time, if the safety feature fulfilled its promise it was retained; otherwise it was scrapped.

Nonprofit industry associations also frequently set safety standards, but these standards still must pass a market test.

Government is typically justified in mandating disclosure of harmful effects of products or working conditions that producers may be aware of, but consumers and workers can not discover until a significant period of time after exposure. There may also be harmful effects from the manufacture or use of some products that fall on the community at large – another case of negative "externalities," comparable to environmental pollution. In all of these cases government can make a useful contribution by disclosing, or requiring firms to disclose, all relevant safety information so that consumers and workers can make informed choices. But it is not clear that government itself is always an efficient provider or mandator of safety. For example, a number of auto safety devices, including seat belts, airbags, collapsible steering columns, and steel side supports, which are now mandated, were already available as options or standard features on many car models. These features would almost certainly have become standard on all cars when consumers became sufficiently aware of the benefits and had incomes high enough to justify their purchase; but that knowledge and acceptance doesn't always come about quickly. In fact, even after seat belts were mandated in the United States it was some years before the public at large began to use them. The Ford Motor Company tried unsuccessfully to introduce seat belts as optional features in 1961, but there were few takers.

The key reasons that government provision of safety may be inefficient are the centralized and inflexible nature of the regulatory process and the perverse incentives at work in the bureaucracies that establish and enforce such rules. For example, regulation of safety in pharmaceutical products by the U.S. government began in 1906 in response to a public demand for protection against unsafe drugs. Safety criteria were tightened over the years and then, in 1962, in response to intense Congressional pressure, a requirement that drugs be shown to be "effective" was added. Today, largely because of regulatory lag, the approval process for new prescription drugs can take 10-15 years and is enormously expensive, approaching $1 billion for some drugs. As a result, the number of new pharmaceutical products introduced each year has fallen sharply. A large part of the delay (four years, on average) is due to the difficulty of establishing "effectiveness." And paradoxically, there is no evidence that the percentage of new drugs that turn out to be effective in actual use is any greater after 1962 than it was before.[22] The Food and Drug Administration (FDA) is apparently no more successful in screening out ineffective drugs than was the unregulated market. That is not entirely surprising, because doctors are not likely to prescribe drugs they do not believe will be effective and patients are not likely to keep buying and taking drugs that do not seem to work.

The long delays in approving new drugs mean that those who could benefit from highly effective drugs clearly suffer – indeed, in many cases die – because of the drugs' unavailability during the approval process. One landmark study calculated that the delay in introducing two highly effective anti-tuberculosis drugs after World War II was responsible for 29,000 deaths per year.[23] One reason for the long approval delays is that for regulatory agency heads the personal and political costs of approving a drug that proves to be unsafe are many times greater than those associated with delaying the approval of a drug that proves to be highly effective. Those who lose their lives because of the delays are often not even aware of the problem. Approved drugs that are later determined to be unsafe or ineffective can lead to highly publicized lawsuits and resignations or dismissal of agency heads.

To address the problem of delays, the FDA has created a "fast track" for very promising drugs or those that treat diseases for which there are many sufferers. The decision to place a drug on fast track is rare and still rests with the agency, however, whose rulings cannot easily be appealed.

The overall efficiency of the approval process would probably be improved if the effectiveness requirement were dropped. Although desirable in principle, the cost of making this a regulatory requirement almost certainly exceeds any benefits, particularly because it may not in fact improve on the unregulated market's ability to asses effectiveness. Other weaknesses in the present system, such as a lack of quality control in drug manufacturing, could be addressed by tightening liability laws for manufacturers.

Education and Welfare

Education and a public "safety net" for the poor are partial public goods, providing benefits both to those who receive these services and to society as a whole. To a considerable extent, however, private producers supply quantities of both of these services, the former by private schools and universities and the latter in the form of charitable giving. In recent years enrollments in private elementary and secondary schools have been rising, while self-help and workfare programs have become more important in providing the social safety net. Introducing greater variety in educational systems, including charter and magnet schools to serve diverse student needs, is one promising but controversial approach to increasing choice, competition, and the quality of schooling.[24] The quality of K-12 schooling is, of course, extremely important in emerging market economies, because literacy and basic quantitative skills have become indispensable in the information age.

All societies assume some responsibility for supporting families and individuals experiencing unforeseen and unavoidable financial difficulties. In the United States, such support comes from both private charities and the government. Government offers cash payments through the program, Temporary Assistance for Needy Families (TANF), formerly known as Aid to Families with Dependent Children. It also provides in-kind benefits, including the food stamps program (which can be electronic transfer benefit cards), Medicaid, and housing subsidies. These "welfare" programs are often criticized because of the perverse incentives they may give recipients. For example, welfare may discourage work effort because benefits are sharply reduced whenever recipients earn any income above some minimum allowable level. The loss of benefits is equivalent to a severe tax on such income earnings. Secondly, welfare is sometimes criticized for its more-or-less automatic character, providing benefits to qualified recipients almost as an "entitlement." This may have the effect of artificially increasing the eligible population.

The first of these concerns has been addressed by offering some aid in the form of the so-called earned-income tax credit. The credit provides cash payments to low-income families, which are only partially and very gradually removed as the families earn income through employment. The second concern brought forth determined efforts by the Clinton administration in the 1990s to require welfare recipients to find jobs and leave welfare after specified periods of time. Aided by the strong economy, these efforts resulted in a substantial reduction of the welfare rolls by the end of the decade.

Although economic growth can not address the immediate plight of the poor, it is probably still the most effective long-term and universal antidote to poverty. The growth of the American economy played an important role in reducing poverty, especially when combined with incentives to join the work force. An improved educational system would, of course, also be highly effective in reducing poverty by providing future workers with marketable skills.

In the transition economies, one factor delaying the liquidation of unprofitable state-owned enterprises in China and the former Soviet Union is that the enterprises provide workers with housing and a broad range of social services, including health care and education. Until public and private sources for these services can be established, independent of any firm or industry, the enterprises will remain as necessary social institutions in these economies.

MACROECONOMIC STABILIZATION POLICIES

Macroeconomic stabilization refers to attempts to minimize unemployment and inflation by smoothing the ups and downs of the business cycle while promoting steady rates of economic growth. Successful stabilization is a public good, first because it tends to benefit everyone (except those few who earn their living speculating on the course of the business cycle or, like economists, giving advice during downturns), and second because only the national government has the size and resources necessary to carry it out. The main instruments of stabilization are fiscal and monetary policy.

Fiscal Policy

Fiscal policy involves setting the overall levels of government spending and revenues (mostly taxes). Taxes reduce private spending but finance an equal amount of government spending. In other words, they shift resources away from the private sector to produce goods and services demanded by government. Ideally, taxes that are raised primarily to pay for government programs (rather than for some other purpose, such as to reduce pollution or the consumption of cigarettes and alcohol) will not affect the relative prices of particular goods and services. A tax on personal income is probably the least disruptive to the pattern of resource allocation because it is not a tax on a specific product or any group of products. Income tax rates can also be set to vary with income, enabling lower income families to pay a lower percentage of their earnings than higher income households. Income taxes that have this redistributive feature are said to be "progressive," whereas sales taxes are "regressive" because they take a higher percentage of earnings from low-income families.

Because taxes reduce private spending, and government spending is a major component of total spending in the national economy, government can manipulate its budget to stimulate or slow down the level of economic activity. For example, if private spending is declining in a recession, government can offset this by increasing its own expenditures, or by reducing taxes so that consumers and businesses have more "disposable" or after-tax income and can increase their spending. Conversely, when the economy is "overheated" or inflationary, government can raise taxes or reduce its own expenditures. These discretionary changes in government spending and tax levels can not be done quickly or flexibly enough to serve as a practical tool during the moderate upswings and downswings of the typical U.S. business cycle. Fluctuations in national income lead automatically, however, to changes in tax revenues and government expenditures on unemployment compensation and assistance to low-income households. These "automatic stabilizers" raise or lower disposable income countercyclically and do a great deal to cushion the impact of the business cycle. In severe periods of unemployment or inflation, the political consensus to adopt discretionary changes in spending or taxes is likely to develop, and develop quickly enough to be helpful.

Monetary Policy

Monetary policy is a far more flexible and immediate instrument of stabilization than fiscal policy, although there are differing opinions on how best to use it. Some economists and policymakers favor frequent policy moves in an effort to "fine tune" the macroeconomy. Others believe that it is only possible to achieve long-term goals effectively, pursuing fixed and rarely changing targets and policies. This group argues that trying to identify and offset short-term changes in the economy is likely to do more harm than good.

The basic ideas of monetary policy are straightforward. Expansionary monetary policies mean that a nation's central bank – in the United States, the Federal Reserve System (or the "Fed" for short) – increases the amount of money and the availability of credit in the economy, which reduces interest rates and promotes additional spending by businesses and households. Contractionary monetary policy is the opposite – the central bank reduces the amount of money, raising interest rates and choking off some business and household spending.

One aspect of the Federal Reserve System that sets it apart from a number of other central banks is its independence, which was formally established in 1951. Its governors are appointed to 14-year terms by the president and confirmed by the senate. Thereafter it operates as an autonomous agency that reports periodically only to Congressional committees, but is not subject to their control or to anyone else's. The Fed is self-financed, earning interest on the government bonds it holds and on the loans it extends to member commercial banks. This structure has worked well for the United States (and other nations whose central banks are relatively independent), enabling the Fed to pursue its own policy goals rather than following the usually short-term wishes of a politically oriented White House and Congress by accommodating their fiscal policies.

Deposit Insurance

Since 1935, federal deposit insurance has been a major factor contributing to the stability of money, the banking system, and the entire U.S. economy. Deposit insurance applies to almost all checking accounts, savings deposits, certificates of deposit, and savings and loan shares. This insurance acts as a public good because it eliminates the incentive for panicked deposit withdrawals ("bank runs") by the public, which historically destabilized the entire economy. Administered primarily by the Federal Deposit Insurance Corporation (FDIC), premiums are paid to this agency by banks and other savings institutions to insure deposits up to $100,000 each. There is some evidence that rapid increases in the 1980s from an insured deposit level of $40,000 to the current $100,000 may have encouraged riskier lending behavior by banks, because banks and their depositors felt that the probability of deposit loss had become effectively zero. In 1986 savings and loan associations in the American southwest were hit particularly hard by the collapse of world oil prices and the resulting default on their loans to the oil industry and related firms. The cost of paying depositors and other creditors of failed S&Ls and other banks exceeded $100 billion, but a substantial portion of this sum was recovered by the sale of salvageable assets. Despite this setback, the principle of deposit insurance remains sound, and has introduced a degree of stability to the monetary system that was not achieved throughout the 19th century or during the first third of the 20th century.

International Economic Institutions

Individual countries generally prefer to control their own domestic monetary and fiscal polices and price levels, which they can do if they have an independent currency and flexible exchange rates. This view has been changing in Europe, however, as the European Union (EU) moved to a single currency, the euro, to promote trade and eliminate the inconvenience of converting currencies at each border crossing. Among EU members, only Britain has not yet adopted the euro, reluctant to give up its pound sterling and its monetary/fiscal independence. The use of a common currency effectively converts Europe into a single economy, much like that of the United States. Most trade barriers within the EU have already been removed and passports and visas for citizens of EU countries are being eliminated.

Three major international economic institutions were created after World War II: the International Monetary Fund (IMF), the World Bank, and the General Agreement on Tariffs and Trade (GATT), which has since been replaced by the World Trade Organization (WTO). The IMF was created to help countries smooth fluctuations in their exchange rates, bring inflation under control, and open their markets to international trade and investment. The World Bank was formed to extend loans for capital projects in developing nations. Opinion is divided on the effectiveness of both the IMF and the World Bank in helping create stability and the infrastructure for economic development. The WTO (and in earlier years GATT), however, is widely credited with substantially reducing trade barriers, opening markets, and stimulating growth throughout the world

LINKS BETWEEN THE ECONOMIC AND POLITICAL SYSTEMS

Ultimately, the success of a market economy depends on the people's acceptance of markets as an effective and reasonably equitable way to allocate goods and services and, by establishing prices for labor and other productive resources, to determine incomes. Government plays an important but limited role enforcing the rule of law and private property rights, maintaining competition, and providing public goods. The latter include national defense, the public infrastructure, macroeconomic stability, and cost-effective levels of education, environmental protection, welfare benefits, and income redistribution.

Any general tendency of government to expand further, providing subsidies and protection to politically influential groups at the expense of the rest of the population, risks encouraging a whole range of nonmarket and divisive political responses. Economies thus afflicted are more likely to experience labor market unrest, nonpayment of taxes, default of private and public debts, bribery and corruption of government officials, unstable governments, and lower levels of investment (domestic and foreign) and economic growth.

Consider a recent extreme example. In 1997 overdue unpaid bills in the Russian economy amounted to a staggering 25 percent of the gross domestic product.[25] Corruption of public officials was widespread. Democracy, though encompassing free elections and many human rights – but not all – was fractious. The Russian Mafia had become active enforcers of property "law" as they interpreted it. This happened in an economy where people were not yet committed to playing by the rules of open markets and respect for private property.

China also still experiences a great deal of government bribery and corruption. Taxes are generally paid, but the legal tax rate is barely sufficient to meet the central government's commitments, including payments to the unprofitable state-owned enterprises. Because China is a political dictatorship that basically enforces most private property rights, misuse of assets and failure to meet contractual obligations are not common. Although the communist party has lost most of its direct control over the economy, it still administers a political system with little regard for human rights other than an individual's right to property income. Free elections at the local level are beginning to take hold, however.

The key question for emerging market economies is whether a viable market economy can emerge from an undemocratic or unstable democratic system. The economic development of the West is not entirely relevant to the answer to this question, because the West's political and economic institutions matured over the course of several centuries. Clearly, there are contemporary examples of flourishing free-market democracies that grew quickly out of political dictatorships, including Franco's Spain and Pinochet's Chile. During Hong Kong's stunning economic development as a British colony, it lacked electoral democracy but enjoyed civil rights. Singapore's flourishing market economy developed under a political system with limited electoral freedom and sharply limited civil rights. India has had complete electoral democracy but a spotty record on civil rights, and until recently was economically stagnant under a system of extensive government economic controls.

There is probably an optimal working relationship between the economy and the political system of every developing country. Democracy in the West, including the United States, evolved along with the evolution of markets. In the early American republic, the right to vote was limited to male landowners and was only gradually extended to the entire adult population as social and economic institutions matured. And from the beginning, government provided political stability and the necessary rule of law (including protection of private property rights), and supplied those public goods that were needed to keep markets functioning efficiently. Not every government intervention was consistent with market efficiency – for example, significant protection from European and other foreign manufactured goods was practiced until shortly after World War II. But the geographical size and population of the country were so vast that internal trade and specialization compensated for any lack of cheap imports.

It seems clearly impossible to separate economic freedom from complete political freedom indefinitely. Even if political freedom is not a necessary causal force at every stage of economic development, the information capability of a modern market economy invariably undermines attempts at media and individual speech controls. And expecting free-market consumers and producers to passively accept limitations on their political freedom for any extended period is wholly unrealistic.

NOTES

1. See Heinz Kohler, "Soviet Central Planning," in D. Kennett and M. Lieberman, eds., *The Road to Capitalism* (Ft. Worth: The Dryden Press, 1992), pp. 5-14; and Ed Hewett, *Reforming the Soviet Economy* (Washington: The Brookings Institution, 1988), pp. 191-196.

2. See the study of the Peruvian economy by Hernando de Soto, *The Other Path* (New York: Harper & Row, 1989).

3. See Yingyi Qian, "How Reform Worked in China," Working Paper 473, The William Davidson Institute (Ann Arbor: University of Michigan, June 2002).

4. See Leon Aaron, "The Strange Case of Russian Capitalism," *AEI Russian Outlook*

(Washington: American Enterprise Institute for Public Policy Research, Winter 1998).

5. See Joseph A. Schumpeter, *Capitalism, Socialism, and Democracy* (London: Allen and Unwin, 1952), pp. 81-86.

6. See N. Gregory Mankiw, *Macroeconomics*, 4th ed. (New York: Worth, 2000), p. 129.

7. See W. Kip Viscusi, John N. Vernon, and Joseph E. Harrington, Jr., *Economics of Regulation and Antitrust* (Lexington, Mass.: D.C. Heath, 1995), p. 290.

8. See Peter Asch, *Industrial Organization and Antitrust Policy* (New York: Wiley, 1983), pp. 275-276.

9. See Asch, *op. cit.*, p. 251.

10. See Asch, *op. cit.*, p. 350, for an analysis of this tendency.

11. See Viscusi et al., *op. cit.*, pp. 492-514, for an account of the history of AT&T regulation.

12. See Harold Demsetz, "Why Regulate Utilities?" *Journal of Law and Economics*, 11 (April 1968), pp. 55-65, and the discussion on franchises in Viscusi et al., chap. 13.

13. See the summaries of the report by Sylvia Nasar, "U.S. Still No. 1 in Something? Yes, Productivity," *New York Times*, Oct. 14, 1992, p. 1; and William Lewis, "The Secret to Competitiveness," *Wall Street Journal*, Oct. 22, 1993.

14. See Lewis, *op. cit.*

15. See Nasar, *op. cit.*

16. See Lewis Evans, Arthur Grimes, Bryce Wilkinson, and David Teece, "Economic Reform in New Zealand 1984-95: The Pursuit of Efficiency," *Journal of Economic Literature* 34 (Dec. 1996), pp. 1856-1902, esp. pp. 1880-1883.

17. See Claudia Goldin, "Labor Markets in the Twentieth Century," in Stanley Engerman and Robert Gallman, eds. *The Cambridge Economic History of the United States*, Vol. III (Cambridge: Cambridge University Press, 2000), p. 584.

18. See David Lipton and Jeffrey Sachs, "Privatization in Eastern Europe: The Case of Poland," *Brookings Papers on Economic Activity*, No. 1, 1990, pp. 75-147.

19. See House, Post Office, and Civil Service Committee, Postal Personnel and Modernization Subcommittee, Electronic Message Service Systems, Hearings, January 29, February 6, 20, March 11, 20, 25, April 1, 1980, U.S. Government Printing Office, Serial No. 96-78, pp. 68-69.

20. See Evans et al., *op cit.*

21. See Gabriel Roth, *Roads in a Market Economy* (Brookfield, VT: Ashgate Publishing, 1996).

22. See Sam Peltzman, *Regulation of Pharmaceutical Innovation: The 1962 Amendments* (Washington: American Enterprise Institute for Public Policy Research, 1974), pp. 58-63.

23. See Peltzman, *op. cit.*

24. See Robert Barro, *Getting It Right: Markets and Choices in a Free Society* (Cambridge, Mass: MIT Press, 1996).

25. See Serguey Braguinsky and Grigory Yavlinsky, *Incentives and Institutions* (Princeton: Princeton Univ. Press, 2000), p. 146.

LESSON ONE
MARKETS AND THE MARKET SYSTEM

LESSON DESCRIPTION

This lesson introduces students to the primary economic institution in a market economy, markets. As described in the introductory essay to this volume, markets are an institution that emerges spontaneously from the interaction of self-interested buyers and sellers, establishing prices for goods and services that provide key incentives and signals. The first activity in this lesson stresses the decentralized nature of decision-making in competitive markets, and shows how self-interested behavior by individuals in these markets regularly leads to efficient outcomes. Next, the links between different types of markets are explored through a circular flow activity. Finally, the importance of prices that are free to rise or fall to achieve market equilibrium is demonstrated.

INTRODUCTION

Adam Smith, considered the father of modern economics, was one of the first to describe the systematic effects of everyday, self-interested behavior by ordinary men and women in organizing economic activity, establishing markets, and systematically answering three fundamental economic questions: what to produce, how to produce, and for whom to produce. Perfectly competitive markets require many "atomistic" buyers and sellers (too small to control prices or market output levels), the free flow of information, protection of property rights, negligible side effects on third parties (those not directly engaged in production or consumption), and enforcement of contracts. When those conditions are met, prices act as important signals in achieving efficient levels of production and consumption for goods and services, by automatically adjusting quantities supplied and demanded whenever an imbalance (shortage or surplus) develops. Later lessons explore what happens when there are problems with property rights, third-party effects, and other problems that can make it impossible for markets to establish efficient levels of production and consumption.

CONCEPTS

    Product markets
    Factor markets
    Allocative efficiency
    Circular flow model
    Shortage
    Surplus
    Market prices
    Law of demand
    Law of supply

CONTENT STANDARDS

Markets exist when buyers and sellers interact. This interaction determines market prices and thereby allocates scarce goods and services.

Prices send signals and provide incentives to buyers and sellers. When supply and demand changes, market prices adjust, affecting incentives.

A nation's overall levels of income, employment, and prices are determined by the interaction of spending and production decisions made by all households, firms, government agencies, and others in the economy.

BENCHMARKS

Market prices are determined through the buying and selling decisions made by buyers and sellers.

Relative price refers to the price of one good or service compared to the prices of other goods and services. Relative prices are the basic measures of the relative scarcity of products when prices are set by market forces (supply and demand).

The market clearing or equilibrium price for a good or service is the one price at which quantity supplied equals quantity demanded.

An increase in the price of a good or service encourages people to look for substitutes, causing the quantity demanded to decrease, and vice versa. This relationship between price and quantity demanded, known as the law of demand, exists as long as other factors influencing demand do not change.

An increase in the price of a good or service enables producers to cover higher per-unit costs and earn profits, causing the quantity supplied to increase, and vice versa. This relationship between price and quantity supplied is normally true as long as other factors influencing costs of production and supply do not change.

Markets are interrelated; changes in the price of one good or service can lead to changes in prices of many other goods and services.

Scarce goods and services are allocated in a market economy through the influence of prices on production and consumption decisions.

When consumers make purchases, goods and services are transferred from businesses to households in exchange for money payments. That money is used in turn by businesses to pay for productive resources (natural, human, and capital) and to pay taxes.

OBJECTIVES

Students will:

♦ Explain that markets operate primarily through uncoordinated, decentralized decisions made by individual buyers and sellers.

♦ Distinguish between product markets and factor markets.

♦ Identify interactions between buyers and sellers across product and factor markets

and trace out both monetary and nonmonetary flows in the circular flow model.

♦ Explain the role of prices in providing incentives and signals in market economies, which are used to answer the basic economic questions: what, how, and for whom to produce.

TIME REQUIRED

Two class periods

MATERIALS

- Visual 1: The Magic of Markets
- Visual 2: What's for Lunch Tomorrow?
- Visual 3: In the Words of Adam Smith…….
- Visual 4: Circular Flow Diagram Without Government Sector, transparency plus one copy per student OR
- Visual 5: Circular Flow Diagram With Government Sector, transparency plus one copy per student
- Visual 6: Discovering the Market Clearing Price
- Activity 1: Menu cards, cut apart to provide one per student
- Activity 2: Circular Flow Descriptions, one copy per student
- Activity 3: Circular Flow Examples, one copy cut into strips
- Activity 4: Buyer Cards, one copy cut apart, and Seller Cards, one copy cut apart

PROCEDURES

1. Explain that a **market** is any kind of arrangement that allows the potential buyers and sellers of a particular good or service to interact. Avoid using the word "place" or implying a location in discussing markets. Although it is true that many markets involve direct face-to-face interaction between buyers and sellers, that is not an essential element of the exchange. Indeed, technology has dramatically altered the manner in which many buyers and sellers complete their transactions.

2. Explain that consumer goods and services – things consumers buy because the goods or services provide them with satisfaction – are exchanged in markets called **product markets**. Markets for inputs used in the production process are called **factor markets.** These markets are where the factors of production (natural resources, labor, capital, and entrepreneurship) are bought and sold.

3. Explain that students and most other people who have grown up in countries like the United States tend to take markets for granted, yet markets accomplish remarkable results every day. Without any centralized coordination or control of individual decisions about what, how, and for whom to produce, markets work to insure the availability of the many types and qualities of goods and services that consumers want by providing incentives for producers to make and offer to sell their goods and services day after day, year after year, in the marketplace.

4. Display Visual 1, The Magic of Markets, and lead a discussion using these questions:
    *   What did you have for breakfast this morning? *(Answers will vary)*
    *   How did this type of food arrive in your house? *(Answers will vary)*
    *   How did someone in the family know what and how much to buy for breakfast? *(Past experience with tastes and eating habits of family members)*
    *   How did the store it was purchased from know someone would buy it? *(Past experience and habits of store customers)*
    *   How does the local fast food restaurant know how many workers to schedule for each shift during the week? *(Again, from past experience or, for a new store, from what they observe from established stores in similar areas, or from competitors who are already operating in this area)*

*   What would happen if a change in consumer preferences and buying patterns significantly reduced the demand for a good or service? *(At first producers might try to avoid cutting their production or prices, but in time prices would fall and, eventually, producers would reduce the amount of the product offered. Example: After September 11, 2001, the decrease in demand for air travel led to massive schedule reductions for major airlines.)*
*   What would happen if higher production costs significantly reduced the supply of a good or service? *(At first, producers may try to absorb the higher costs and not raise prices – particularly if it is also costly for them to implement higher prices, for example in an expensive restaurant that would have to reprint an extensive menu. If the higher production costs persist, however, producers will ultimately reduce the amounts they are willing and able to sell at a given price. That will lead to a price increase, causing consumers to reduce the amount of the good or service demanded. Example: Higher oil and gasoline prices will reduce highway travel for vacations and the demand for cars that are less fuel efficient, such as SUVs.)*
*   For most goods and services, is a central authority needed to decide what, how, and for whom to buy and sell in competitive markets? *(No – the results come from thousands of decentralized or individual decisions of consumers and producers)*

5. Display Visual 2, What's for Lunch Tomorrow? showing four menu options. Ask each student to rank his or her menu preferences by showing their first, second, third, and fourth choices. (For this activity, no ties are allowed.) Tell students to write down these rankings to record their choices.

6. Randomly distribute one menu card from Activity 1 to each student. Ask all of the students to stand up, then have only the students who received a card with their top menu choice sit down.

7. To begin Part 2 of the activity, tell the students who are still standing to attempt to trade menu cards ONLY with other students who are still standing. Students should trade cards ONLY if a trade improves the satisfaction of BOTH students, by moving them higher up on their menu rankings. Allow at least five minutes for students to trade. Then ask for a show of hands to see how many of these students were able to improve their satisfaction by moving up on their ranking of menu items by trading. Then have all of the students who now hold their first menu choice sit down.

8. Lead a discussion of the activity, beginning with the following two questions:
    *   Is it likely that a random distribution of menu items, such as demonstrated at the beginning of Part 1, will fully satisfy all consumers? *(No – there is no mechanism for revealing tastes, preferences, dietary restrictions, etc., and no method for allowing people to make individual choices.)*
    *   Did the trading in Part 2 of the Activity increase total satisfaction of the consumers? *(Yes, assuming some trading did occur, because the traders were better off and the students who did not trade stayed at the same level of satisfaction. No, if no trades were completed.)*

9. Introduce the concept of **allocative efficiency**. One way to describe allocative efficiency (assuming that all individuals' preferences are accepted and counted) is to say that resources are allocated efficiently when it is NOT possible to benefit one person without making someone else worse off. Then continue the discussion of Activity 1 with the following questions:

*   Was the initial distribution of menu items allocatively efficient? *(Not if, as most likely, there were trades during Part 2. The trades indicate that it was possible to benefit some students without harming others. If there were no trades during Part 2, the initial allocation was efficient.)*
*   After the trading round was complete, was the new distribution of menu items allocatively efficient? *(Yes. After all of the possible trades had been made, it was impossible to improve the satisfaction of any student without harming someone else.)*
*   Does allocative efficiency guarantee that everyone has maximum satisfaction? *(No, it is possible for some students to be "stuck" with their 2nd, 3rd, or even 4th menu choice.)*
*   How do markets contribute to allocative efficiency? *(Resources are directed toward their best uses because consumers are willing to pay for the things they like, and producers are willing to pay for inputs that help them produce goods and services profitably – in other words as long as they can produce goods and services for less than what consumers are willing to pay for them.)*

10. Display Visual 3, In the Words of Adam Smith. Allow students five minutes to read and consider this famous passage from *The Wealth of Nations* individually. Then put students in small groups (3–4 students) to discuss the quote and have them paraphrase the main ideas in modern terms. Ask a student from each group to report. Stress the importance of "self-love" (self-interest) in the quote. Emphasize that Smith was a strong proponent of "natural liberty," a system in which individuals are left alone ("laissez faire") to pursue and advance their own interests, but in competition with others doing the same thing. Smith staunchly believed that self-interest is the main and most reliable engine of economic growth and

progress. That implies that market systems will be efficient because, in market transactions, if I want something from you, I must provide something you want in exchange. In Activity 1 and in the routine exchanges that students see at all kinds of stores, both buyers and sellers gain by agreeing to trade even in making routine and repeated trades. Smith also advocated a limited role for government, as noted in the following passage from *The Wealth of Nations*:

"The uniform, constant, and uninterrupted effort of every man to better his condition, the principle from which public and national, as well as private opulence is originally derived, is frequently powerful enough to maintain the natural progress of things toward improvement, in spite both of the extravagance of government, and of the greatest errors of administration." Adam Smith, *An Inquiry into the Nature and Causes of the Wealth of Nations*, 1776, (Book II, Chapter II, passage 31).

11. Explain that the **circular flow model** is a diagram that demonstrates the systematic linkages between markets for goods and services (product markets), and markets for resources used in production (input or factor markets). Stress that although many people before Adam Smith had written about the efficiency of individual markets and the key role of self-interest, Smith was one of the first to show how a wide range of markets for different kinds of goods and services, each seemingly independent, were actually linked together in a market *system*, and that a system of competitive markets would be very efficient because all of the individual buyers and sellers in those markets knew what they wanted, and used the resources they controlled very carefully, to achieve their own goals.

12. Display either Visual 4 or 5. If class time is limited or student backgrounds and abilities in economics are low, use the two-sector circular flow model, showing households and businesses, in Visual 4. If time and student

background and ability permit, use Visual 5, which is a three-sector model including government. Explain that this Visual and activity will show the basic economic connections and flows among households, businesses, and (optional) government in both product and factor markets. Ask students to identify examples of households (their own, neighbors', friends', relatives', their teacher's), businesses (fast food restaurants, grocery stores, etc), and (optional) government (federal, state, and local agencies). Review the difference between product and factor markets.

Referring to Visual 4 or 5, note that the arrows with odd numbers will represent real or non-monetary flows of goods, services, and inputs or productive resources. The complete non-monetary circular flow of the economy will be shown with arrows 1, 3, 5, and 7. On the other hand, the even-numbered arrows will represent monetary flows. A complete monetary flow of the economy will be shown by arrows 2, 4, 6, and 8. (In economics classes, you may also want to point out that in any given year the monetary flow measures the dollar value of the real flow in the overall economy, so the circular flow model also demonstrates how the prices for goods, services, and factors of production that are studied in microeconomics can be used to measure the overall level of economic activity that is studied in macroeconomics.)

13. Distribute one copy of Activity 2, Circular Flow Descriptions, and one copy of either Visual 4 or 5 to each student. Review each numbered item on the handout and assign each one to an arrow on the Circular Flow Diagram. If Visual 4 is used, copy and use only the top portion of Activity 2 (numbers 1-8). If Visual 5 (3 sectors, including government) is used, use items 1-16.

14. Cut apart Activity 3, Circular Flow Examples, to form individual slips. Fold the slips in half and place all of the slips in a container. Have students take turns drawing a slip, reading it aloud, and determining the

correct arrow reference number. When a student provides an incorrect answer, encourage classmates to offer corrections. Be careful to use the starred (*) slips only when working with the circular flow model that includes the government sector (Visual 5).

Answers:

- *Olivia chooses a beautiful sweater for her grandmother's Christmas present (1)*
- *Henry paints houses as a summer job (3)*
- *Jorge receives income from rental properties (4)*
- *David pays for tickets to a rock concert (2)*
- *General Motors produces SUVs for sale to consumers (7)*
- *The Green Bay Packers receive money from season ticket sales (8)*
- *Exsalonce Beauty Parlor hires another hairdresser (5)*
- *Abs-of-Steel Fitness Center pays its personal trainers each Friday (6)*
- ** Sona Corporation pays $5,000 in income taxes to the state of Wisconsin (12)*
- ** Irene receives $400 each month from the government because she has low income (14)*
- ** A Pentagon worker receives $60,000 per year for her work as a translator (14)*
- ** A recent police academy grad applies for a job with the municipal police department (13)*
- ** A homeowner's city government provides curbside garbage pickup (15)*
- ** 3Squares Company produces MREs (meals-ready-to-eat) for U.S. army troops (9)*

15. When students have demonstrated an understanding of linkages between different kinds of markets shown in the circular flow, extend the discussion to include the role of prices. Prices send signals and provide incentives to buyers and sellers. Scarce goods and services are allocated in a market economy through the influence of prices on production and consumption decisions.

Specifically, an increase in the price of a good or service encourages people to look for substitutes, causing the quantity demanded to decrease, and vice versa. This relationship between price and quantity demanded, known as the **law of demand**, normally holds as long as other factors influencing demand do not change.

An increase in the price of a good or service allows producers to cover higher per-unit costs of production to earn profits, causing the quantity supplied to increase, and vice versa. This relationship between price and quantity supplied, called the **law of supply**, normally holds as long as other factors influencing costs of production and supply do not change.

Market prices are determined through the decisions made by buyers and sellers. The market clearing or equilibrium price for a good or service is the one at which quantity demanded equals quantity supplied. If a price does not clear the market, either a **shortage** (quantity demanded exceeds quantity supplied) or **surplus** (quantity supplied exceeds quantity demanded) will occur. Shortages trigger upward pressure on price, as disappointed demanders make it known that they would be willing to pay more than the current price. Surpluses trigger downward pressure on price, as disappointed suppliers learn that consumers will buy more only if they offer their goods and services at a lower price.

16. Tell students that Activity 4 will demonstrate the important role of prices in clearing the market, using eight sellers and eight buyers. The buyers and sellers will act in their own self-interest, with buyers attempting to buy a good at the lowest possible price, and sellers attempting to sell the good at the highest

possible price. Tell students that the game is played in several rounds, with a price announced by the teacher at the beginning of each round.

In each round, buyers should seek a seller willing to trade at that price. Likewise, sellers seek a willing buyer at the announced price. An "exchange" pairing between buyer and seller occurs when trade at the announced price is mutually agreeable to both. The prices on the cards are NOT required to be equal for an exchange pairing to occur.

17. Explain that at some prices, some buyers and sellers are unwilling to trade at all. For example, if the announced price is $2, a seller holding a card stating "you are willing to sell the good if the price is $12 or more" is not willing to trade during this round. Similarly, if the announced price is $14, a buyer holding a card stating "you are willing to buy the good if the price is $8 or less" is not willing to trade. Because identifying who might be "unwilling" to trade in a given round can be confusing to students, the teacher should demonstrate (using prices of $14 and $2) with a few buyer and seller cards distributed to students before the actual simulation begins.

18. Tell students that after they create their initial buyer/seller exchange pairings, there will be time for "bumping". Any unpaired buyers or sellers can "bump" a buyer or seller already in an exchange pairing under the following circumstances. An unpaired buyer can bump an already paired buyer IF he/she is willing to pay the seller a higher price than the paired buyer. Likewise, an unpaired seller can bump an already paired seller IF he/she is willing to offer the good at a lower price than the paired seller. Students who are unpaired should check all the exchange pairs to see if they can bump. Tell students they should try to bump other buyers and sellers until all possible bumps have been exhausted. For most of the prices announced, however, there will be a "mismatch" between

willing buyers and willing sellers, even after bumping is exhausted.

19. Select 16 students and distribute one buyer or seller card to each. Each student will use the same card throughout all rounds of the game. (Note: the game is easier to monitor if buyer and seller cards are printed on different colors of paper.) Explain that the game involves 8 buyers, 8 sellers, and seven rounds, with prices announced at the beginning of each round by the teacher. When each round is complete, the 16 students will each fit into one of three categories: 1) unwilling buyer/seller; 2) exchange pair buyer/seller; or 3) willing but unpaired buyer/seller. Instruct students who are unwilling buyers or sellers (due to the price announced during a particular round) to stand off to the side or sit down during that round. The remaining willing buyers and sellers should attempt to form exchange pairs during the round.

20. Begin by announcing that in round 1 the price will be $3. Help buyers and sellers determine whether they are willing or unwilling buyers/sellers at that price. Remind unwilling buyers/sellers to move to the side of the trading area or sit down. Allow enough time for initial exchange pairings, then allow time for "bumping". There should be only one exchange pair because there is only one willing seller at a price of $3. Lead the class in counting the numbers in each group: (unwilling sellers: 7; unwilling buyers: 1; exchange pairs: 1 buyer/seller pair; willing but unpaired sellers: 0; willing but unpaired buyers: 6). Display Visual 6 and record these results for the $3 price round. Record additional results as each remaining price round is completed, but first conclude the debriefing for the price of $3.

21. Ask students to identify whether there is a shortage or surplus in the market at this price. *(There is a shortage: more willing buyers than willing sellers.)* What do the unwilling sellers have in common? *(Each is willing to sell only at prices higher than the announced price.)*

Explain that this will happen if the current market price is too low relative to a producer's costs for it to produce and sell its product at a profit. What do the willing but unsuccessful buyers have in common? *(Each is willing to buy at a price higher than the current market price.)* Given these conditions, ask students to predict what will happen to price. *(There will be upward pressure on price from the six disappointed, "wannabe" consumers.)*

22. Continue the activity with price rounds of $5 and $7, counting the numbers of willing and unwilling buyers and sellers, and exchange pairs at that price. Record these data for each price round on Visual 6. Discuss whether a shortage or surplus exists, and ask students to predict the direction of price, given the conditions of that round. Be sure to discuss the results of each round before moving on to the next price round. (The shortage condition continues, but becomes smaller as the price rises.)

23. Complete additional rounds in the following order: $15, $13, $11, and finally $9. The final round demonstrates the equilibrium or market clearing price. At the earlier prices ($11–$15) there will be a surplus, with the quantity demanded less than the quantity supplied. The market clearing price is the only price at which the quantity demanded equals the quantity supplied. In other words, there are no willing buyers left unsatisfied and no willing sellers holding produced goods. A price of $9 clears the market of both buyers and sellers, and is the only price at which there are neither willing buyers nor willing sellers who are unable to form an exchange pair. Note that at prices below equilibrium, there are only willing but disappointed buyers. At prices above equilibrium, there are only willing but disappointed sellers. These conditions influence the movement of prices in unregulated markets, with prices rising when there are unsatisfied buyers willing to buy the goods, and falling when there are unsatisfied sellers willing to sell

their surplus goods, but no available buyers at the current price.

24. The table below summarizes the results at all prices:

Price	Unwilling Buyers	Unwilling Sellers	Exchange Pairs	Willing Unpaired Buyers	Willing Unpaired Sellers
$3	1	7	1	6	0
5	2	6	2	4	0
7	3	5	3	2	0
15	7	1	1	0	6
13	6	2	2	0	4
11	5	3	3	0	2
9	4	4	4	0	0

25. Ask students to explain how the results of the simulation reinforce the ideas of Adam Smith. *(Buyers and sellers act in their own self-interest, exchanges occur when there are mutual benefits, and prices are key signals for both buyers and sellers.)* Emphasize that in the competitive markets described by Smith, equilibrium price is achieved through powerful market forces, without any government intervention or central planning.

CLOSURE

1. Review the important points of this lesson by discussing the following questions:

- What is a market? *(The interaction of self-interested buyers and sellers, with prices acting as incentives and signals to both groups.)*
- How are the basic economic questions (what, how, and for whom to produce) answered in a market economy? *(Consumers signal what they are willing and able to pay for goods and services, and producers who are able to make a profit at those prices determine the most efficient way to produce products, competing against other producers.)*
- How are households, businesses, and government linked together in a market economy? *(The circular flow model shows the connections in terms of both monetary flows and "real" flows of goods and services from these sectors to*

and from the product market, where goods and services are produced, and to and from the factor market, where productive resources or inputs are bought and sold.)

- What is the role of prices in a market economy? *(Prices act as important signals of how scarce a good or service is. That affects the behavior of both buyers and sellers, with buyers wanting to consume more at low prices, and sellers willing to produce and sell more at high prices. In competitive markets adjustments occur automatically, with prices falling to eliminate surpluses and rising to eliminate shortages.)*

ASSESSMENT

(Correct answers are in **bold**)

1. Markets determine what, how, and for whom to produce primarily through:
   a. laws passed by the legislature.
   b. centralized committee decisions.
   c. elected officials.
   d. **interactions of buyers and sellers.**

2. Which of the following represents a factor market interaction?
   a. A young mother buys a health club membership.
   b. A real estate agent sells a home in your neighborhood.
   c. **A local farmer hires students for crop harvesting.**
   d. A high school senior buys a class ring.

3. Which of the following represents a product market interaction?
   a. **A bride-to-be purchases postage stamps for wedding invitations.**
   b. A college student works in a computer lab.
   c. A local restaurant hires more waitstaff.
   d. A post office employs more staff in the mail sorting room during holidays.

4. If quantity demanded = 15 and quantity supplied = 8 when the price is $10, in this market there is currently:
   a. an equilibrium.
   b. a market clearing.
   c. **a shortage.**
   d. a surplus.

5. When a surplus of a good or service exists at a given price, we expect price to
   a. **fall.**
   b. rise.
   c. remain the same.
   d. We cannot tell what price might do.

EXTENSION ACTIVITIES

1. For higher ability students, use the supply and demand cards from Activity 4 as the basis for a graphing assignment: Construct the demand and supply curves, showing price on the vertical axis and quantity demanded/supplied on the horizontal. Verify that equilibrium occurs at a price of $9.

2. Reinforce student understanding of market forces with other National Council on Economic Education lessons. See www.e-connections.org/lesson7/Tlesson7.html for "Demand Shifters" activity, or www.e-connections.org/lesson11 for lesson entitled, "Lowell Workers and Producers Respond to Incentives."

Visual 1
The Magic of Markets

What did you have for breakfast this morning?

How did this type of food arrive in your house?

How did someone in the family know what and how much to buy for breakfast?

How did the store it was purchased from know that someone would buy it?

How does the local fast food restaurant know how many workers to schedule for each shift during the week?

What would happen if a change in consumer preferences and buying patterns significantly reduced the demand for a good or service?

What would happen if higher production costs significantly reduced the supply of a good or service?

Is a central authority needed to decide what, how, and for whom to buy and sell in competitive markets?

From *Focus: Institutions and Markets*, © National Council on Economic Education, New York, NY

Visual 2
What's for Lunch Tomorrow?

Menu 1: Veggie pizza

Menu 2: Cheeseburger

Menu 3: Chef salad

Menu 4: Chicken nuggets

Visual 3
In the Words of Adam Smith...

"But man has almost constant occasion for the help of his brethren, and it is in vain for him to expect it from their benevolence only. He will be more likely to prevail if he can interest their self-love in his favour, and show them that it is for their own advantage to do for him what he requires of them. Whoever offers to another a bargain of any kind, proposes to do this. Give me that which I want, and you shall have this which you want, is the meaning of every such offer; and it is in this manner that we obtain from one another the far greater part of those good offices which we stand in need of. It is not from the benevolence of the butcher, the brewer, or the baker, that we expect our dinner, but from their regard to their own interest. We address ourselves, not to their humanity, but to their self-love, and never talk to them of our own necessities but of their advantages."

Adam Smith, *An Inquiry into the Nature and Causes of the Wealth of Nations*, 1776, (Book I, Chapter II, passage 2)

From *Focus: Institutions and Markets*, © National Council on Economic Education, New York, NY

Visual 4
Circular Flow Diagram (Without Government Sector)

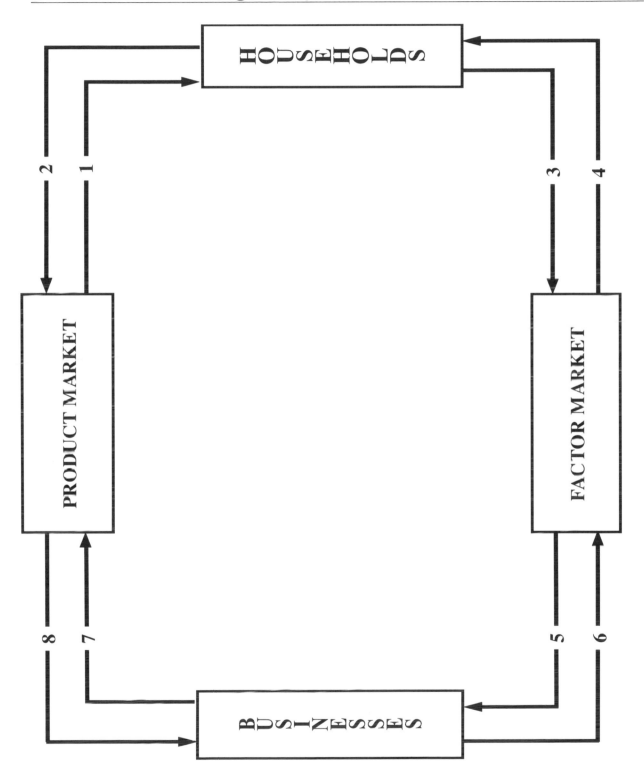

Visual 5
Circular Flow Diagram (With Government Sector)

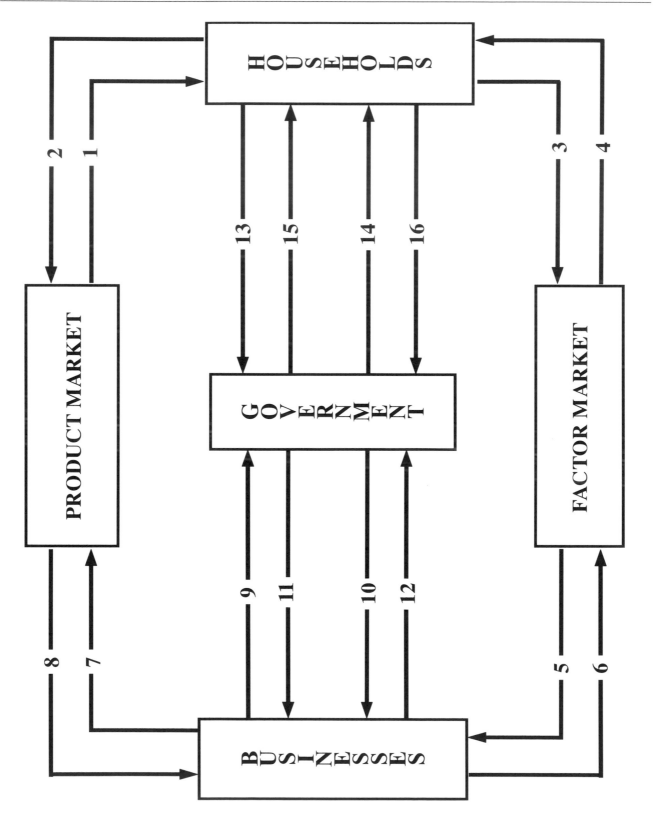

Visual 6
Discovering the Market Clearing Price

Round	Price	Unwilling Buyers	Unwilling Sellers	Exchange Pairs	Willing Unpaired Buyers	Willing Unpaired Sellers
1	$3	____	____	____	____	____
2	$5	____	____	____	____	____
3	$7	____	____	____	____	____
4	$15	____	____	____	____	____
5	$13	____	____	____	____	____
6	$11	____	____	____	____	____
7	$9	____	____	____	____	____

Activity 1
Menu Cards

VEGGIE PIZZA	VEGGIE PIZZA	VEGGIE PIZZA
VEGGIE PIZZA	CHEESEBURGER	CHEESEBURGER
CHEESEBURGER	CHEESEBURGER	CHEESEBURGER
CHEF SALAD	CHEF SALAD	CHEF SALAD
CHEF SALAD	CHEF SALAD	CHICKEN NUGGETS
CHICKEN NUGGETS	CHICKEN NUGGETS	CHICKEN NUGGETS

From *Focus: Institutions and Markets*, © National Council on Economic Education, New York, NY

Activity 2
Circular Flow Descriptions

1. Households receive and consume goods and services produced by businesses. Example: Jo buys CDs, haircut, pizza.
2. Households pay for the goods and services they purchase. Example: cash payment for cheeseburger, check written for college tuition.
3. Households offer labor and other factors to businesses in the factor market. Example: labor provided in factory, land provided to grow crops.
4. Households earn income as payment for labor and other factors used by business. Example: wages from job.
5. Businesses hire labor and other factors to produce goods and services. Example: summer jobs for college students.
6. Businesses pay the owners of the factors used in production. Example: payroll check issued to worker, or interest paid on a loan to build a new factory.
7. Businesses produce goods and services to sell in the product market. Example: Dell makes computers for consumers.
8. Businesses receive revenues from the sales of their goods and services. Example: restaurant tallies its receipts for meals served.

The following flows are used if the government sector is added to the model (Visual 5):

9. Businesses produce goods and service for purchase by government. Example: Boeing makes airplanes for the federal government.
10. Government pays businesses for goods and services purchased. Example: Department of Defense pays for paper bought from Office Max.
11. Government provides goods and services for business use. Example: roads and police protection.
12. Businesses pay taxes to federal, state, or local government. Example: property tax paid by an insurance company.
13. Households provide labor services to government. Example: switchboard operator at The White House.
14. Government pays its employees and military or makes transfer payments to low-income families. Example: paycheck to civil service worker, Social Security benefits paid to senior citizens.
15. Government provides goods and services that benefit households. Example: education, parks, justice system.
16. Households make tax payments to government. Example: income, sales, and property taxes.

Activity 3
Examples

Olivia chooses a beautiful sweater for her grandmother's Christmas present.

Henry paints houses as a summer job.

Jorge receives income from rental properties.

David pays for tickets to a rock concert.

General Motors produces SUVs for sale to consumers.

The Green Bay Packers receive money from season ticket sales.

Exsalonce Beauty Parlor hires another hairdresser.

Abs-of-Steel Fitness Center pays its personal trainers each Friday.

* Sona Corporation pays $5,000 in income taxes to the state of Wisconsin.

* Irene receives $400 each month from the government because she has low income.

* A Pentagon worker receives $60,000 per year for her work as a translator.

* A recent police academy grad applies for a job with the municipal police department.

* A homeowner's city government provides curbside garbage pickup.

* 3Squares Co. produces MREs (meals-ready-to-eat) for U.S. army troops.

Note: use the items marked with the * only if you are using Visual 5, which includes the government sector.

From *Focus: Institutions and Markets*, © National Council on Economic Education, New York, NY

Activity 4
Buyer Cards – (duplicate on white paper)

YOU ARE WILLING TO BUY THE GOOD IF THE PRICE IS $ 16 OR LESS	YOU ARE WILLING TO BUY THE GOOD IF THE PRICE IS $ 14 OR LESS
YOU ARE WILLING TO BUY THE GOOD IF THE PRICE IS $ 12 OR LESS	YOU ARE WILLING TO BUY THE GOOD IF THE PRICE IS $ 10 OR LESS
YOU ARE WILLING TO BUY THE GOOD IF THE PRICE IS $ 8 OR LESS	YOU ARE WILLING TO BUY THE GOOD IF THE PRICE IS $ 6 OR LESS
YOU ARE WILLING TO BUY THE GOOD IF THE PRICE IS $ 4 OR LESS	YOU ARE WILLING TO BUY THE GOOD IF THE PRICE IS $ 2 OR LESS

Activity 4 (continued)

Seller Cards – (duplicate on colored paper)

YOU ARE WILLING TO SELL THE GOOD IF THE PRICE IS $ 2 OR MORE	YOU ARE WILLING TO SELL THE GOOD IF THE PRICE IS $ 4 OR MORE
YOU ARE WILLING TO SELL THE GOOD IF THE PRICE IS $ 6 OR MORE	YOU ARE WILLING TO SELL THE GOOD IF THE PRICE IS $ 8 OR MORE
YOU ARE WILLING TO SELL THE GOOD IF THE PRICE IS $ 10 OR MORE	YOU ARE WILLING TO SELL THE GOOD IF THE PRICE IS $ 12 OR MORE
YOU ARE WILLING TO SELL THE GOOD IF THE PRICE IS $ 14 OR MORE	YOU ARE WILLING TO SELL THE GOOD IF THE PRICE IS $16 OR MORE

From *Focus: Institutions and Markets,* © National Council on Economic Education, New York, NY

LESSON TWO
PROPERTY RIGHTS AND CONTRACTS AS ECONOMIC INSTITUTIONS

LESSON DESCRIPTION

Students consider the importance of a system of defining, recording and protecting property rights in a market-based economy. Students differentiate between private and communal property, they consider various methods for recording property ownership, and they examine one institution – The United States Patent and Trademark Office – created to define and protect property rights. Finally, students examine a timely case involving questions of property rights – Napster vs. Metallica.

INTRODUCTION

As stressed in the introductory essay to this volume, clearly defined and enforced property rights are essential in a market economy. Without some guarantee that property rights are, in practice as well as theory, both exclusive and transferable, people and firms have little incentive to accumulate property to improve their own economic position, and by doing that make the economy as a whole grow wealthier over time. What business, for example, would take the risk of producing a new product if its new product design could be immediately used by its competitors?

Whenever businesses and individuals must use resources to protect their property from others (for example, the use of private police or security forces and alarm systems), those resources cannot be used in other productive ways. Keeping the costs of enforcing property rights reasonably low further supports the idea

that government should define and enforce property rights, and provide the legal and judicial institutions for doing so. The idea of property rights was clearly important to the drafters of the U.S. Constitution. They specifically referred to the need to protect intellectual property and to the U.S. Patent and Trademark Office, which is a federal agency that is almost exclusively devoted to recognizing and legally assigning intellectual property rights.

CONCEPTS

Private property
Communal property
Intellectual property
Market economy
Incentives
Legal foundations of a market economy
Contracts

CONTENT STANDARD

Institutions evolve in market economics to help individuals and groups accomplish their goals. Banks, labor unions, corporations, legal systems, and not-for-profit organizations are examples of important institutions. A different kind of institution, clearly defined and enforced property rights, is essential to a market economy.

BENCHMARK

Property rights, contracts, standards for weights and measures, and liability rules affect incentives for people to produce and exchange goods and services.

OBJECTIVES

Students will:

♦ Define private property and identify the major characteristics that differentiate private property from communal property.

♦ Briefly describe the benefits to individuals and society as a whole of clearly defined property rights, and contrast that with the costs of poorly defined property rights.

♦ Identify some of the major government agencies and institutions responsible for determining and enforcing property rights.

TIME REQUIRED

Two or three class periods

MATERIALS

- Visual 1: Thoughts on Private Property
- Visual 2: The Tragedy of the Buffalo
- Visual 3: Symbols of Ownership
- Activity 1: *Zimbabwe's Wildlife Ranches Help Save the Black Rhino*, one copy per student; 100 3" × 3" squares of black construction paper
- Activity 2: Recording Our Property Ownership, one copy per student
- Activity 3: Patents, Trademarks, and Copyrights…Oh My!!, one copy per student
- Activity 4: A Case of Trademark Piracy? Napster vs. Metallica, one copy per student
- masking tape

PROCEDURES

1. Display Visual 1 and have students compare and contrast the quotations. Discuss the following questions: How do Locke's and Adams' views on private property differ from those expressed in the Cuban Constitution? How does the U. S. Constitution reflect Locke's and Adams' ideas? What are some benefits to having only commonly held property (in the case of Cuba, by the government)? What are some drawbacks to commonly held property? (As students suggest benefits and drawbacks, record these on the board.)

2. Ask students if there might be some benefits in having individual families and companies be entirely responsible for protecting their own private property? What would be the major drawbacks to that arrangement? (As

students suggest advantages and disadvantages, record these on the board.) Explain that students will now participate in an activity that will help them distinguish between privately owned and communal property. Tell students that as they participate, they should think about the lists of drawbacks and benefits they have already listed on the board and be prepared to add to the lists.

3. Display Visual 2. After briefly discussing students' initial reaction to the plight of the American buffalo versus American cattle, ask students if they can think of other examples of animals that are being (or have been) hunted close to extinction. What, if anything, do these animals have in common with the American buffalo? (*The idea of private ownership of cattle vs. common or no ownership of such animals as buffalo during the 19th century, and whales and fish that live in the oceans today, should emerge in the discussion. Point out that private ownership of domesticated pets, such as cats and dogs, has also insured their survival, just as much as chickens, pigs, and other animals valued for commercial uses.*)

4. To develop these ideas further, inform students that they will have the chance to engage in a simulation of hunting for black rhino. Hunting here can mean catching the rhinos live to sell to zoos, not necessarily killing the rhinos for trophies or other uses. Take 100 3" × 3" squares of black construction paper and randomly scatter these around the room (with some flourish!). Tell students each of these squares represents one black rhino, and that you will conduct three one-minute hunting periods in which they can 'hunt' rhinos anywhere in the room. Announce that you will pay a different price for any rhinos that are hunted in each of the three rounds:

Round	Price per rhino
1	$ 500
2	$1,000
3	$1,500

Stress that once they pick up or even touch a rhino square, it must be turned in during that round, for whatever the price is in that round. In other words, they can not pick or scoop together rhinos in the first round, then hold them to turn in until the third round.

5. Conduct the three rounds of the simulation, collecting all of the black squares, and record earnings of students at the end of each round.

6. Announce that the class will now repeat the simulation, but with one key difference. Using masking tape or some other system, divide a large part of the room into squares approximately 3' × 3'. (HINT: If you have linoleum tile in your room, each tile is probably a 1' square.) Assign ownership of one square to each student, and announce that you will enforce that ownership by penalizing anyone who takes anything from somebody else's square. Distribute the black rhinos again, more or less randomly, but making sure that there are more rhinos in some students' property squares than others. Repeat the instructions from procedure 5 concerning the price you will pay for a rhino in each round – which will be the same table of prices used before. Also, remind students not to pick or scoop up the rhinos until the round in which they decide to sell them.

7. Debrief the simulation. Begin by asking: In the first part of the activity, before the floor was divided up into squares, why were most rhinos captured in the first (or first and second) rounds, even though the price per rhino went up in rounds two and three? (*Without well - defined and recognized property rights, students had no guarantee that any rhinos would be left after the first round. As a result, the rhinos disappeared very quickly.*) In the second version of the simulation, when students could only capture rhinos located on their own property, why were more rhinos left until the third round ? (*Because students owned the rhinos on their land, they had incentives to*

capture and sell their rhinos when it was most advantageous to them.)

8. Distribute copies of Activity 1, and give students time to read the newspaper article *"Zimbabwe's Wildlife Ranches Help Save the Black Rhino,"* which explains how private property rights are now helping to protect the black rhino in Africa.

9. Discuss Activity 2 and relate it to the simulation by reviewing how property rights create incentives to protect and preserve property. On the other hand, experience shows all too well that there is little incentive to protect communally held property. Discuss how these factors explain both the decrease in the buffalo herds in the 1880s and why cattle are not extinct today.

10. Explain to students that in order for private property to be clearly defined and well protected, societies must have some mechanism for recording the ownership of property, and a police force and judicial system. These institutions are very old. For example, historians have discovered records of land ownership dating back to 3000 B.C.E. and legal 'deeds' to property that date to the time of Hammurabi, approximately 1750 B.C.E.

11. Have students complete Activity 2. Discuss with students the range of records for 'proof of ownership' of their property. Do they have documentation for all the property they own? Discuss examples of family property. Is there a relationship between the value of some kinds of property (for example, a house or car) and the nature of the proof of ownership (for example, a deed or title)? Why is such proof of ownership necessary for a market to work well? What might happen if no proof of ownership of property could be established?

12. Display Visual 3. Ask students if they have seen these symbols before.
What do they symbolize? ® stands for registered, © stands for copyrighted and ™

stands for trademark. *(Students should know that these symbols appear on many of the products we buy.)* Discuss how these symbols are related to property rights. These symbols document ownership of **intellectual property.** This can include artwork, computer software, music, literature and brand names that are used to identify the particular producer of almost any kind of goods and services.

13. Stress that for property rights to have any real effect in the economy they must be enforced as well as clearly defined, and therefore many social institutions and government agencies have evolved to clearly define and effectively enforce property rights. The United States Patent and Trademark Office (USPTO) is one such institution, created under explicit provisions in the U.S. Constitution. The USPTO promotes industrial and technological progress in the United States and strengthens the national economy by administering laws relating to patents and trademarks; advising the Secretary of Commerce, the President of the United States, and other government agencies on patent, trademark, and copyright protection; and advising the Secretary of Commerce, the President of the United States, and other government agencies on the trade-related aspects of intellectual property. (NOTE: If your students have access to Internet, have them take a quick tour of the USPTO web site: http://www.uspto.gov/. The site also has a number of interesting games for students at http://www.uspto.gov/web/offices/ac/ahrpa/opa/kids/kidgames.html.)

Discuss with students the role of intellectual property rights in the global economy. For example, although no international patent office comparable to the USPTO exists, sections of the World Trade Organization's Agreement on Trade-Related Aspects of Intellectual Property Rights (TRIPS) requires the 144 member nations to recognize patent and trademark rights. However, not all nations of the world are WTO members and so problems can arise if non-member countries or some member countries

(e.g., countries of the former Soviet Union and other transition economies) do not recognize or actively enforce those rights.

14. Use Activity 3 to introduce students to the definitions of patents, copyrights, trademarks and service marks. Discuss several examples of each of these types of property right with students, and have them find more examples of each symbol on products they own or use during the rest of the school day and at home this evening. List these examples on the board or a transparency in the next class and use the list to discuss how important property rights of all kinds are to the overall economy. Have students complete the "Test Your Knowledge Quiz" from Activity 3.

Answers:
1. *False. Many sounds and smells are trademarked. For example, NBC's three-tone chime is trademarked.*
2. *True. This is a benefit from defining property rights, which is what patents do.*
3. *False. Owens-Corning has trademarked its "pink" insulation.*
4. *False. Only the symbol - ® - means that a trademark has been registered.*
5. *False. The USPTO does not offer patents on people.*
6. *True. This is exactly what a patent gives you.*
7. *False. Copyrights established legal ownership of intellectual property, and can be sold or transferred.*
8. *True. With permissions and negotiated fees, the holder of a patent can give or sell the production or publication rights to whomever he chooses, just as someone who owns a house, car, or land can transfer it to someone else.*
9. *False. A servicemark refers to a service (e.g., Roto-Rooter) as opposed to a good (e.g., The Whopper).*

15. Have students complete Activity 4. After reading the introductory text, have students complete the chart. Discuss their responses using the answers shown below. It is important to stress the nature of the differences in music formats and how these formats make it easier or more difficult to define property rights and protect against copyright violations.

16. Have students read or act out the fictitious debate between Shawn Fanning (creator of Napster) and Lars Ulrich (drummer for the band Metallica). Discuss the questions posed by the moderator, Fred Mediator, to the audience. You may wish to have students draft a letter to the editor or create an essay outlining their own position on this issue.

	Music Format		Explanation
	Traditional (Tapes, CDs)	Digital (MP3 files)	
Can Metallica own its music in this format?	YES	YES	The 'music' is owned by the band in both formats.
Does Metallica have exclusive control of its music in this format?	Most of the time	NO	Both CDs and MP3s can be illegally created and distributed, but it is much easier to illegally distribute MP3s over the Internet.
Can Metallica exchange the property right (i.e., sell it or give it away) to their music in this format?	YES	NO	A CD sale requires a transfer of payment from a buyer to the holder of copyright (or the holder's designee), MP3 file transfers are beyond the band's control.
Can Metallica's music be easily protected from illegal use or theft in this format?	Most of the time	NO	It is illegal to duplicate both CDs and MP3s for sale. But it is much harder to enforce the illegal sale or use of MP3s.

Ask students what is different about listening to a swapped MP3 file on their computer compared to listening to the same song on the radio or on MTV? Explain that copyright protection also exists for recordings played over the radio or cable systems. Royalties are paid to an artist each time a song is played. The quality of a copy from the radio or from cable TV has until recently, however, been substantially less than the recorded versions people bought. This shows again how some laws and regulations that worked well with old technologies do not work as well with new technologies.

CLOSURE

Review with students the importance of defining, recording, and protecting property rights. Ask students to work in pairs or groups of three to think about these questions: What would our society be like without property rights? How would your lives be different today? Why do individual markets and a market system require a system of property rights to function effectively?

ASSESSMENT

Have students discuss or write a short paper on the following quotation:

"Finally, after enduring a decade of economic disruption that followed the end of communism, Russia may have grasped the key to economic success. People in advanced capitalist nations already have found the key to success. They've taken it for granted for so long that they hardly know it exists, even though it touches them in numerous ways every day. It makes possible a modern economy that creates opportunity for millions of people to improve their lives.

The key is a coherent system of property laws."
--Editorial, *Columbus Dispatch*, July 23, 2001 (http://www.dispatch.com/news/editorials01/july01/776716.php)

Questions for discussion:

1. What is the "key" to economic success in Russia? Why might the writer believe this to be true? Why do you believe it to be true? Why do you think "people in advanced capitalist nations" have taken property rights for granted? Explain some ways in which well-defined and enforced property rights impact your life. Why do we take these for granted? How might your life (or the lives of students in Russia, for example) be different without well-defined property rights?

Visual 1
Thoughts on Private Property

"Property must be secured, or liberty cannot exist."
    --John Adams, 1790?

Government's main purpose "is the mutual preservation of the lives, liberties and estates, which I shall call by the general name property."
    --John Locke, 1690

"Congress shall have the power to...Promote the progress of science and useful arts by securing for limited times to authors and inventors the exclusive right to their respective writings and discoveries."
    --The Constitution of the United States of America (Article 1, Sec. 8, Clause 8)

...goods cannot be transmitted as property to common...people, except in exceptional cases in which the partial or total transmission of some economic objectives is destined to the end of development of the country and do[es] not affect the political, social and economic fundamentals of the state, [without] prior approval of the Council of Ministers or its Executive Committee.
    --Cuban Constitution (Article 15)*

* Source: http://www.cubapolidata.com/gpc/gpc_constitution_1992.html, Constitución de la República de Cuba (Reformas de 1992), Capítulo XV. Special thanks to Professors Mark Schug and Solomon Flores University of Wisconsin at Milwaukee, for providing the translated version,

Visual 2
The Tragedy of the Buffalo

Throughout history, human beings have used livestock for food, tools, and clothing. A modern example is the cow. Used for beef, leather, and other important goods, cows and cattle thrive on farms across the United States and the world.

Much as we depend on cows today, Native and European Americans depended on the buffalo for food, tools, and clothing. However, the buffalo were hunted to near extinction, as the chart below shows:

Year	Number of Buffalo
1870	14,000,000
1874	1,500,000
1878	525,000
1882	245,000
1886	5,000
1889	150

Why did hunters in the 1870s and 1880s nearly destroy a resource they depended on?

Source: F.G. Roe, *The North American Buffalo,* Toronto: University of Toronto Prss, 1951, p. 490.

VISUAL 3
Symbols of Ownership

                  TM

Where have you seen these symbols?
What do these symbols represent?
How are they different?
How are they related to property rights?

Famous Examples:

®	©	TM
Edison's light bulb	The movie *Star Wars*	The Whopper
TEFLON	TV series *Dragnet*	Cincinnati Bengals
John Deere's plough	*Hey Jude* by the Beatles	Hostess cupcakes
Philo Farnsworth's TV	James Barrie's *Peter Pan*	Domino sugar

Activity 1
Article: Zimbabwe's Wildlife Ranches Helps Save the Black Rhino[1]

By Staff Reporter – The Financial Gazette of West Lafayette

A report released by The Center for Private Conservation, a Washington-based wildlife research group, says the Zimbabwe system of wildlife management – based primarily on privatizing *common land resources – has made it one of the best wildlife nations in the world. The report indicates wildlife management in Zimbabwe's private animal conservancies were considered to have important wildlife management lessons for the rest of the world.*

The report also said that research, conducted by Kay Muir-Leresche and Dr. Robert Nelson, stressed that Zimbabwe was one of only a handful of countries in the world that had given more-or-less full control of the use of wildlife and wildlife preserves to private owners, leading to better wildlife management.

The researchers stated that even developed countries such as the United States, which have a strong history of free economies, still strictly regulated wildlife on both public and private land alike. This policy often results in poor management and the subsequent dwindling of animal populations. This is due to what economists refer to as the "tragedy of the commons." Property that is held in common, like grazing land or wilds herds of animals, is often mistreated or over-used because no real "owner" exists. Every person who has access to such a common resource will tend to overuse it because the consequences of such overuse do not transfer directly back to each user.

The Center's report indicates that, as a result of Zimbabwe's particular concept of wildlife ranching, the country had seen an increase in the population of several species once threatened with extinction.

It said other benefits of the scheme included the reduction of state subsidies to the beef industry and an increase in Zimbabwe's tourism industry.

"In Zimbabwe, a majority of many desirable species—including 94 percent of kudu, 63 percent of giraffe, 56 percent of cheetah and 53 percent of both sable and impala—are found on the commercial ranch properties," it said. The report concludes that "private conservancies such as the Bubiana and Chiredzi River conservancies have been introduced. In these areas the black rhino, well on its way to extinction in Africa, are coming back and poaching has been virtually eliminated."

The Center also praised Botswana, Namibia, South Africa and other countries that were taking wildlife ranching seriously.

---

[1] The content for this article was drawn from several online sources including:
"Wildlife Researchers Hail Zimbabwe," The Financial Gazette Online, accessed on October 14, 2002 at http://www.fingaz.co.zw/fingaz/2001/ Janruary/Janruary31/488.shtml; the BBC (http://www.bbc.co.uk); and a report by Michael De Alessi entitled "Private Conservation and Black Rhinos in Zimbabwe: The Savé Valley and Bubiana Conservancies" (available from http://www.openrepublic.org/policyanalyses/Environment/20000101_PRIVATE_CONSERVATION_AND_THE _BLACK_RHINO_IEA.htm)

Activity 2
Recording Our Property Ownership

Using the data retrieval chart below, first list property that you own. Remember that property can take on many forms: books, computers, CDs, cars, clothing, and houses are all examples of property. Once you have listed your property, indicate how you document your ownership of that property. For example, when you buy a CD from the music store, you are given a receipt that shows clearly what you bought and what you paid for it. This receipt documents your ownership and you are required to have it if you need to return the CD to the store.

Once you have listed your own property, take the sheet home and work with your family to list examples of property your family owns. How is ownership of this property documented?

My Property:	Ownership Documented By:
My Family's Property	Ownership Documented By:

Activity 3
Patents, Trademarks, and Copyrights...Oh My!!

A *patent* is given by the United States Patent and Trademark Office (USPTO) for a new and unique invention. The patent grants property rights to the inventor for 20 years from the date the application for the patent was filed in the United States. Inventors must pay a fee to register their patent with the USPTO and U.S. patent grants are valid in U.S., U.S. territories, and U.S. possessions. It is interesting to note that what the USPTO grants the inventor is not the right to make, use, offer for sale, sell or import, but the right to <u>exclude</u> others from making, using, offering for sale, selling or importing the invention.

The USPTO defines a *trademark* as a word, name, symbol or device that is used in trade with goods to indicate the source of the goods and to distinguish them from the goods of others. In other words, the trademark communicates to the potential consumer who made the product. A *servicemark* provides the same information as a trademark except that it identifies and distinguishes the source of a service rather than a good. Unlike patents, *trademark* and *servicemark* rights may be used to prevent others from using a confusingly similar mark, but not to prevent others from making the same goods or from selling the same goods or services under a clearly different *trademark* or *servicemark*.

Copyright is a form of protection provided to the authors of original works of authorship such as music, literature, artworks and other forms of intellectual work. *Copyrights* may be granted to both published and unpublished works. The 1976 Copyright Act generally gives the owner of copyright the exclusive right to reproduce the copyrighted work. That is, only the author, artist, or musician can legally re-print or perform the work. According to the USPTO, the copyright protects only the form of expression and not the subject matter of the writing. For example, a description of a machine could be copyrighted, but this it would not prevent others from writing a description of their own or from making and using the machine. Copyrights are registered by the Copyright Office of the Library of Congress.

Use the chart below to find examples of a patented, trademarked, and copyrighted items from around school or around your house.

Patented	Trademarked	Copyrighted

Activity 3 (continued)

Test Your Knowledge	Circle one
1. You must be able to see a trademark.	True / False
2. Patents provide incentives to invent, invest in, and disclose new technology worldwide.	True / False
3. A color may not be part of a trademark.	True / False
4. The use of ™ next to a brand name means that it has been registered as a trademark with the U.S. Patent and Trademark Office.	True / False
5. You can get a patent on your brother.	True / False
6. A patent gives you the right to exclude anyone else from making your product.	True / False
7. Intellectual property is imaginary and therefore cannot be owned or sold.	True / False
8. Someone can sell a product that has a patent, a trademark or a copyright on it.	True / False
9. A servicemark is the same as a trademark.	True / False

Activity 4
A Case of Trademark Piracy? Napster vs. Metallica

© 2001 Jimmy Margulies The Record (NJ)
Reprinted by Permission

© Tribune Media Services, Inc. All Rights Reserved.
Reprinted with permission.

Look carefully at the two cartoons above. What is the issue portrayed in both? Does this issue have anything to do with property rights? In 1999, 18-year-old Shawn Fanning developed software that allowed users to create and trade MP3 files (a digital music format) that contained popular music. Fanning made this software available via a website he called Napster. (NOTE: read more about Shawn Fanning and Napster at http://www.cnn.com/ALLPOLITICS/time/2000/10/02/napster.html) Millions of teenagers across the United States and around the world began to happily copy and share their favorite music. Unfortunately, the artists whose music was being copied and shared weren't quite so happy. In fact, many artists felt that they were becoming victims of computer piracy. Musicians felt their privately owned and copyrighted work was being stolen in a way not so different from shoplifting a CD from a local music store.

Was Napster encouraging piracy? Were violations of copyright law occurring? How did MP3 files (compared to CDs) allow this to occur? The heavy metal band Metallica brought these issues into the public spotlight because a large proportion of the MP3s Napster users were copying and sharing Metallica songs. In 2000, the band brought a lawsuit against Fanning and Napster claiming that Napster had "devised and distributed software whose sole purpose is to permit Napster to profit by abetting and encouraging piracy." Napster was also sued by the Recording Industry Association of America on behalf of a number of record labels for enabling piracy on an "unprecedented scale." The lawsuits eventually led to the removal of the first Napster web site, but similar services are still available. (Read more about the Metallica/Napster lawsuit at http://www.forbes.com/2000/04/14/mu4.html).

Recall that one key issue related to providing and protecting any private property right is whether or not that right can be clearly defined. The following chart asks you to compare the traditional musical formats of CDs and tapes with the new digital MP3 format and determine how property rights in one format might be more difficult to define and protect than in another.

Activity 4 (continued)

Questions	Music Format		Explanation
	Traditional (Tapes, CDs)	Digital (MP3 files)	
Can Metallica own its music in this format?			
Does Metallica have exclusive control of its music in this format?			
Can Metallica exchange the property right (i.e., sell it or give it away) to their music in this format?			
Can Metallica's music be easily protected from illegal use or theft in this format ?			

"Shawn Fanning Debates Metallica's Drummer Lars Ulrich"
(NOTE: This debate is based on quotes from both people and language from Metallica's lawsuit, but it is only a fictional account of a possible debate between the two major figures in the Napster lawsuit.)

Scene: An MTV studio in New York City. Lars Ulrich, the drummer for Metallica is seated on the left; Shawn Fanning, founder of Napster, on the right. In the middle is the moderator for today's debate, Fred Mediator.

Mediator: Good evening. Let me begin by asking Mr. Fanning, why did you start Napster in the first place?

Fanning: I'm glad I have the chance to set the record straight. It was frustrating surfing the Net for good music, with so many sites claiming to offer good music only leading to dead ends. I figured that if I could develop software that allowed kids to swap music directly, without going through some middleman server, great music would be busting out all over the Net! This is what the Internet was supposed to be about: it builds communities of listeners, it breaks down barriers, its scalable…

Ulrich: That's what I'm afraid of! It's going to 'scale' us right out the music business!!

Mediator: Mr. Ulrich, please wait until I ask you a question to respond. We need some level of decorum…in spite of our location at MTV. I take it you disagree with Mr. Fanning's motives?

Ulrich: Completely! These 'dead ends' he's referring to were really those sites that were legally entitled to sell our music, that we had given permission to sell and that were paying us our commission. We own our music because it's copyrighted and we have the final say over who has the right to sell it or give it away. Mr. Fanning has devised software whose sole purpose is to permit Napster to profit by encouraging piracy.

Mediator: How do you respond to these charges – brought in Metallica's lawsuit – that your software allows users to essentially steal copyrighted music?

Fanning: First, it is perfectly legal – under the Audio Home Recording Act of 1992 – to make personal copies of music for home use, if it's not done for profit. Second, from the beginning, we have stated that the program is not for illegal downloading. And we don't post pirated songs at our homepage. In fact, we have no MP3 files on our home server, no copyrighted music. We only help people share music they already have.

Activity 4 (continued)

Mediator: Mr. Ulrich, I assume you disagree here?

Ulrich: While Mr. Fanning claims that Napster is not guilty of copyright violations because of the Audio Home Recording Act, I say this is like claiming the driver of the getaway car in a bank holdup isn't guilty because he didn't hold the money! And 99% of the files that are shared using Napster are illegally pirated.

Mediator: Mr. Fanning, you believe that your site actually helps artists?

Fanning: I think struggling musicians benefit, yeah. If you're an indie band, you can't afford the press kits and marketing of these mega-bands – like Metallica – and so we provide a service. We can get bands noticed, more so than the traditional recording industry. Also, if established bands learn about Napster, and know how to work with us, there is value in that. Fans will still buy CDs. In fact, in 2000 – while Napster was supposedly breaking into the music industry's vault – CD sales went up over $500 million. How else can you explain it, except that fans get a taste of a band's music using Napster and then go out and buy the CDs.

Ulrich: I can't sit by anymore…this is ridiculous! He's stealing artists' intellectual property! This can only hurt music in the long run. Now I'm no money-grubbing capitalist – I'm from Sweden, after all – but why would I want to write a song and record it knowing that I'll never see a dime of the royalties? Where's the incentive to create new music…

Fanning: …the incentive is in the music itself! That's the problem with you sellout rock stars…you forget about the kid who got you those multi-million dollar record deals in the first place…this freedom is what the Internet is about, not the centrally planned, government-controlled thing it's become.

Mediator: Gentlemen, gentlemen…please calm down. Let's get back to our questions. Mr. Ulrich can you sum up your concerns for us please.

Ulrich: This case, our lawsuit, will define the role of copyrights and intellectual property. It's already defining new approaches to content on the Internet. This case is about the violation of copyrights – our copyrights – clear and simple.

Mediator: Mr. Fanning, can you sum up please.

Fanning: Napster has simply provided a service to other users, we have never stored copyrighted material and we discourage illegal downloads. This case is about user access to information and how far the government can go in limiting that.

Mediator: As we conclude this debate, I ask you, the viewer, to decide: Who is right? What are the consequences? Why are copyrights (and patents) so closely guarded? What benefits are there to a strong system of intellectual property rights? Costs?

LESSON THREE
BUSINESS
ORGANIZATIONS

LESSON DESCRIPTION

Students first look at a list of business names and discuss what the various abbreviations that are often used as part of businesses' names mean. In a reading, students learn about three types of business organizations – sole proprietorships, partnerships, and corporations. They compare the advantages and disadvantages of each type of business organization, including problems that arise when the objectives of a firm's owners' (principals) differ from the objectives of the firm's managers (agents) and other employees.

INTRODUCTION

Different legal forms of business organizations – proprietorships, partnerships, and corporations – are key economic institutions in a market economy. They establish the legal rules and methods used to produce all of the goods and services that are sold to consumers in private markets. Corporations allow people to limit the economic risks they face in forming a business and make it easier to obtain financial capital when large investments in factories and equipment are necessary to take advantage of economies of scale. These advantages have contributed to the growth and development of many large businesses in market economies, and to the overall level of production and income in those economies.

CONCEPTS

Corporations
Partnerships
Sole proprietorships

Limited liability
Principal-agent problems
Economic institutions
Economies of scale

CONTENT STANDARD

Institutions evolve in market economies to help individuals and groups accomplish their goals. Banks, labor unions, corporations, legal systems, and not-for-profit organizations are examples of important institutions. A different kind of institution, clearly defined and well-enforced property rights, is essential to a market economy.

BENCHMARK

Incorporation allows firms to accumulate sufficient financial capital to make large-scale investments and achieve economies of scale. Incorporation also reduces the risk to investors by limiting stockholders' liability to the value of their shares of ownership in the corporation.

OBJECTIVES

Students will:

♦ Define corporations, partnerships, and sole proprietorships.

♦ Compare the advantages and disadvantages of organizing a business as a corporation, partnership, or sole proprietorship.

♦ Explain and give examples of the principal-agent problem.

♦ Explain limited liability.

♦ Give examples of laws and regulations that affect how corporations and other forms of businesses are formed and operate.

TIME REQUIRED

One to two class periods

MATERIALS

- Access to reference books or Internet
- Visual 1: Names of Businesses
- Visual 2: Principal-Agent Model
- Activity 1: The Ant and the Grasshopper's Big Adventure, one copy per student
- Activity 2: Grasshopper and Ant Debate, one copy per student
- Activity 3: Business Organizations: Advantages/Disadvantages, one copy per student
- Activity 4: Data on Businesses, Sales and Profit, one copy for each pair of students

PROCEDURES

1. Display a transparency of Visual 1. Explain that each listing on the transparency is the name of a business. Discuss the following:

   A. How could we categorize or sort these businesses into groups? (*Answers will vary, but might include by type of product produced, by alphabetical order, level of sales or profits, number of employees, etc.*)

   B. Some of the businesses have abbreviations following their name, and some include words like "Associates". What do these abbreviations and words mean? (*Answers will vary.*)

2. Explain that these abbreviations and words refer to how the business is legally organized to operate. Divide students into groups. Allow time for groups to work with reference materials and/or Internet to determine what each of the various abbreviations on the list of company names mean.

3. When students have completed work, have them identify what each abbreviation means. (*Ltd.or LTD refers to limited liability, Co. is company, Corp. is corporation, Inc. is incorporated, PC is professional corporation, LLC is limited liability company, SA is anonymous society, p.l.c. refers to publicly limited company*)

4. Explain that many of these abbreviations, such as SA, LTD, LLC, PC, reflect the idea that incorporation means, literally, recognition as a legal body separate from the owners. For example, SA – anonymous society – implies that the owners are anonymous and separate from the identity of the corporation, which has the legal right to enter into contracts as a separate entity. Ltd. refers to **limited liability**. This abbreviation also emphasizes the legal separation of owners and the corporation.

5. Point out that many of the businesses listed did not have abbreviations as part of their names, but nevertheless they must legally operate as a particular kind of business.

6. Refer students to the transparency and tell them that their next task will be to learn more about the three major types of businesses, corporations, partnerships, and sole proprietorships.

7. Distribute a copy of Activity 1 to each student. Tell students to read Part I of the story.

8. When students have completed Part I of the reading, distribute a copy of Activity 2.

9. Divide the class into groups representing Ant and Grasshopper. Allow time for students to debate/discuss the best options for Grasshopper and Ant. When students have decided, have them continue reading Part II of Activity 1.

10. When students finish reading Part II of Activity 1, distribute a copy or Activity 3 and tell them to complete the first two rows of the activity.

11. Have students read Part III of the story. Tell them to complete the last two rows of Activity 3. Discuss the following:

A. Initially the grasshopper was operating a **sole proprietorship**. A sole proprietorship is a business operated by an individual or a married couple, without legal documents issued by a state government recognizing the company as a corporation or partnership. Many businesses are operated this way.

B. Based on the experience of the grasshopper, what are some advantages of organizing a business as a sole proprietorship? (*get to keep the profit from the business, could operate as he wanted, easy to open*)

C. Based on the experience of the grasshopper what are some disadvantages of organizing a business as a sole proprietorship? (*limited access to financial capital, unlimited liability, little free time*)

D. When the ant and the grasshopper became partners, the business organization changed to a partnership. A general **partnership** is a business operated by two or more people. The ant and the grasshopper met with an attorney to draw up a partnership document. What types of things did the document specify? (*how the business would operate, how the business would be managed, how profit or loss would be distributed between the two partners, and who had*

authority to conduct business on behalf of the business)
Note: Limited partners are sometimes referred to as silent partners. Limited partners are not involved in the day-to-day operations of a business. If a limited partner becomes involved in the day-to-day operations of the business, the partner loses his or her status as a limited partner, along with any legal benefits that come with that status. For example, in some states liability for limited partners is limited to the amount that the partner has invested or agreed to invest in the partnership. If the partner takes an active role in the business, he or she loses this status and the protection of limited liability.

E. Based on the experiences of the ant and the grasshopper, what are some advantages of organizing a business as a partnership? (*partners can specialize, more than one person with access to financial capital, possibility of more time off*)

F. Based on the experiences of the ant and the grasshopper, what are some disadvantages of organizing a business as a partnership? (*unlimited liability, must share profits, hard to transfer ownership, decision-making/ management decisions must often be shared*)

G. Later, the ant and the grasshopper felt they had to change the business organization in order to continue growing. They decided to form a corporation. A **corporation** is a legal entity wholly separate from the shareholders who own it. Most large businesses in the United States operate as C-corporations. These are usually large, publicly held companies, but they also include small and even single-owner companies. C-corporations may have more than one class of stock, such as preferred stock and common stock.

H. Businesses may also organize as S-corporations. S-corporations are different from C-corporations because the profits and losses of an S-corporation are not taxed at the corporate level. Instead, earnings are reported on the owner's personal tax returns in much the same way as sole proprietorships and partnerships. S-corporations are limited to one class of stock and shareholders are limited in number and by U.S. residency.

I. What are some advantages of organizing a business as a C-corporation? (*limited liability, easier to raise financial capital and to transfer ownership than for proprietorships and partnerships – the corporation can even continue to operate long after the original owners are dead*)

J. What are some disadvantages of organizing a business as a C-corporation? (*more forms and regulations than with proprietorships and partnerships; corporate tax rates are often higher than personal tax rates for owners of partnerships and proprietorships, and double taxation in that corporations pay taxes on profits, and owners also pay taxes on any dividends that are paid to shareholders out of after-tax profits*)

K. What are some advantages of organizing a business as an S-corporation? (*limited liability,*

easier to raise financial capital and to transfer ownership than for proprietorships and partnerships, no corporate taxes)

L. What are some disadvantages of organizing a business as an S-corporation? (*more regulations and forms than for proprietorships and partnerships*)

12. Explain that all of the different forms of business organizations – proprietorships, partnerships, and corporations – represent an important kind of economic institution in market economies. An **economic institution** is an established custom or practice or an organization in the economy. Economic institutions evolve in market economies to help individuals and groups accomplish their goals.

13. Explain that corporations are institutions that allow people to organize large-scale businesses more easily by making it easier to obtain financial capital and take advantage of economies of scale. **Economies of scale** occur when the long-run average total cost of producing goods and services declines as the output level of a firm increases.

14. Explain that corporations also reduce the risk to investors by limiting stockholders' liability to the value of their shares of stock in the corporation. These advantages have contributed to the growth and development of many large businesses in market economies, and to the overall level of production and income in those economies.

15. Tell students that after careful consideration, the ant and the grasshopper decided to form a C-corporation. They found investors interested in owning stock in the corporation, but they also discovered many rules and regulations that they had to follow.

Sometimes those rules and regulations made Ant and Grasshopper fondly recall the "good old days" when running their business was a lot simpler. Discuss the following:

A. Stockholders are the legal owners of a corporation. The stockholders elect a board of directors. The board of directors is supposed to watch over the management of the corporation and look out for the stockholders' interests.

B. The CEO and other managers of a corporation make the day-to-day decisions about hiring workers or buying equipment. Top management usually makes major strategic decisions about expansion or downsizing the firm, or changing the type or mix of products it produces, in close consultation with the board of directors.

C. As officers of the corporation Ant and Grasshopper had to file articles of incorporation and adopt by-laws. They had to observe corporate formalities such as holding regular board of directors and stockholders meetings, including an annual election of officers.

D. Corporate officers are responsible for regularly filing various kinds of forms with local, state, and federal government agencies, including taxes and reports on other kinds of activities. All of these reports and meetings take considerable time and may require the services of an attorney, accountants, and other business consultants. If the corporate officers don't comply with all reporting requirements, the corporation could lose its status as a corporation.

E. Ant and Grasshopper had to adhere to local business regulations and requirements, such as acquiring appropriate permits and licenses. Of course, they had to do some of this as partners and Grasshopper had to do some of it as a sole proprietor, too.

16. Explain that Ant and Grasshopper expanded slowly. Over five years, they added four additional locations. As the corporation grew, Ant and Grasshopper encountered more new challenges. They were owners and managers of the corporation; however, they employed managers at each store. Ant and Grasshopper weren't certain that all of the managers kept the interests of the owners in mind when making decisions. Sometimes they let employees go home early when business was slow, or skip sweeping and cleaning up the store, to be more popular with the employees they supervised. They often bought new computers and desks and furniture for their offices. In short, it wasn't clear whether managers were interested in maximizing profits so that owners' stocks appreciated or the owners received large dividends. Sometimes it appeared that the managers were making decisions to protect their own interests.

17. Point out that these are difficult problems to consider. Explain that when economists study problems such as these, they usually use a principal-agent model.

18. Display a transparency of Visual 2 and discuss the following.

A. In the principal-agent model, managers are viewed as agents for the owners. **Agents** are individuals who act on behalf of others. The owners are viewed as principals. **Principals** are the parties on whose behalf agents are acting. Sometimes agents are even called agents, for example when somebody represents actors, singers, or other entertainers. But in many cases people represent others directly or indirectly, even though they are not called agents. For example, union members elect shop stewards and bargaining committees to represent their interests, and politicians are elected or appointed to represent their constituents. All employees of a business can be considered agents of the firms' owners, but especially top managers who make key decisions about investments and competitive strategies.

B. Store managers and other employees at *StarHops* are expected to represent the interests of the owners of *StarHops*.

C. Problems often arise when the objectives of the principal and the agent are different. It is important that managers (agents) have incentives to make decisions that are in the best interest of the owners (principals).

D. One method that firms use to provide these incentives is profit sharing. This gives the managers a stake (not direct ownership, unless it is a stock option) in the performance of the firm, and therefore stronger incentives to make decisions that are in the best interest of the owners. Firms might also tie manager bonuses to the company's level of profits.

19. Explain that Ant and Grasshopper, along with the board of directors, were considering ways in which to provide incentives for managers to act in the best interest of the owners of *StarHops*.

20. Ask students which type of business organization they think is most prevalent in the United States, which type accounts for the greatest level of sales, the greatest level of employment, and the greatest overall level of profits. (*Answers will vary.*)

21. Divide students into pairs. Distribute a copy of Activity 4 to each pair of students. Explain that one set of data shows the total number of businesses in the U.S. and the number that are organized as sole proprietorships, partnerships, corporations, and employment levels. The other set of data shows the total sales revenue and profits generated by sole proprietorships, partnerships, and corporations.

22. Discuss the following:

A. Which type of business organization represents the greatest number of firms in the U. S.? (*sole proprietorship*)

B. Which type of business organizations employs the greatest number of people? (*C-corporation*)

C. Which type of business organization has the greatest receipts? (*C-corporation*)

D. What is the average level of profits for each type of firm? (*sole proprietorships–$187 billion/ 17,176,000 = $10,887.28; partnerships–$168 billion/1,759,000 = $95,508.81; corporations– $915billion/4,710,000 = $194,267.51*)

E. What is the average level of employment for each type of firm? (*sole proprietorships–5,699/1467 = 3.9; partnerships–3,918/341 = 11.5; S-corporations–21,446/1,517 = 14.1; C-corporations 70,982/1870 = 38.0*)

F. In which type of firm would you prefer to work? (*Answers will vary. Students might prefer to work for a sole proprietor or a partnership because these organizations might be smaller with fewer layers of management. Students might prefer to work for a corporation because there's greater opportunity for advancement or perhaps better benefits.*) Which type of firm would you prefer to own or manage? (*Students might prefer to own sole proprietorships or partnerships because they have more control. On the other hand, they may prefer corporations because there is liability protection.*)

G. Would a large manufacturing firm more likely be a corporation or a proprietorship? A law firm? A small restaurant? Why? (*The advantages and disadvantages of some types of business are more important in some types of businesses than others. For example, huge capital investments make corporations the dominant form of business in manufacturing; but running a business with less regulation and the way the owners want to run it, while avoiding principal-agent problems, is more important in many small restaurants.*)

CLOSURE

Review the important points of the lesson by asking the following questions.

1. What is a sole proprietorship? (*a business operated by an individual or a married couple that has not been legally registered or recognized as a corporation or partnership*)

2. What is a partnership? (*a business operated by two or more people that has not been legally registered or recognized as a corporation*)

3. What is a corporation? (*A corporation is a business recognized by state government as a legal entity, separate from the shareholders who own it.*)

4. What are some advantages of operating as a sole proprietorship? (*A sole proprietor gets to keep all the profit earned from the business, can operate the business as he or she wants to. Sole proprietorships are relatively easy to open.*)

5. What are some disadvantages of operating as a sole proprietorship? (*A sole proprietor must personally raise all financial capital for the business. Sole proprietors incur all losses. Sole proprietors have unlimited liability.*)

6. What are some advantages of operating as a partnership? (*Partners can specialize, access more financial capital, and have the possibility of more time off.*)

7. What are some disadvantages of operating as a partnership? (*Each partner may be fully liable for any debts of the business, but must share profits and decision-making; hard to transfer ownership.*)

8. What are some advantages of operating as a corporation? (*limited liability, greater ability to specialize and divide management and labor tasks, easier to raise financial capital and transfer ownership*)

9. What are some disadvantages of operating as a corporation? (*more rules and regulations, more paper work, corporations pay corporate income tax rates on earnings, owners also pay tax on dividends*)

10. What is limited liability? (*Owners of a corporation are only liable for the amount they have invested in shares of stock for the corporation.*)

11. What are economies of scale? (*situations in which long-run average total cost declines as the output of a firm increases*)

12. What is an agent? (*An agent is an individual who acts on behalf of others.*)

13. In a corporation, who are agents? (*managers and employees*)

14. What is a principal? (*A party on whose behalf an agent is acting.*)

15. In a corporation, who is a principal? (*an owner/stockholder*)

16. What is the principal-agent model? (*A model that describes the interaction between two individuals in a contractual relationship where the objectives of the two individuals may differ.*)

17. What are some rules and regulations that affect small corporations? (*C-corporations – officers of the corporation must file articles of incorporation and adopt by-laws. They must hold regular board of directors and stockholders meetings, including an election of officers. Corporate officers must file various forms concerning taxes and the firm's business activities. They must observe federal, state, and local business regulations and requirements, such as acquiring all appropriate permits and licenses. S-corporations – must follow rules regarding citizenship/residency of owners and the maximum number of owners. They must complete and file articles of incorporation and observe tax regulations.*)

ASSESSMENT

1. Tell students that they will play the role of business consultant. In this role, they have been hired to advise a partnership on the advantages and disadvantages of incorporating. They must write a letter to their client outlining these benefits and costs.

2. Have students read the following scenario and answer the questions.

Andrew owns an ice cream shop. He hires Lisa to work at the shop. Lisa receives an hourly wage. Andrew isn't always around to supervise Lisa, but he expects Lisa to put in a full day's work, be personable with customers, and minimize waste of ice cream, cones and so forth. In other words, he wants Lisa to do everything that she can to maximize the profit the ice cream store earns. Lisa is married and has three kids. She has a lot on her mind. Sometimes she closes a little early to get home and help her kids with homework, get dinner on the table and so forth. She isn't always as friendly as she could be, but she does enough to earn her wages and keep her job.

   a. Who is the principal in this situation?

   b. Who is the agent in this situation?

   c. What is the conflict between the goals of the principal and the agent?

   d. Is their anything Andrew could do that might alleviate the problem?

3. Have students research the rules and regulations that determine the environment for new business development in their local communities. They should answer questions about licenses, fees, taxation, and other regulations, and decide whether these rules and regulations serve to inhibit or promote new business development.

EXTENSION

1. Teach Lesson 3, "What is a Stock? Or Who Owns McDonalds?" from *Learning from the Market: Integrating the Stock Market Game™ across the Curriculum*, National Council on Economic Education, New York, NY, 1997.

2. Have students work in teams to interview a sole proprietor, members of a partnership, and someone from a corporation in their community. Students should ask interviewees to identify advantages and disadvantages they note for their type of business organization, to identify the main types of rules and regulations that affect the business (local, state, and federal), and to explain how these rules and regulations inhibit or promote their ability to succeed and expand in the community.

3. Have students locate data for different types of businesses (corporations, partnerships and proprietorships), including the number of each type of business and total sales, profits, and employment levels for their city, county, or state. Have them compare this data to the national data presented in the lesson.

Visual 1
Names of Businesses

Schnurbusch & Assoc., LLC

Brandvein & Co. PC

Cummings Oberkfell & Ristau

Adjusters, Inc.

Superior Heating and Cooling

Rhymes Corporation

Beckmann Brothers

Chiodini Associates

Dawdy & Associates, Inc.

Kodner Watkins Muchnick & Dunne LLC

Bridal Inspirations, Ltd.

Earl Scheib Paint & Body

Miller Plumbing

Mesa Cycles

McDonald's Corporation

Daimler Chrysler Corporation

Baco Itaú, S.A.

Odebrecht of America, Inc.

TimAir Limited

Kongsberg Automotive

B. P. p.l.c.

Repsol YPF

Ballast Nedam Corporate

Goldman Sachs Group

Abdul Latif Jameel Group

Galmiche and Sons Heating and Cooling

Toyota Motor Corporation

Boeing Corporation

France Télécom

AOL Time Warner

Visual 2
Principal-Agent Model

The **principal-agent model** describes the interaction between two individuals in a contractual relationship where the objectives of the two individuals may differ. The principal wants some action on the part of the agent, who has been hired to carry out this action.

Agents are individuals who act on behalf of others.

Principals are the parties on whose behalf agents are acting.

When agents and principals have different goals, it is often necessary or helpful to provide incentives that encourage agents to act in the best interests of principals.

Activity 1
The Ant and the Grasshopper's Big Adventure

Part I

When you were a child, you probably read a fable about an ant and a grasshopper. At that time in their lives, Ant was a very responsible saver. She was always putting something away for the future. Grasshopper didn't have the discipline to save. He seemed to spend everything as soon as he got it. Of course, you probably haven't heard much about what happened to Grasshopper and Ant when they grew up.

Ant and Grasshopper both went on to college. Ant earned a degree in accounting with a minor in computer science. She landed a terrific job. Grasshopper earned a business degree. He read about a red hen that opened a baking business. This gave him a great idea for *StarHops*, a coffee shop and bakery. He borrowed from his family and was able to secure a small loan from a local bank to start the business. He opened his shop with little difficulty.

His business was really successful, and he was enjoying himself. He was earning a profit each year and he was free to operate as he chose (as long as he didn't break any laws). He thought he could be even more successful by expanding into neighboring communities. However, he just didn't have the financial capital he needed to buy or rent other locations and equipment, and he couldn't get additional loans from the bank. Liability was a big issue, too. As the owner of the business, he was personally responsible for all obligations, debts, and other liabilities the business incurred. If the business failed, he'd have a lot of problems. He also knew it would be very difficult to manage more than one location. He was already working 60 to 70 hours per week, and was often at his shop from 5:00 a.m. to 6:00 p.m. He really hadn't had a day off for three years!

Grasshopper began to think it might be a good idea to take on a partner. He knew that he could show how successful his shop was, and he thought he could demonstrate how successful another location would be. He even had a partner in mind. He put together a business plan for the expansion and called his old friend Ant.

Ant and Grasshopper met to discuss the possibilities. Grasshopper knew that Ant's computer and accounting skills would really be valuable for the business. Both Ant and Grasshopper agreed that with two of them they could specialize in various tasks, they could share time at the two locations, and they could both earn a living from the business. Both were concerned about problems that might arise. For example, Ant remembered Grasshopper in his younger days, so Ant was very concerned that Grasshopper wouldn't do his share of the work. On the other hand, Ant knew that Grasshopper had been operating a successful business for three years. Grasshopper was concerned about making decisions for the business. He knew that Ant could be pretty pushy sometimes. That might make it difficult to make decisions. On the other hand, Ant had a lot of savings that she was willing to invest to expand the business.

Grasshopper and Ant went to see an attorney, Ms. Centi, to learn more about partnerships. She explained that Ant and Grasshopper would be general partners. This meant that each partner could conduct business on behalf of the partnership and that both could participate in the day-to-day operations of the business. Ant and Grasshopper had some trouble agreeing about profit sharing.

Activity 1 (continued)

Grasshopper had started the business and wasn't sure he wanted to share profits equally with Ant. Ant wasn't willing to invest her hard-earned savings if she didn't receive a fair share of the profit. Ms. Centi explained that before the contract could be written, Ant and Grasshopper would have to negotiate a decision about whether Ant would be a partner, how much money Ant would put into the business, and what share of the profits Ant would receive if she became a partner.

Part II

After much discussion Grasshopper and Ant decided that Ant would be a partner. She would invest a large portion of her savings into the business. In return, Ant would receive 40% of the business. Ms. Centi explained that this would be included in the contract. Ant and Grasshopper also asked the attorney about liability and taxes, and what would happen if either one of them left the business. Ms. Centi explained that each partner was fully liable for all obligations and debts incurred by the business even when the liabilities were incurred by the actions and decisions of the other partner. She also explained that profits from the partnership would be taxed only once, and that profits or losses from the partnership would be reported on the partners' individual tax returns and taxed at each individual partner's rate. Ms. Centi pointed out that if either Ant or Grasshopper left the partnership or died, the business would have to be reformed and registered with the government, listing all existing partners. She pointed out that the rights and assets given each partner in the contract could not be transferred to anyone else without the consent of the other partner – this would make it harder for Ant or Grasshopper to sell or transfer ownership of the business.

Grasshopper used the information Ms. Centi provided to compare the advantages and disadvantages of sole proprietorship and partnership. Ant reflected on the information Ms. Centi provided in order to decide whether she wanted to become Grasshopper's partner.

Part III

Even though they had some concerns about working together, Ant and Grasshopper both thought it was a good idea. They went back to see Ms. Centi who drew up the partnership contract for them. Grasshopper and Ant were relieved to have everything spelled out carefully.

Wow! What a success the partnership was. Ant worked just as hard as Grasshopper. They were able to share ideas and specialize, too. Ant handled the accounting tasks, inventory, and so forth. Grasshopper handled personnel and customer relations. Often Grasshopper provided entertainment by fiddling familiar tunes at each location one evening a month. Every once in a while each of them was able to enjoy a day off! Occasionally, they had disagreements, but they were able to work things out and the business thrived.

Soon other ants and grasshoppers were interested in being a part of the *StarHops* phenomenon. Ants and grasshoppers in neighboring communities wanted a *StarHops* shop located near them. Grasshopper and Ant were considering expanding the business even more. After all, there were other people interested in the business, but Ant and Grasshopper weren't sure that adding partners was the best thing to do.

Activity 1 (continued)

Ant decided to investigate some other options for organizing their business. She used her computer skills to search online. She discovered that another option open to them was forming a corporation. She learned that they could form a C-corporation or an S-corporation. First, she decided to focus her research on C-corporations. She found that one major advantage to forming a C-corporation is that liability is limited to the loss of a shareholder's investment. With a C-corporation financial capital of others can be brought to the business through the sale of stock, and stock makes it easy to transfer ownership because stock is easy to transfer or sell from one person to another. Ant also learned that tax payments for her and Grasshopper would change if they formed a corporation. Owners of C-corporations do not report their share of corporate profits on their personal tax returns. The corporation pays corporate taxes on earnings. Owners pay taxes on profits paid out to them in the form of bonuses and dividends. Of course, Ant and Grasshopper would have a lot more forms to fill out, and they would have to pay annual filing fees in the states where they opened *StarHops*. There were also many reporting regulations that had to be met. The idea of forming a C-corporation was sounding more and more complicated.

Ant decided to take a closer look at the S-corporation. She learned that with an S-corporation, liability is also limited to the loss of a shareholder's investment. As with a C-corporation, it is easier for S-corporations to raise capital because stock can be sold to investors, and transfer of ownership is easily done through the sale of stock. She discovered that with an S-corporation, income is reported on shareholders' personal tax returns. The S-corporation itself does not pay any income tax. This eliminates the double taxation that can exist with a C-corporation. Of course there were still fees for incorporating and many reporting regulations. Ant also learned that not every business could qualify as an S-corporation. Only those businesses that are domestic, have only one class of stock, have no more than 75 shareholders, and operate on a calendar tax year can incorporate as S-corporations. Also, all shareholders in an S-corporation must be citizens or residents of the United States.

Ant put together a chart listing the advantages and disadvantages of the S-corporation and the C-corporation and went to meet with Grasshopper.

Activity 2
Grasshopper and Ant Debate

Grasshopper and Ant are considering whether to become partners in the *StarHops* business. If you were Grasshopper, would you make Ant a partner? What share of the profits from the business would you be willing to give Ant?

If you were Ant, would you want to put your savings into Grasshopper's business? What share of the profits would you want?

Consider the following.

- Grasshopper has operated the business successfully for several years and has kept all of the profit earned from the business.

- Grasshopper could hire Ant as an employee and pay Ant a salary higher than what she currently earns.

- Grasshopper could hire Ant at a somewhat lower salary and offer Ant profit sharing. This means that if the business is successful, Ant would receive a bonus or additional payment based on the level of success.

- Grasshopper could make Ant a partner if Ant agrees to buy into the business with some of her savings. But Grasshopper probably wouldn't want to give Ant an equal share in the business. Maybe he would offer her a 30% partnership in the business.

- Ant already has a job and is successful. She may not be willing to leave her rather secure position to work for Grasshopper unless she has a strong incentive to do so.

- Ant will only put her savings into the *StarHops* business if she thinks that the return she will receive is greater than what she currently earns on the financial investments she has.

What type of agreement should Grasshopper and Ant have?

Activity 3
Business Organizations: Advantages/Disadvantages

Type of Business Organization	Advantages	Disadvantages
A sole proprietorship is		
A partnership is		
A C-corporation is		
An S-corporation is		

From *Focus: Institutions and Markets*, © National Council on Economic Education, New York, NY

Activity 4
Businesses, Sales and Profits

Employer and Nonemployer Firms by Legal Form of Organization, 1997

Legal Form of Organization	Employers Number of Firms (thousands)	Employees (thousands)	Nonemployers
All types of firms	5,295	103,360	15,527
C-Corporations	1,870	70,982	520
S-Corporations	1,517	21,446	462
Partnerships	341	3,918	885
Individual Proprietorships	1,467	5,699	13,655
Other, including cooperatives, estates, receiverships, and businesses classified as unknown legal forms of organization.	99	1,315	3

Source: U.S. Bureau of the Census, 1997, *Economic Census*, Company Summary.

Number of Returns, Receipts, and Net Income by Type of Business, 1997

Item	Number of Returns (1000)			Business Receipts (billions of dollars)			Net Income (billions of dollars)		
	Nonfarm propri-etorships	Partner-ships	Corpora-tions	Nonfarm propri-etorships	Partner-ships	Corpora-tions	Nonfarm propri-etorships	Partner-ships	Corpora-tions
1997	17,176	1,759	4,710	870	1,297	15,890	187	168	915

Source: U.S. Census Bureau, *Statistical Abstract of the United States*, 2000, Table No. 855.

LESSON FOUR
FINANCIAL SYSTEMS

LESSON DESCRIPTION

Students participate in a brief simulation to demonstrate the important role financial intermediaries play in promoting investment and economic growth in market economies. Through direct instruction, students learn some specialized terms related to financial markets. Then students participate in an activity to help them identify other financial institutions in a market economy.

INTRODUCTION

In a market economy, one important role that financial institutions play is to channel savings into investments. Individual savers and investors have strong incentives to make good and careful decisions. Savers are setting money aside to protect themselves against "rainy days" – including the risks of unemployment, illness, or even death, and perhaps several decades of retirement when their incomes may be lower than while they are working. They also save to purchase expensive, "big ticket" items such as cars, homes, vacations, and education. Borrowers, on the other hand, must pay interest. Most of the interest they pay is used to make the interest payments to the savers and other depositors who actually provide the funds that are used to make loans. The rest of the interest payments are a source of income to lending institutions, used to pay other expenses and, if the firm is successful, with some fraction remaining as profits.

Banks provide a place for individuals to keep checking and savings accounts, and must compete for these deposits by providing convenient ways for customers to make deposits and withdrawals, and by paying competitive interest rates on these accounts. They must compete for borrowers, too, partly by charging competitive interest rates on loans that they consider to be "good risks." This process of channeling funds from one group of people to others is important to the overall economy because the loans are used by some people to start or expand businesses; to help larger and established businesses invest in new factories, machines, and technologies; and to help individuals invest in their human capital through education and training programs, or to purchase homes and expensive durable goods such as cars and large appliances.

Other specialized financial institutions, such as the stock market and bond market, also play a key role in promoting good investment and business practices in a market economy. Millions of individuals, usually working through brokerage firms, compete to invest their funds, hoping to earn the highest future profits at an acceptable level of risk. Different investors may view different levels of risk as acceptable or unacceptable, and may disagree about which firms or industries are likely to be more profitable in the future. But eventually, as in any competitive market, each individual must decide where to place their money and which risks to accept or avoid.

CONCEPTS

Saving
Investment
Financial institutions
Interest rate
Financial/personal investment
Primary market
Secondary market
Economic growth
Technological change

CONTENT STANDARDS

Institutions evolve in market economies to help individuals and groups accomplish their goals. Banks, labor unions, corporations, legal systems, and not-for-profit organizations are examples of important institutions. A different kind of institution, clearly defined and well-enforced property rights, is essential to a market economy.

Investment in factories, machinery, new technology, and the health, education, and training of people can raise future standards of living.

BENCHMARKS

Saving is the part of income not spent on taxes or consumption.

Banks and other financial institutions channel funds from savers to borrowers and investors.

Economic growth is a sustained rise in a nation's production of goods and services. It results from investments in human and physical capital, research and development, technological change, and improved institutional arrangements and incentives.

Investments in physical and human capital can increase productivity, but such investments entail opportunity costs and economic risks.

OBJECTIVES

Students will:

♦ Define saving, investment, and personal/financial investment.

♦ Define economic growth, stocks, bonds, and financial institutions.

♦ Give examples of financial institutions in a market economy.

♦ Explain some of the key roles of financial institutions in the economy.

♦ Explain that personal investments in stocks, bonds, and other financial

securities may or may not fund additional real investments in capital goods, depending on whether those investments are made in primary or secondary financial markets.

TIME REQUIRED

One or two class periods

MATERIALS

- Visual 1: An Interest in Interest
- Visual 2: Investment and Growth
- Activity 1: Where's the Money, cut apart to provide one card per student
- Activity 2: Financial Institutions, cut apart to provide one card for twelve students
- Three pieces of construction paper labeled Investment Banker, Stockbroker, and Commercial Banker
- Activity 3: From Saving to Investment, one copy per student
- masking tape

PROCEDURES

Note: Before beginning this lesson, complete the information on Visual 1, An Interest in Interest, by calling a local bank or checking a local newspaper.

1. Explain that students will participate in an activity that demonstrates a role for savings in the economy. Each student will receive a card. Some students will want to borrow money, while others will have savings that they may be willing to lend. Students should follow the instructions on their cards.

2. Distribute a card from Activity 1 to each student. Allow time for students to read their card and make sure they understand what they are supposed to do. Explain that students who are borrowers should find people who want to lend. Those who are lenders should find people who want to borrow. Tell students they should try to negotiate a

lending/borrowing deal at an interest rate acceptable to both lender and borrower. As a reference point, using information from Visual 1, announce the interest rate for one-year CDs; but do not display the Visual at this point.

3. Tell students they may begin. Allow students to interact for about 10 minutes. Discuss the following.

A. How many of you wanted to borrow money? (*four or more*)

B. Were you able to find people to lend you the amount that you wanted to borrow? (*Answers will vary.*) If yes, how many people did you have to interact with to accomplish this? (*Answers will vary.*)

C. Were you able to find people to lend you the amount you wanted to borrow at the interest rate that you wanted? (*Answers will vary.*) If not, why not. (*couldn't find people willing to lend at this rate*)

D. How many of you wanted to earn interest on your savings and were willing to lend to do so? (*remainder of the class*)

E. Were all of you able to lend as much as you wanted to? (*Answers will vary.*) If not, why not? (*couldn't find people who wanted to borrow or who wanted to borrow as much as I had to lend*)

F. Were all of you able to lend at the interest rate you wanted? (*Answers will vary.*) If not, why not? (*couldn't find people who wanted to borrow at that interest rate*)

G. What exists in our economy that would make it easier for borrowers and lenders to meet? (*banks and other financial institutions*)

H. What do banks and credit unions do that makes the borrowing/lending process easier? (*Banks accept deposits from those who want to save and pay interest to these savers. Banks lend money to those who want to borrow and charge interest to these borrowers.*)

4. Explain that banks and credit unions are examples of financial institutions that develop in market economies. Display Visual 1 and explain that an **interest rate** is the price people pay to borrow money and the price lenders receive for lending money.

5. Explain that Visual 1 lists interest rates that are available for different types of loans. The prime rate is the interest rate lenders charge their very best customers – large corporations and other businesses that borrow significant amounts of money. These are customers in whom the lenders have great confidence regarding repayment. The less confidence lenders have that they will be repaid, the higher the interest rate charged. This higher interest rate protects the lender against the risk of loss that results when some borrowers fail to repay.

6. Point out that interest rates vary based on collateral, too, because the collateral is another way of protecting banks and other lenders against failure to repay a loan. Therefore, if a borrower secures a loan with collateral, the interest rate will be lower. For example, the interest rate is lower on a home loan because the house is a valuable asset. If the borrower doesn't repay the loan, the lender can sell the house to recover the funds it loaned. A new car is a less valuable asset than a house, and riskier because it can may be driven away or destroyed in an accident; but a new car is usually more valuable than a used car. As a result, the interest rates for loans to purchase a new car are often higher than the

interest rates on a home loan, but lower than the interest rates for purchasing a used car.

7. Point out that the interest rate for "passbook" savings is lower than the interest rate for a one-year certificate of deposit and that the interest rate for a one-year certificate of deposit is lower than the interest rate for a five-year certificate of deposit. Explain that when savers buy certificates of deposit, they are required to leave the money in the account for the designated period of time or they must pay a penalty. Higher interest rates are the incentive for agreeing to keep the money in the account for the designated length of time. In practice, a "passbook" savings account has no such time requirement, so the interest rate is lower. A one-year certificate of deposit requires a shorter time commitment than a five-year certificate, so the interest rate is lower.

Savers accept the risk that the value of the account or certificate of deposit will not increase as rapidly as the rate of inflation. Therefore, if they are "locked in" for a particular amount of time, they expect to earn higher interest rates to protect against this inflation risk.

8. Display Visual 2 and explain that **financial institutions** are intermediaries that help channel savings to economic investment. The ability to efficiently channel savings into economic investments affects a nation's rate of economic growth, because the investments increase a nation's capacity to produce goods and services in the future.

9. Explain that **economic growth** is a sustained rise in a nation's production of goods and services. Historically, economic growth has been the primary means by which market economies reduce poverty and raise standards of living. Economic growth results from several factors, including capital formation (building new factories and machines), investment in human capital, technological change, and improved institutional arrangements.

10. Explain that economic growth also depends on the level of saving and investment in capital goods and human capital. To show why, first explain that physical capital refers to goods produced to be used in producing other goods and services. Physical capital includes factories, machines, tools, and inventories of finished goods, raw materials, and other inputs. Human capital refers to the quality of labor resources, which can be improved through investments in education, training, and health. Discuss the following.

A. If business owners have trouble finding people who will lend them money for investment, how will it affect the economy? (*Business owners will be unable to expand existing businesses or start new businesses. As a result, there will be less production and fewer jobs.*)

B. If individuals and households have trouble finding people who will lend them money to purchase large items, such as cars or appliances, how will it affect the economy? (*Individuals and households will buy fewer of these goods. As a result, businesses will sell fewer goods. This will hurt the economy.*)

C. What improved institutional arrangements could develop to improve the lending/borrowing interaction in the activity? (*financial intermediaries*)

D. How would these arrangements contribute to economic growth? (*make it easier for borrowers to find the money needed for investment*)

E. How would investment in capital goods contribute to economic growth? (*More and better factories, machines, and equipment lead to more and better production of goods and services in the future.*)

F. How would investment in human capital contribute to economic growth? (*People who are more skilled and better educated are usually more productive.*)

11. Explain that **technological change** is the introduction of new methods of production or new products intended to increase the productivity of existing inputs. Technological change is the result of research and development and can lead to economic growth.

12. Explain that when people **save**, they do not consume all of their current income. Discuss the following.

A. Why do people save? (*Answers will vary but should include that people save because they wish to purchase something expensive in the future, such as a car, house, or college education. People also save for protection against unforeseen problems, such as illness, lay-offs, or disability. Many people also try to save for their retirement.*)

B. When people save, does anyone benefit other than the savers? (*If everything produced today is consumed, there can be no investment. Therefore, saving also benefits people who want to borrow to invest, and therefore the economy as a whole. Saving also benefits those who want to borrow to consume more than they could based only on their current income – for example, someone who wants to borrow money to purchase an automobile.*)

13. Display Visual 2 again and explain that in economics, a distinction is made between saving and investment. **Saving** means not consuming all current income. **Investment** entails the production of capital goods, such as machines, buildings, and equipment that can be used to produce more goods and services in the future.

14. Explain that **personal investments** are made when individuals buy financial securities, such as stocks and bonds. Stocks and bonds are riskier than savings accounts because their value fluctuates up *and down* far more than the value of savings accounts. However, in the long run, they usually pay a higher rate of return than the interest earned on savings accounts.

Note: Savings accounts and the interest paid on these accounts are usually insured by the federal government. This makes these accounts relatively very safe. However, the real value of funds held in savings accounts is still affected by the rate of inflation, and over time by the interest rates that are paid on these accounts.

15. Explain that in the next activity students will learn more about financial institutions that develop in market economies. These include the stock and bond markets. Explain that 12 students will participate in the activity, while the rest of the class observes. All members of the class will participate in the discussion that follows.

16. Select three students and give them the investment banker, stockbroker, and commercial banker cards from Activity 2. Have these students tape the investment banker, stockbroker, and commercial banker signs on their desks. Explain that the other students will be seeking help from these three different kinds of financial institutions. When

a student asks for help from one of the institutions (investment banker, stockbroker, or commercial banker), the student playing that role must check his or her cards to determine if he or she is able to provide the kind of assistance requested.

17. Select nine students and distribute one card from Activity 2 to each of them. Tell these students to read their cards and decide which of the three financial institutions would provide the service they want. If a student selects an institution that does not provide that service, the student should record that on his or her card, and go to one of the remaining two institutions for help. Students should visit institutions until they find the service they want.

18. Allow time for students to complete the activity. When all nine students have found the appropriate institution have each of the nine students report the following to the class:

- Who are they? What type of financial product or service were they seeking?
- Which institution did they contact first? Did that institution provide the product or service? If not, why?
- Which institution provided the product or service, and why?

19. Distribute a copy of Activity 3 to each student. Explain that the three students who had roles as the investment banker, stockbroker, and commercial banker will read their role-cards to the class. As other students listen, they should begin to write the answers on Activity 3.

20. When the three students have finished reading their cards, discuss the following. Tell students they may record answers to the questions on Activity 3 as they hear them during the discussion.

A. A bond is a legal promise to repay money loaned to a business or government agency, with interest, on a specified date or dates.

B. A stock is a share of ownership in a corporation.

C. Often, people don't know that stocks and bonds traded on markets like the New York Stock Exchange are actually secondary securities traded in secondary markets. In the activity, who participated in **secondary markets**? (*John McQuerry, Tara Rau, and Tim Smith*)

D. From whom did they receive assistance? (*stockbroker*)

E. Why is this secondary market activity? (*They were buying previously issued stocks or bonds.*)

F. Newly issued corporate stocks or bonds or newly issued state or municipal bonds can be purchased in the **primary market**. In this activity, who participated in the primary market? (*Jeff Leonard, Jessica Schults, and Teresa Sanchez*)

G. From whom did they receive assistance? (*investment banker*)

H. Why is this called a primary market? (*They were selling newly issued corporate stocks or bonds or newly issued state or municipal bonds, which means that most of the funds used to purchase these securities created new funds for private firms or state and local governments to use.*)

I. Who received assistance from the commercial banker? (*Susan LaGrone, Sandy Snow, and Joe Doe*) Why? (*They were consumers or businesses seeking loans or depositing money in regular checking or savings accounts.*)

J.   Note that all of these financial institutions help channel savings to investments.

21. Explain that a distinction is made between new issues of stock made available through investment banks (primary market) and the reselling of shares of stock through stock markets (secondary market). Likewise, a distinction is made between new issues of bonds from corporations made available through investment bankers (primary markets) and bonds that are resold through bond markets (secondary markets).

22. Explain that corporations can raise money to begin operations or raise money to expand operations by offering new issues of stocks or bonds to investment bankers in the primary market. Investment banks purchase these securities from the firms (this is the primary transaction) and then sell them to the public at a price somewhat higher than the price they paid the issuing companies. After that, whenever these stocks or bonds are traded, the trades are handled in the secondary markets, such as the New York Stock Exchange or NASDAQ.

23. Explain that when individuals buy stocks and bonds, they may or may not provide additional funds for investment in capital goods, such as factories and machines. That simply depends on whether the purchases of stocks and bonds were made in primary or secondary markets.   However, it is only because there is an active secondary market for trading existing shares of stocks and bonds that the primary market can operate as efficiently as it does, making it possible for firms to acquire funds for investments with new issues of stocks and bonds.

CLOSURE

Review the following points:

A. Financial institutions are intermediaries that have developed in market economies that channel savings to investment.

B. Saving is income not spent on current consumption.

C. Interest is the price lenders receive and the price borrowers pay for lending and borrowing money.

D. Investment is the production of capital goods, such as machines, buildings, and equipment that can be used to produce more goods and services in the future.

E. Banks accept deposits from savers. Savers earn interest on their savings. Banks use the deposits to make loans to other people and to businesses. The borrowers agree to repay the loans with interest.

F. Corporations issue new shares of stock when the companies are first formed. They may also issue new shares of stock when they want to expand the business by building new facilities or equipment. These transactions are conducted through financial intermediaries – investment banks – in the primary market.

G. Corporations can also raise funds to expand by issuing bonds. Federal, state, and local governments also issue bonds to finance various projects. These transactions are conducted through financial intermediaries – investment banks – in the primary market.

H. In secondary stock and bond markets, people buy and sell previously issued stocks or bonds through stockbrokers. Those who buy stocks in the stock market are purchasing shares of ownership in a corporation. They hope that the share price will increase and that the firm will pay higher dividends, resulting in a financial gain.

I. By channeling savings to investment, funds are provided for research and development that can lead to new technologies, and more human and physical capital are created to increase the future production of goods and services. All of this contributes to the national level of economic growth.

J. Economic growth is a sustained rise in a nation's production of goods and services. Economic growth helps raise standards of living.

ASSESSMENT

1. Ask students to explain the difference between the primary and secondary markets for stocks and bonds.

2. Ask students to explain why banks and other financial institutions are important to economic growth.

3. Ask students to explain how banks and other financial institutions channel savings to investment.

EXTENSION

1. Teach the lesson, "Saving, Investing, and the Invisible Hand" from *Focus: High School Economics, Second Edition*, National Council on Economic Education, New York, NY, 2001.

2. Teach the lesson, "Showtime on Wall Street" from *Learning from the Market:*

Integrating The Stock Market Game™ across the Curriculum, National Council on Economic Education, New York, NY, 1997.

Visual 1
An Interest in Interest

Prime rate   _____

Interest rate on "passbook" savings account   _____

Interest rate on one-year CD   _____

Interest rate on five-year CD   _____

Interest rate on a 15-year fixed mortgage   _____

Interest rate on a 30-year fixed mortgage   _____

Interest rate on a loan for a new car   _____

Interest rate on a loan for a used car   _____

Visual 2
Investment and Growth

Economic Growth: A sustained rise in a nation's production of goods and services. Economic growth results from investments in human and physical capital, research and development, technological change, and improved institutional arrangements and incentives.

Capital Goods: Goods produced and used to produce other goods and services.

Human Capital: The quality of labor resources, which can be improved through investments in education, training, and health.

Saving: Income not spent on current consumption.

Investment: The production of capital goods, such as machines, buildings, and inventories that can be used to produce more goods and services in the future.

Personal Investment: Purchasing financial assets and securities, such as stocks and bonds, which are riskier than savings accounts because they might fall in value. In most cases stocks and bonds will pay a higher rate of return in the long run than the interest paid on savings accounts.

Activity 1
Where's the Money?

You own a web site technology firm. You want to borrow $50,000 to buy new computer equipment and software for your firm. You are willing to pay interest on the loan. Find individuals who are willing to lend you the money required to make this investment.	You have saved $10,000. You would like to earn interest on your savings. You are willing to lend the $10,000 if the borrower(s) will pay interest on the loan. See if you can find someone who wants to borrow your money.
You want to buy a new car, but will have to borrow $20,000. You are willing to pay interest on the loan. Find individuals who are willing to lend you the money required to make this purchase.	You have saved $15,000. You would like to earn interest on your savings. You are willing to lend the $15,000 if the borrower(s) will pay interest on the loan. See if you can find someone who wants to borrow your money.
You want to open a restaurant in your community. You will have to borrow $100,000 for new equipment. You are willing to pay interest on the loan. Find individuals who are willing to lend you the money required to make this investment.	You have saved $25,000. You would like to earn interest on your savings. You are willing to lend the $25,000 if the borrower(s) will pay interest on the loan. See if you can find someone who wants to borrow your money.
You want to buy a new refrigerator for your home. You have to borrow $1,000 to make this purchase. Find an individual who is willing to lend you the money required to make this purchase.	You have saved $10,000. You would like to earn interest on your savings. You are willing to lend the $10,000 if the borrower(s) will pay interest on the loan. See if you can find someone who wants to borrow your money.
You have saved $2,000. You would like to earn interest on your savings. You are willing to lend the $2,000 if the borrower(s) will pay interest on the loan. See if you can find someone who wants to borrow your money.	You have saved $15,000. You would like to earn interest on your savings. You are willing to lend the $15,000 if the borrower(s) will pay interest on the loan. See if you can find someone who wants to borrow your money.
You have saved $5,000. You would like to earn interest on your savings. You are willing to lend the $5,000 if the borrower(s) will pay interest on the loan. See if you can find someone who wants to borrow your money.	You have saved $15,000. You would like to earn interest on your savings. You are willing to lend the $15,000 if the borrower(s) will pay interest on the loan. See if you can find someone who wants to borrow your money.

Activity 1 (continued)

You have saved $5,000. You would like to earn interest on your savings. You are willing to lend the $5,000 if the borrower(s) will pay interest on the loan. See if you can find someone who wants to borrow your money.	You have saved $2,000. You would like to earn interest on your savings. You are willing to lend the $2,000 if the borrower(s) will pay interest on the loan. See if you can find someone who wants to borrow your money.
You have saved $5,000. You would like to earn interest on your savings. You are willing to lend the $5,000 if the borrower(s) will pay interest on the loan. See if you can find someone who wants to borrow your money.	You have saved $2,000. You would like to earn interest on your savings. You are willing to lend the $2,000 if the borrower(s) will pay interest on the loan. See if you can find someone who wants to borrow your money.
You have saved $5,000. You would like to earn interest on your savings. You are willing to lend the $5,000 if the borrower(s) will pay interest on the loan. See if you can find someone who wants to borrow your money.	You have saved $1,000. You would like to earn interest on your savings. You are willing to lend the $1,000 if the borrower(s) will pay interest on the loan. See if you can find someone who wants to borrow your money.
You have saved $10,000. You would like to earn interest on your savings. You are willing to lend the $10,000 if the borrower(s) will pay interest on the loan. See if you can find someone who wants to borrow your money.	You have saved $25,000. You would like to earn interest on your savings. You are willing to lend the $25,000 if the borrower(s) will pay interest on the loan. See if you can find someone who wants to borrow your money.
You have saved $2,000. You would like to earn interest on your savings. You are willing to lend the $2,000 if the borrower(s) will pay interest on the loan. See if you can find someone who wants to borrow your money.	You have saved $1,000. You would like to earn interest on your savings. You are willing to lend the $1,000 if the borrower(s) will pay interest on the loan. See if you can find someone who wants to borrow your money.
You have saved $5,000. You would like to earn interest on your savings. You are willing to lend the $5,000 if the borrower(s) will pay interest on the loan. See if you can find someone who wants to borrow your money.	You have saved $5,000. You would like to earn interest on your savings. You are willing to lend the $5,000 if the borrower(s) will pay interest on the loan. See if you can find someone who wants to borrow your money.
You have saved $5,000. You would like to earn interest on your savings. You are willing to lend the $5,000 if the borrower(s) will pay interest on the loan. See if you can find someone who wants to borrow your money.	You have saved $8,000. You would like to earn interest on your savings. You are willing to lend the $8,000 if the borrower(s) will pay interest on the loan. See if you can find someone who wants to borrow your money.

Activity 2
Financial Institutions

Investment Banker You are an investment banker. You are able to sell new issues of corporate stock – this is stock newly issued by a corporation to raise funds to begin new operations or to expand existing operations. You are also able to sell newly issued corporate bonds. You do not make consumer loans or business loans. You do not buy and sell previously issued and owned stock. In other words, if someone wants to buy previously issued shares of stock, you can't help them.	**Commercial Banker** You are a commercial banker. You accept deposits from your customers and make loans. You lend money to businesses and to consumers. You do not sell stocks and bonds.
Stockbroker You are a stockbroker. You do not sell newly issued corporate stocks and bonds for businesses. You do help individual clients who want to buy or sell previously issued shares of stock. You also sell previously issued corporate bonds, municipal bonds, and federal bonds and bills. You do not make loans to consumers or businesses.	You are Joe Doe. You want to borrow $15,000 to buy a new car.
You are Sandy Snow. You own a restaurant. You want to borrow $50,000 to invest in new equipment for your business.	You are Jeff Leonard, the President of a corporation that manufactures computer hardware. You want to issue new corporate bonds. You will use the revenue generated from the sale of these bonds to invest in a new office building and new equipment.

Activity 2 (continued)

You are Jessica Schults, the Mayor of Whatsville. You and members of the City Council have approval to issue new municipal bonds. Revenue generated from these bonds will be used to repair roads and develop two new parks in the city.	You are John McQuerry. You have a portfolio of stocks and bonds. You want to sell 1000 shares of stock in a fast-food chain and purchase shares of stock in an athletic equipment company.
You, Susan LaGrone, received a bonus from the company for which you work. You want to place the money in a savings account.	You are Teresa Sanchez, the CEO of Sunshine Interiors. You want to issue new shares of stock in your company, and use the funds to build a new assembly line and add laser cutters.
You are Tim Smith. Your portfolio includes U.S. Treasury Bills. You are interested in selling these securities.	You are Tara Rau, you want to purchase corporate bonds for your portfolio.

Activity 3
From Saving to Investment

1. What is a bond?

2. Who issues bonds?

3. What is a stock?

4. What is a secondary market?

5. Give an example of a secondary transaction.

6. What is a primary market?

7. Give an example of a primary transaction.

8. What are financial institutions?

LESSON FIVE
MAINTAINING COMPETITION

LESSON DESCRIPTION

This lesson introduces the rationale for maintaining and strengthening competition, and illustrates the U.S. experience with antitrust laws and other government regulations and agencies. But there are costs and limits to the scope of these government programs, too. A classroom simulation is used to illustrate how difficult it is to maintain collusion designed to limit competition, even in a market where there are only a few producers and no anti-trust enforcement.

INTRODUCTION

To promote economic efficiency and protect consumers, governments in market economies strive to maintain open and competitive markets. No nation has been more active in this regard than the United States, especially beginning with the Sherman Antitrust Act in 1890. Institutions that maintain and strengthen competition can pay significant dividends in the form of increased productivity growth and economic efficiency. Nevertheless, not all nations have embraced the U.S. approach of aggressively enforcing antitrust laws, and even some U.S. economists are skeptical about the likely benefits of many kinds of antitrust laws and enforcement activities

CONCEPTS

  Collusion
  Oligopoly
  Antitrust legislation and enforcement
  Economies of scale
  Mergers (horizontal, vertical, and
    conglomerate)
  Herfindahl-Hirshman Index
  Concentration ratios

CONTENT STANDARD

Competition among sellers lowers costs and prices and encourages producers to produce more of what consumers are willing and able to buy. Competition among buyers increases prices and allocates goods and services to those people who are willing and able to pay the most for them.

BENCHMARKS

The pursuit of self-interest in competitive markets generally leads to choices and behavior that also promote the national level of economic well being.

Collusion among buyers or sellers reduces the level of competition in a market. Collusion is more difficult in markets with large numbers of buyers and sellers.

OBJECTIVES

Students will:

♦ Analyze the role of governmental and nongovernmental institutions in preserving competition in the marketplace.

♦ Identify types of mergers and their relationship to competition.

♦ Experience the dynamics of competition in imperfect markets.

TIME REQUIRED

Two class periods. Day one – procedures 1-8. Day two – procedures 9-11 and Assessment.

MATERIALS

• Visual 1: Competition and the Economy
• Visual 2: Adam Smith Speaks
• Visual 3: Types of Mergers
• Visual 4: The Sherman Act of 1890
• Visual 5: U.S. Department of Justice Guidelines

- Activity 1: What Type of Merger Is It?, one copy per student
- Activity 2: Calculating the Herfindahl-Hirshman Index, one copy per student
- Activity 3: Will the Government Likely Oppose a Merger?, one copy per student
- Activity 4: The Oligopoly Game, one copy per student
- Activity 5: Examples of Anticompetitive Behavior, one copy per student

PROCEDURES

1. Display Visual 1. Ask the class to react to Henry Clay's statement. Do they agree that competition is a great positive force in the economy? What are the benefits of competition? (*lower prices, higher output and a more rapid rate of innovation*)

2. Display Visual 2 and read Adam Smith's view that business people would naturally try to restrain competition. Ask students to identify the benefits of such behavior to producers. (*higher prices and profits*)

3. Explain that one technique that firms have used to limit competition is to buy out or merge with each other. In other cases, however, mergers and acquisitions can be used to make firms more efficient by lowering costs of production. In fact, in markets that were competitive both before and after a merger, a merger can actually increase the level of competition, because the competition takes place between more efficient firms. That means policymakers and those who enforce laws designed to maintain competition – such as the Antitrust Division of the U.S. Department of Justice – have to evaluate whether a particular merger reduces, increases, or does not significantly affect competition.

4. Display Visual 3, which defines three types of mergers: horizontal, vertical, and conglomerate. Explain that each type of merger might reduce competition in some markets, but in other cases there may be benefits from

mergers in the form of lower costs of production and economies of scale.

5. Mergers may strengthen competition if the combined firms are more efficient, and may even help consumers by allowing products to be sold at lower prices. One possible source for this improved efficiency is a decrease in average costs of production that sometimes occurs as production levels increase, called **economies of scale**. Economies of scale can be related to production technology if larger firms benefit from greater specialization and more efficient equipment, or they may involve financial economies such as being able to get quantity discounts for larger orders from suppliers (who may well enjoy economies of scale in production), or getting better credit terms on loans because the larger firm is a better credit risk. Whatever the underlying reason for the economies of scale, the implication is that a merger can sometimes lower costs and thereby strengthen competition in the marketplace. At some point a tradeoff may set in, however, as mergers reduce the number of competitors in the marketplace.

6. To check students' understanding of mergers distribute Activity 1, What Type of Merger Is It? Answers are 1. *H*; 2. *V*; 3. *C*; 4. *H*; 5. *H*; 6. *V*; 7. *V*; 8. *H*; 9. *C*; 10. *V*. 11. *H*

7. Display Visual 4, and explain that the landmark legislation authorizing the U.S. government to use lawsuits to maintain competition in markets for goods and services produced in the United States is the Sherman Act of 1890. The Sherman Act and later laws, such as the Clayton Antitrust Act of 1914, make it a federal crime to collude with competitors, or to buy up competing firms if the effect is to reduce the level of competition in a market.

8. Given that some mergers can reduce competition, whereas others can actually increase competition or have no major effect on the level of competition in some markets, ask students to discuss how the government might

decide whether or not to oppose a specific merger as anticompetitive. *(Students will probably mention several factors, such as effects on price and profit levels, that can only be judged after the merger takes place. Other factors, such as how many firms are currently producing the good and service, and how big a share of the market the largest firms in the industry currently control, can be considered before the merger takes place.)* As students suggest factors, put them in two columns, with one column including factors that can be evaluated before the merger, and others that cannot be evaluated until after the merger takes place. Don't label the two columns right away, and after you have a few items listed in each column, see if the students can tell why you put items into the two different columns. Then label the two columns "Before the Merger" and "After the Merger," and see if students can add any additional items.

9. Explain that lawsuits under antitrust acts are very costly and time consuming both for firms that have merged or want to merge, and for the Department of Justice. That means it is very useful if firms can tell, in advance, whether the Department of Justice is likely to challenge a merger under the antitrust laws or not. For that reason, in 1982 the Antitrust Division published merger guidelines based on something called the Herfindahl-Hirshman Index (HHI).

10. Distribute copies of Activity 2 and show students how to calculate the HHI index. *(The answers in Activity 2 are: 1) $50^2 + 30^2 + 10^2 + 10^2 = 3600$ and for 2) $50^2 + 30^2 + 20^2 = 3800$.)* Point out again that higher HHI values indicate a higher degree of market concentration, with a pure monopoly having an HHI of 10,000.

11. Explain that prior to using the HHI, the Department of Justice relied on simpler kinds of **concentration ratios**, calculated by adding together the market shares (usually measured as dollars of sales) for the largest four, eight, 16 or 32 firms in an industry. One major problem with these ratios was their inability to account for differences in the distribution of market shares. For example, in two industries with only four firms, both industries would have a 4-firm concentration ratio of 100. But an industry where three firms each had only five percent market shares while the largest firm had 85 percent of the market would quite likely be less competitive than a market in which each of the four firms had a 25 percent market share. The HHI reflects that difference – to demonstrate that have students calculate Herfindahl-Hirshman Indexes for those two markets. *(25²+ 25² +25² +25² = 2500 versus 5² + 5² +5² + 85² = 7300)*

12. Now that students can calculate a Herfindahl-Hirshman Index, show them the guidelines used by the U.S. Department of Justice to determine when a merger is likely to be challenged as anticompetitive. Display Visual 5. The Justice Department is only likely to intervene if the Index rises above 1000 as a result of a horizontal merger. Even then, the change in the HHI must be greater than 100 points if HHI is in the 1000 to 1800 range, or 50 points if HHI is greater than 1800.

13. Continue to display Visual 5 while you put the class into small groups and distribute copies of Activity 3. Have each group analyze the problem as if they were a team of Justice Department economists recommending action to the federal attorneys. Have the groups report their results to the entire class. *(Answers for Activity 3: 1) HHI = 1466. 2) HHI = 1538 after the merger. 3) No challenge likely because the increase in the HHI is only 72 points, which falls below the 100-point threshold for an HHI value between 1000 and 1800. 4) The Justice Department would likely challenge a merger between firms #4 and #5 because the HHI rises 240 points, from 1466 to 1706.)*

14. Explain that while the U.S. government enforces antitrust legislation to help maintain competition in markets, it is also important for students to understand how

powerful competitive forces are, even in some markets with only a few competitors. In fact, historically, it has proven difficult for firms to collude, or to maintain any collusion, even if the collusion is not illegal under a nation's antitrust laws. Ask them how easy they think it is for firms to collude. *(Many students are likely to feel that firms collude frequently.)* Tell the students that you are going to give them the opportunity to test their theories about collusion by giving them an extra credit test or quiz.

15. Divide the class into nine groups (be sure to have an odd number of groups) and tell them they are going to play the role of oligopolists. An **oligopoly** is an industry with a relatively small number of competing firms, in this case nine. Distribute Activity 4 and explain the rules for the activity, answering any questions the students may have. Have each group designate one member as their spokesperson. That is the person who will signal, by raising an open hand or a closed fist, whether their company is going to compete or collude in each round. Explain that in an oligopoly, firms' profits are interdependent, which means they are affected by the decisions made by other firms in the industry. In this simulation, if a majority of firms choose to collude, they will try to raise prices by reducing the overall level of industry output, to earn higher profits. If all firms collude they each get 20 points, compared to only 10 points if all firms compete by lowering prices and selling more output. However, if a majority of firms vote to collude while a minority vote to compete, any firm that competes (open hand) gains even higher profits (40 points), because they sell more output than the colluding firms, at a price that is higher than the competitive price but probably somewhat less than the collusion price.

16. Begin the simulation and do not allow discussion between different teams for the first two rounds. Usually, a few firms try to collude and earn zero points while the majority chose to compete and earn 10 points. You may want to

allow some discussion between teams at this point to see if the firms can collude, or even "dictate" a collusion round where each firm earns 20 points, and then see if they can maintain the collusion making independent choices again. Generally, the collusion breaks down quickly with some good natured acrimony, because individual firms do better if they compete regardless of whether the other firms try to collude or cheat. This simple model fits many oligopolistic markets and accounts for their competitive behavior even without the threat of government intervention. Collusion is very difficult to maintain if there are strong incentives for individual firms to cheat on the collusion, especially if there are more than a few firms (which makes it harder to identify cheaters and enforce collusive agreements).

17. Explain that because competitive forces are so powerful even in industries with a relatively small number of firms, some economists feel that it is not necessary, or cost effective, for national governments to have an extensive antitrust program. You may also want to discuss some cases in which antitrust laws and regulations have been misused with the result of reducing effective competition, as discussed in the introductory essay to this volume. Note that many other countries are not nearly as aggressive as the United States in using antitrust laws to maintain competition. Still, most economists agree that the government has some role to play in this area, because monopoly power can develop in some markets, and the benefits of competition to consumers and the economy as a whole are so important.

CLOSURE
Review the major points of the lesson by asking the following questions.

- What is a merger? *(two or more firms joining together)*

- What are the three basic types of merger? (*horizontal, vertical, conglomerate*)

- How and when did the Federal Government get involved in insuring competition in the marketplace? (*Sherman Antitrust Act in 1890 followed by the Clayton Antitrust Act and the Federal Trade Commission Act, which were both passed in 1914*)

- Why did the Federal Government get involved in insuring competition in the marketplace? (*Competitive markets generally result in lower prices and higher output.*)

- Is there any reason to believe that some mergers can promote economic efficiency and help consumers? (*Yes, if they result in a more competitive firm that can take advantage of economies of scale.*)

- Is it easy for firms in an oligopoly to collude? (*No. First, collusion is illegal in the United States. Second, firms that choose to ignore collusive agreements will often be more profitable than firms in the same industry that attempt to collude, so attempts at collusion are often unsuccessful.*)

ASSESSMENT

Distribute Activity 5 and ask students to locate an article from a newspaper, magazine, or the internet that illustrates anticompetitive behavior, or at least behavior that is alleged to be anticompetitive. Allow students to use the Internet and search engines to find these articles. The articles may deal with mergers or collusion, or with government laws or interventions designed to maintain competition. Once they locate the news item, students are to cite it and answer the questions in Activity 5.

Visual 1
Competition and the Economy

"Of all human powers operating on the affairs of mankind, none is greater than that of competition."

Henry Clay, 1832
Quoted in *World Development Report 2002*,
New York: Oxford University Press

Visual 2
Adam Smith Speaks

"People of the same trade seldom meet together, even for merriment and diversion, but the conversation ends in a conspiracy against the public, or in some contrivance to raise prices."

Adam Smith, 1776
Wealth of Nations,
Book I, Chapter 10.

Visual 3
Types of Mergers

1. Horizontal Merger – combines directly competing firms producing and/or selling similar products.

2. Vertical Merger – combines two firms involved in different stages of producing a good or service

3. Conglomerate Merger – combines unrelated firms

From *Focus: Institutions and Markets*, © National Council on Economic Education, New York, NY

Visual 4
The Sherman Act of 1890

Section 1. "Every contract, combination in the form of trust or otherwise, or conspiracy in restraint of trade or commerce among the several States, or with foreign nations, is hereby declared to be illegal."

Section 2. "Every person who shall monopolize, or attempt to monopolize, or combine or conspire with any other person or persons to monopolize any part of the trade or commerce among the several States, or with foreign nations, shall be deemed guilty of a misdemeanor...

Visual 5
U.S. Department of Justice Guidelines

When Will the Government Probably Oppose a Merger
Between Two Firms in the Same Industry/Market?

Herfindahl-Hirshman Index (HHI) for the Industry/Market	Likely to Challenge the Merger if It Causes the HHI to Rise by
Above 1800	50 points or more
1000 to 1800	100 points or more
1000 or less	Unlikely to challenge the merger

 From *Focus: Institutions and Markets*, © National Council on Economic Education, New York, NY

Activity 1
What Type of Merger Is It?

Classify each of the following hypothetical mergers as:

> H for Horizontal
> V for Vertical
> C for Conglomerate

____ 1. Two toy companies decide to merge because they believe they will be able to develop more ideas for new toys and produce and sell them faster, at lower costs.

____ 2. A major producer of automobiles buys a large rental car company.

____ 3. A life insurance company merges with a major telecommunications company.

____ 4. A large producer of business and personal computers buys a company that produces computers for the home market.

____ 5. A commercial bank buys a credit union.

____ 6. A natural gas producer buys a company that owns natural gas pipelines that transport gas to major urban areas.

____ 7. A corporation that specializes in computer operating systems merges with a company that produces software for word processing and spreadsheets.

____ 8. A cable television company merges with a company that uses satellite dish technology to provide television service to consumers.

____ 9. An automobile manufacturer buys a baseball team.

____ 10. A cable television "super station" buys a motion picture corporation that owns thousands of classic movies.

____ 11. All the pizza companies in your community are bought up by one person.

Activity 2
Calculating the Herfindahl-Hirshman Index (HHI)

Since 1982 U.S. antitrust policy has used the Herfindahl-Hirshman Index (HHI) to help decide whether the Justice Department should oppose specific horizontal mergers. The index is calculated using the market shares (S) of firms in the relevant market, with market share usually measured as the percent of total sales in the industry for each firm. To calculate the HHI, the shares of all "n" firms in an industry are squared, and then those squared values are added up. In other words, the formula is:

$$HHI = S_1^2 + S_2^2 + S_3^2 + \ldots + S_n^2$$

The HHI is one indicator of the degree of competition and concentration in an industry. For example, for a monopoly, where there is only one firm in the industry, the HHI would equal 100^2, or $10,000$.

In an industry where there are only two firms with equal market shares of 50%, the HHI is $50^2 + 50^2 = 5,000$.

To make sure you understand how to calculate the HHI, suppose there were only four firms in an industry, with the following market shares:

Firm 1	50%
Firm 2	30%
Firm 3	10%
Firm 4	10%

1. Calculate the Herfindahl-Hirshman Index (HHI) for this industry

$$HHI = \underline{\hspace{2cm}}$$

2. Now calculate the HHI if the two smallest firms (#3 and #4) merged, so that their market shares are added together and now there are only three firms in the industry.

$$HHI \text{ after merger } = \underline{\hspace{2cm}}$$

From *Focus: Institutions and Markets*, © National Council on Economic Education, New York, NY

Activity 3
Will the Government Likely Oppose a Merger?

Firms in Industry	Firms' Market Share
Firm 1	20%
Firm 2	20%
Firm 3	15%
Firm 4	12%
Firm 5	10%
Firm 6	10%
Firm 7	9%
Firm 8	4%

Use the U.S. Department of Justice Merger Guidelines and the data in the table above to answer the questions below.

1. What is the Herfindahl-Hirshman Index (HHI) in this industry? _____.

2. What would the HHI equal if the two smallest firms in this industry merged? _____

3. How would the Justice Department respond to these mergers using its antitrust guidelines? Explain your answer using the post-merger change in the HHI.

4. Determine the Justice Department position if the merger involved Firms #4 and #5 rather than Firms #7 and #8. Would the government be likely to oppose the merger?

Activity 4
The Oligopoly Game

Name _____

		"Other Firms in the Industry"	
		Compete	Collude
"Your Company"	Compete	10	40
	Collude	0	20

- The table above illustrates the points you will receive in each round based on your behavior and the behavior of other firms in the industry. Your objective is to maximize your profits (total points) during a five-round game. In each round you must decide whether you want to compete or collude. If you choose to compete, that means you will offer lower prices to try to get customers to buy your product. If you choose to collude, that means that you will cooperate with the other firms and charge the same price they do. Figure out how many points you will receive if all firms collude, if all firms compete, if you compete when other firms collude, and if you try to collude when other firms compete. Then decide whether you will collude or compete.

- In each round, at the time your teacher indicates, the spokesperson for your firm will indicate your decision to collude by raising a clenched fist, or your decision to compete by raising an open hand.

- Your competitors must also decide whether to compete or collude. That response will be the strategy that receives the majority of all votes in the class.

- You can not talk to other groups/firms, unless your teacher decides to let you do that.

- Record your points for each round based on the following example. If you vote to compete in the first round (open hand), and more than half of the class votes to collude (more than 50 percent hold up a clenched fist), you will receive 40 points. If you had voted to collude (clenched fist) in that situation, you would receive 20 points. There will be time after each round for you to record your points. You will receive a grade on this exercise after 5 rounds.

    Minimum Points Needed for Grade
    90 = A
    80 = B
    70 = C
    60 = D
    below 60 = F

1.   Points earned in each round.
     ROUND I ___ ROUND II ___ ROUND III ___ ROUND IV ___ ROUND V ___

2.   Total points from all five rounds: _____ .

 From *Focus: Institutions and Markets*, © National Council on Economic Education, New York, NY

Activity 5
Examples of Anticompetitive Behavior

Name _____

Find a news article in a newspaper, magazine, or on the Internet that deals with potentially anticompetitive behavior by business firms, or government policies or actions designed to maintain competition. Make a copy of the article to turn in, and provide a complete bibliographic citation to show where you found the article, where and when it was published, etc. Using the article, answer the questions below.

1. What is the title of the article, and when and where was it published?

2. What are the key points in the article dealing with how actions by firms or government agencies might either reduce competition, or try to maintain and increase competition in a particular market?

3. In your opinion, should the federal government intervene in this market, perhaps under antitrust laws, to try to maintain or increase competition? Or, is there enough competition at work in the market already, and therefore no need for the government to get involved? Explain your answer.

LESSON SIX
TOO MUCH REGULATION?

LESSON DESCRIPTION

In this lesson, students first read an excerpt from *The Jungle,* written by Upton Sinclair in 1906. Then they learn about the numerous regulations that govern the production and sales of a hamburger today, and about some government regulatory offices and agencies. Finally, they consider the question: How much regulation is enough?

INTRODUCTION

Is there too much government regulation or too little? Who answers that question, and on what basis? Many critics have cited the total cost of government regulation and claimed that there is too much regulation. The U.S. Office of Management and Budget recently provided a report to Congress on the overall costs *and* benefits of federal regulations suggesting that the critics have failed to accurately consider all of the benefits resulting from regulation. The report goes on to emphasize the importance of applying cost-benefit analysis when making changes in regulatory policy – in other words comparing the expected costs of a new policy or a change in an existing policy to the expected benefits.

CONCEPTS

Government regulation
Costs
Benefits
Cost-benefit analysis

CONTENT STANDARDS

Costs of government policies sometimes exceed benefits. This may occur because of incentives facing voters, government officials, and government employees, because of actions by special interest groups that can impose costs on the general public, or because social goals other than economic efficiency are being pursued.

Effective decision-making requires comparing the additional costs of alternatives with the additional benefits. Most choices involve doing a little more or a little less of something; few choices are all-or-nothing decisions.

BENCHMARKS

A government policy to correct a market imperfection is not justified economically if its expected costs exceed its expected benefits.

To determine the optimal level of a public policy program, voters and government officials must compare the marginal benefits and marginal costs of providing a little more or a little less of the program's services.

OBJECTIVES

Students will:

◆ Define costs, benefits, marginal cost, marginal benefit, and opportunity cost.

◆ Explain that there are costs and benefits of government regulations.

◆ Apply cost-benefit analysis to review policy decisions.

TIME REQUIRED

One class period

MATERIALS

- Visual 1: Federal Regulatory Agencies
- Visual 2: Big Brother Is Watching Your Hamburger
- Visual 3: The Price of Life
- Activity 1: Making Sausage in 1906, one copy per student
- Activity 2: Flow Chart, two copies for each group of 4-5 students, and one transparency of the activity
- Activity 3: Problem Cards, cut apart to provide one card for each group of 4-5 students

PROCEDURES

1. Explain that students will read a passage from *The Jungle*, written by Upton Sinclair in 1906. Sinclair describes the working conditions that existed in the meat packing plants of Chicago and the decidedly unappetizing and unhealthy way in which various meats were processed and prepared in these plants.

2. Distribute a copy of Activity 1 to each student. Discuss the following:

A. Would eating sausage that was prepared as described in the reading make people sick? (*probably*)

B. If you suspected sausage and other meat were being prepared this way, what would you do? (*Stop buying sausage and other meat, ask government to intervene, or both.*)

C. In recent years, have you heard about cases of people who became sick from eating meat? (*Answers will vary. However, students may have heard about local cases of food poisoning. They may have heard about people who became sick or died from meat that contained* e. coli *bacteria. They may have heard about mad cow disease or*

wasting disease in deer and other animals.)

3. Explain that the images that Sinclair portrayed were so awful that President Theodore Roosevelt ordered an independent investigation to determine whether what the book portrayed was accurate. The federal investigation, the Neill-Reynolds Report, confirmed that both the working conditions and the meat preparation were as hideous as Sinclair described. For additional information, visit www.boondocksnet.com/editions/jungle/. The public was so outraged that the book is given major credit for passage of the Meat Inspection Act and the Pure Food and Drug Act of 1906. This act led to the establishment of the Food and Drug Administration – the FDA.

4. Point out that new regulatory agencies and new regulatory laws in the United States are often the outgrowth of crises. Discuss the following:

- In the 1950s, a European drug called thalidomide was sold as a sleeping pill. When pregnant women took the drug, it produced horrible birth defects in some babies. As a result, Congress quickly increased the FDA's authority to control the entry of new drugs onto the market.
- In 1965, Ralph Nadar wrote a best-seller, *Unsafe at Any Speed*. This book was an attack on a General Motors product, the Chevrolet Corvair. Nadar argued that the flaws in the car's design made it a death trap, and his book is often credited for federal legislation that established the National Highway and Traffic Safety Administration (NHTSA), which led to a number of automobile safety regulations. Point out that later NHTSA conducted a two-year study of the Corvair. In

1972, NHTSA concluded, "The handling and stability performance of the 1960-1963 Corvair does not result in an abnormal potential for loss of control or rollover and it is at least as good as the performance of some contemporary vehicles both foreign and domestic. The last Corvair was built in 1969, so the results of the study were too late to help save the line. For additional information visit www.nhtsa.dot.gov.

- Cases of children sleeping in flammable pajamas and of children eating paint chips that contained lead brought about additional legislation. This legislation led to the establishment of the Consumer Product Safety Commission (CPSC). In two well-known cases, the CPSC introduced regulations regarding maximum widths for slats on baby cribs and the number of wheels on ATV's.

5. Display Visual 1. Explain that this is a list of some of the major regulatory agencies of the federal government. Explain that when tax dollars are used to operate these agencies and to enforce the various regulations established, the tax dollars can't be used to provide other goods and services.

6. Ask students the following two questions:

A. How many of you ate a fast-food hamburger during the previous week? (*Answers will vary.*)

B. Government regulations govern the production and sales of fast-food hamburgers. How many regulations do you think there are? (*Answers will vary.*)

7. Display Visual 2. Point out that these are just some of the regulations related to the production and sale of fast-food hamburgers in the United States. Most consumers are shocked to learn that there are some 41,000 regulations that govern the production and sale of a fast-food hamburger in the United States today. These laws and regulations add to the cost of producing hamburgers and, therefore, to the price consumers pay for hamburgers. On the other hand, they reduce – but do not eliminate – the risk of sickness or even death from consuming the hamburgers. Given the price students pay for hamburgers, ask them to discuss whether the costs of these regulations is justified by the benefits. They are likely to say yes, but push the discussion to have students consider what would happen if there were no regulations. Would people stop buying hamburgers, or would they just shop more carefully, at businesses that were clean and maintained their reputations for selling clean, healthy, and tasty food? In other words, would market forces alone be enough to insure that the level of product safety would be as high, or almost as high, as it is with all of the regulations and regulatory costs we pay for today?

8. Note that most other products are also subject to some regulation, and in some cases very extensive regulation. Ask the following questions, and discuss students' answers:

A. Give some examples of regulations that affect you. (*speed limits, requirement to wear seatbelts, requirement to attend school, and so on*)

B. Give examples of other products you consume that are in some way regulated. (*gasoline, eggs, milk, packaged food, medications, and so on*)

C. How do regulations regarding the additives in gasoline affect the price people pay for gasoline? (*makes the price of gasoline higher*)

D. How do special packaging requirements for over-the-counter medication affect the price people pay for the medications? (*makes the prices higher*)

9. Point out that, as with fast-food hamburgers, gasoline, and medication, regulations generally cause the prices consumers pay for these products to increase, because the regulations result in higher production costs.

10. Many people argue that the overall costs of regulation are very high, with estimates of the cost for the establishment and enforcement of government regulations at the federal, state, and local levels running as high as $1.1 trillion a year, or approximately $4,000 per man, woman, and child in the United States. Other estimates suggest that federal expenditures on regulatory activity have increased 2.7 times faster than the overall growth in the U.S. economy since 1960. For more information, see: http://mwhodges.home.att.net/regulation_a.htm.

11. Point out that this all sounds pretty shocking, and that this type of information might be used to try to eliminate all government regulation. Is that what we really want? A purely emotional response to this data isn't very helpful when people try to decide whether to implement a specific new regulatory policy, or whether to expand or contract an existing regulatory policy.

12. Explain that there are both costs and benefits of regulation, as with any kind of economic choice. The **costs** are all of the things that have to be sacrificed or given up when a policy is implemented or a choice is made. **Benefits** are any improvements that make people more satisfied when a policy is implemented or a choice is made. Costs are negative; benefits are positive – but you don't get benefits unless you pay some costs. The idea is not to pay too many costs for too few benefits.

13. Explain that when deciding whether to adopt a new regulation, or to expand or contract existing regulatory policies, economists and policy makers apply **cost-benefit analysis**. What that means is that they consider the marginal costs of implementing or changing a policy, compared to the marginal benefits. **Marginal costs** are the extra or additional costs of implementing a policy or of making a choice to do a little more or a little less of something. **Marginal benefits** are the extra or additional benefits of implementing a policy or of making a choice to do a little more or a little less of something. Consumers, businesses, and government agencies all face these kinds of decisions. For example, at a fast-food restaurant, a consumer's decision to super-size a meal involves weighing the extra or additional cost, in dollars and cents but also extra calories (especially for someone on a diet), compared to the extra benefits of the additional food. Notice that some days the extra benefits may exceed the extra costs, but on other days they may not. It just depends on how hungry a person is on any given day.

14. Explain that when using cost-benefit analysis, it is important to consider the broad idea of opportunity cost, not just direct dollar measures of expenditures. **Opportunity cost** is the highest-valued alternative forgone when a choice is made, and that often means that someone must

consider nonmonetary costs. For example, in the example above, even if a salad costs more than a hamburger and fries, a person on a diet may well choose to buy a salad, even if they think the hamburger and fries taste better. Applying that idea to government regulations, when resources are used to provide and enforce additional regulations in some area, those resources can't be used in another way. As a result, society gives up or forgoes those things the resources would have been used to produce, which might have been more spending for schools or national defense, or lowering taxes so that individual consumers would have more money to purchase food, clothing, and other items. But it is also important to consider the expected benefits of regulations, not just the costs.

15. Explain that the economic way of thinking assumes that people's actions as individuals and as policymakers for business and government are based upon a comparison of costs and benefits. (Remember that economists do not claim that money or material goods are the only costs and benefits that people care about.) People choose to do more of an activity or undertake new activities and implement new policies as long as the marginal (additional) benefits of the activity or policy exceed the marginal (additional) costs. People choose to do less of activity or not implement a new policy if the marginal benefits are less than the marginal costs. The optimal level for any activity occurs when the marginal benefits of doing more of the activity are equal to the marginal costs of doing more.

16. Point out that even though there are many rules and regulations regarding safety for automobiles, such as padded dashboards, seat belts, collapsible steering columns, antilock brakes, air bags and so forth, there are still many, many automobile accidents

with serious injuries. Suppose a congressperson from the new state of Confusion has proposed a solution to this problem: reducing the speed limit to zero. Display a transparency of Activity 2 and discuss the following.

A. What are the marginal benefits of a zero speed limit? (*many fewer deaths and injuries due to automobile accidents*) Enter this into box 1a on the flow chart.

B. What are marginal costs of a zero speed limit policy? (*people can't travel via car to work, school, or for enjoyment; people can't move goods via trucks*) Enter these into boxes 2a and 3a of the flow chart.

C. If people can't travel via car to work, school, or for enjoyment, what might happen? (*people would spend much more time traveling to and from work, people wouldn't take as many trips*) Add two boxes below 2a on the diagram. Write one of these results in each of the two boxes. The completed example is shown.

D. If people can't move goods on the highways, what will happen to the cost of moving goods. (*the costs will increase a lot*) Add a box below box 3a on the diagram. Write this information in the box. The completed example is shown.

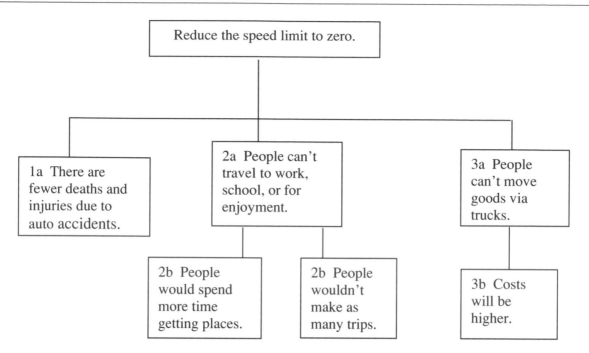

17. Continue adding boxes to the flow chart as needed. When students have added as many results to the chart as they want to, tell them to consider which of these results are benefits of the policy and which are costs.

18. Point out that many lives might be saved and fewer people would suffer serious injury as a result of this policy; that is, the benefits of this policy are great. Ask students if they and others would support such a policy? (*No.*) Why? (*The costs are also great and the expected costs exceed the expected benefits.*)

19. Ask the students if they think that this means people put a dollar value on life. (*Answers will vary.*) Explain that people do place a dollar value on life. Although this seems controversial, it is inevitable. If the value of life is infinite, then society would have to put all of its resources into saving one life whenever possible. Obviously, this isn't done. People also accept risks every day in eating unhealthy foods, drinking unhealthy beverages, smoking, driving, biking, and even walking. The fact that

people take these risks indicates that individuals do not put an infinite value on their own lives, so why should regulatory agencies? Also, if the price of life were infinite, people and nations would not engage in war for any reason, or fireworks displays, space exploration, air or automobile travel, and many other ordinary as well as daring endeavors.

20. Display Visual 3. Explain that this table shows the value of life applied in various studies. (Actuaries calculate risks and life expectancies to set insurance premiums.) The table demonstrates that it is necessary to determine the value of life for a variety of purposes, e.g., determining the value of life lost as a result of unsafe working conditions or unsafe vehicles.

21. Point out that the zero speed limit suggestion is an extreme example used to illustrate the notion that it is benefits relative to costs that must be considered when making policy decisions. Discuss the following:

   A. The FDA allows up to 30% of ground coffee to consist of unripe, moldy beans, gravel, or other noncoffee impurities. Why is this allowed? (*It isn't possible to eliminate all of the unwanted things when the coffee is ground. The extra cost of eliminating all of the impurities is too great relative to the extra benefits.*)

B. The FDA allows a certain amount – many parts per million – of rodent hair, rat droppings, and insect parts in candy bars. Why is this allowed? (*The extra cost of having zero pollutants is too high relative to the extra benefits.*) Source: *Wall Street Journal*, November 19, 2002.

22. Divide students into groups of 4-5. Distribute two copies of Activity 2 and a problem card from Activity 3 to each group. Tell students to read the problem statement and identify two reasonable (not extreme) possible solutions to the problem. Then they should use the flow charts to analyze the costs and benefits of each of the solutions. They should be prepared to present the solution they think has the greatest net benefits.

23. Allow time for students to work on their problems. Tell members of each group to read the information on the group's card to the class, identify the two solutions the group proposed, present the group's choice to the class. and explain why the group decided this was the best choice between the two options. Discuss the following.

A. How easy was it to identify possible solutions to the problems presented? (*Answers will vary.*)

B. Did members of the group usually agree regarding the costs and benefits of the policy choices? (*Answers will vary.*)

C. Will your solution completely eliminate the problem identified? (*Probably not.*) Why? (*The costs of completely eliminating the problem are too great relative to the benefits.*)

24. Explain that in the 1970s and 1980s, there were initiatives to deregulate various industries. These initiatives were developed in response to economic analysis that indicated problems with too much regulation in various industries. There are many examples, such as the airline industry, banking industry, trucking industry, and AT&T. This deregulation came about because economists and policymakers came to recognize that these industries were burdened by too much regulation and that some individual firms, through regulation, had acquired too much economic power. Point out that the predicted goals of deregulation were decentralization of economic power and, as a result of increased competition, a better allocation of resources, lower prices and higher quality for consumers.

25. Explain that advancements in telecommunication technology led to the development of new firms, products, systems, and hardware. In the late 1960s the Federal Communications Commission opened access to previously restricted telecommunications markets. AT&T saw this as a violation of its status as a natural monopoly. AT&T's reaction to the competition led to antitrust discussions – in 1974, the Department of Justice brought an antitrust suit against the company. AT&T was the largest private telephone company in the world and it operated as a natural monopoly in both local and long distance telephone markets until January 1, 1984. At that time, it was dismantled and became 23 local (Bell) operating companies and a much smaller AT&T competing against other

companies (such as MCI and GTE Sprint) selling long-distance calling services. Since then, many of the local Bell companies have merged or been taken over by other companies.

26. Explain that traditional regulatory policies involve government setting standards or mandating some required process or program. More recently, particularly in the case of environmental regulation, there has been a move toward market-based policies that provide greater flexibility. These include pollution permits or marine fishery permits that allow people to hold some volume and trade or sell what they hold or buy additional permits. For additional information on this topic, see Lesson 7 from this volume.

27. Point out that the movements toward market-based approaches have resulted in part from the cost-benefit analysis process applied by economists, from which they were able to demonstrate the net benefits of alternative approaches to traditional regulatory policy.

CLOSURE

Review the major points of the lesson by asking the following questions.

1. What is a cost? (*everything sacrificed or given up when a policy is implemented or a choice is made*)

2. What is a benefit? (*Benefits are things gained when a policy is implemented or a choice is made.*)

3. What are marginal costs? (*The extra or additional costs associated with a decision to do a little more or a little less of something – whether buying one more cola or raising gas efficiency regulations on SUVs by one mile per gallon.*)

4. What are marginal benefits? (*The extra or additional benefits associated with a decision to do a little more or a little less of something.*)

5. What is opportunity cost? (*The highest forgone alternative when a choice is made.*)

6. A school principal has $5,000 to spend. She is considering whether to add computers to the computer lab or to upgrade equipment for the drama department, such as lighting and sound equipment. What are some of the additional costs and benefits associated with each alternative? (*Computer: costs – give up extra equipment for the drama department, more staff time required to regulate the use of computers by students, extra costs of hook-ups and connections; benefits – students will have access to additional computers for research and projects, more students can be in the lab using computers at one time. Sound and lighting equipment: costs – give up extra computers, additional installation costs; benefits – improved quality for performances.*)

ASSESSMENT

1. Present the following problem to students. Ask them to identify a possible solution to the problem and to analyze the costs and benefits of their solution.

Many people are seriously injured in bicycle accidents each year. Members of the state medical association and other concerned citizens are lobbying state legislators for a law that would require all bicycle riders to wear helmets.

2. Some things are recycled at a very high rate. Some things are recycled at lower rates. Some things aren't recycled at all. Aluminum cans are recycled at a very high

rate. Disposable diapers contain several parts that are recyclable; however, disposable diapers aren't recycled. Explain why.

EXTENSION

1. Teach "The Costs and Benefits of Independence," from *United States History, Eyes on the Economy*, Vol. I.

2. Teach "Improving Transportation," from *United States History, Eyes on the Economy*, Vol. I.

3. Have students select one of the regulatory agencies listed on Visual 1 of this lesson. Tell them to conduct research to identify when the agency was established and why, and what type of products or services the agency regulates. Instruct students to select one product or service that the agency regulates and analyze the impact of the agency's regulations on consumers and producers of the good or service.

4. Have students read the following quote and respond to questions A through D.

"Nobody in the United States is forced to buy fast food. The first step toward meaningful change is by far the easiest: stop buying it. The executives who run the fast food industry are not bad men. They are businessmen. They will sell free-range, organic, grass-fed hamburgers if you demand it. They will sell whatever sells at a profit. The usefulness of the market, its effectiveness as a tool, cuts both ways. The real power of the American consumer has not yet been unleashed. The heads of Burger King, KFC, and McDonald's should feel daunted; they're outnumbered. There are three of them and almost three hundred million of you. A good boycott, a refusal to buy, can speak much louder than words. Sometimes the most irresistible force is the most mundane."

Source: Eric Schlosser, *Fast Food Nation*, Boston: Houghton Mifflin, 2001, p. 269

A. How could consumers use their economic power to create healthier food? (*Stop buying the high-cholesterol foods currently served.*)

B. Why don't consumers stop buying the fast foods that are so unhealthy? (*Many consumers prefer the taste of salty and fatty foods.*)

C. Do consumers have all of the information they need to make decisions about fast food? (*Maybe, or maybe not – especially debatable for young consumers.*)

D. What could government do to help consumers have the information they need? (*Mandate full disclosure of information regarding the ingredients found in fast food and the ingredients used to cook/prepare fast food.*)

Visual 1
Federal Regulatory Agencies

Animal and Plant Health Inspection Service

Atomic Energy Commission

Bureau of Alcohol, Tobacco, and Firearms

Consumer Product Safety Commission

Defense Nuclear Facilities Safety Board

Department of Energy

Employment Standards Administration

Environmental Protection Agency

Equal Employment Opportunity Commission

Federal Aviation Administration

Federal Communications Commission

Federal Mine Safety and Health

Federal Trade Commission

Fish and Wildlife Service

Food and Drug Administration

Food Safety and Inspection Service

Immigration and Naturalization Service

Interstate Commerce Commission

National Labor Relations Board

National Transportation Safety Board

Nuclear Regulatory Commission

Occupational Safety and Health Administration

Securities Exchange Commission

Small Business Administration

U.S. International Trade Commission

Visual 2
Big Brother Is Watching Your Hamburger

Cattle are often given growth-stimulating drugs. Use of these drugs must stop at least two weeks before the cattle are slaughtered. The burger must be made from fresh or frozen chopped beef and not contain added water, binders or extenders. There cannot be more than 30 percent fat content in the burger.

Lettuce – The lettuce must be fresh, not soft, overgrown, burst, or "ribby."

Pickles – Slices must be between 1/8 and 3/8 inches thick.

Tomatoes – The tomato must be mature but not overripe or soft.

Cheese – The cheese must contain at least 50 percent milk fat and, if made with milk that is not pasteurized, must be cured for 50 or more days at a temperature of at least 35 degrees Fahrenheit.

Bun – The bun must be enriched with thiamin, riboflavin, and iron.

Mayonnaise The mayonnaise may be seasoned or flavored as long as the substances do not color it to look like egg yolk.

Ketchup – To be considered Grade A fancy, the ketchup must flow no more than 9 centimeters in 30 seconds at 69 degrees Fahrenheit.

Meat Processing Inspections – As many as six inspections can occur under the Federal Meat Inspection Act. The meat is checked before and after slaughter and at boning, grinding, fabrication, and packaging stages.

Source: Michael C. Lemay, *Public Administration,* Belmont, CA: Wadsworth Thomson Learning, 2002, p. 234.

Visual 3
The Price of Life

Author/Year	Risk Variable Calculated by	Implicit Value of Life ($ millions)
Smith (1976)	Bureau of Labor Statistics (BLS)	4.0
Thaler and Rosen (1976)	Society of Actuaries	0.7
Viscusi (1979)	BLS	3.6
Arnould and Nichols (1981)	Society of Actuaries	5.7
Dillingham (1985)	U.S. Department of Labor	5.9

Source: W. Kip Viscusi, John M. Vernon, and Joseph E. Harrington, Jr., *Economics of Regulation and Antitrust*, Lexington, Mass: D. C. Heath, 1992, p. 641.

Activity 1
Making Sausage in 1906

It was only when the whole ham was spoiled that it came into the department of Elzbieta. Cut up by the two-thousand-revolutions-a-minute flyers, and mixed with half a ton of other meat, no odor that ever was in a ham could make any difference. There was never the least attention paid to what was cut up for sausage; there would come all the way back from Europe old sausage that had been rejected, and that was moldy and white – it would be dosed with borax and glycerine, and dumped into the hoppers, and made over again for home consumption. There would be meat that had tumbled out on the floor, in the dirt and sawdust, where the workers had tramped and spit uncounted billions of consumption germs. There would be meat stored in great piles in rooms; and the water from leaky roofs would drip over it, and thousands of rats would race about on it. It was too dark in these storage places to see well, but a man could run his hand over these piles of meat and sweep off handfuls of the dried dung of rats. These rats were nuisances, and the packers would put poisoned bread out for them, they would die, and then rats, bread, and meat would go into the hoppers together. This is no fairy story and no joke; the meat would be shoveled into carts, and the man who did the shoveling would not trouble to lift out a rat even when he saw one – there were things that went into the sausage in comparison with which a poisoned rat was a tidbit. There was no place for the men to wash their hands before they ate their dinner, and so they made a practice of washing them in the water that was to be ladled into the sausage. There were the butt-ends of smoked meat, and the scraps of corned beef, and all the odds and ends of the waste of the plants, that would be dumped into old barrels in the cellar and left there. Under the system of rigid economy which the packers enforced, there were some jobs that it only paid to do once in a long time, and among these was the cleaning out of the waste barrels. Every spring they did it; and in the barrels would be dirt and rust and old nails and stale water – and cart load after cart load of it would be taken up and dumped into the hoppers with fresh meat, and sent out to the public's breakfast. Some of it they would make into "smoked" sausage – but as the smoking took time, and was therefore expensive, they would call upon their chemistry department, and preserve it with borax and color it with gelatine to make it brown. All of their sausage came out of the same bowl, but when they came to wrap it they would stamp some of it "special," and for this they would charge two cents more a pound.

Source: Upton Sinclair, *The Jungle*, New York: Grosset & Dunlap, 1906, p. 161-162.

Activity 2
Flow Chart

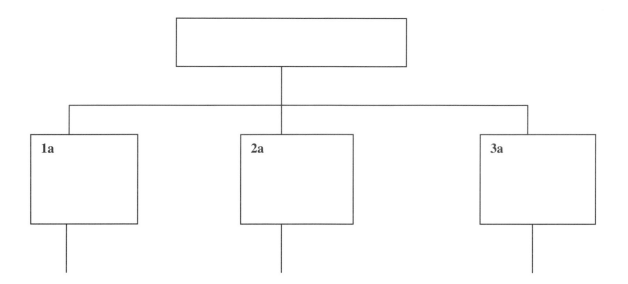

Activity 3
Problem Cards

Higher concentrations of harmful chemicals and residues such as lead are being found in the nations' drinking water. Consumers and environmental groups are very concerned. Congress is considering possible policies to alleviate the problem. You've been asked to recommend solutions to this problem.

The national parks are becoming more and more crowded. As more people visit the parks, landmarks, trees, and other natural features are being damaged or destroyed. The National Parks Commission is considering possible policies to alleviate the problem. As members of the Commission, you've been asked to recommend solutions to this problem.

Although there are fines for littering in your community, the roadsides are covered with trash and debris. Citizens in the community are concerned because the trash is unsightly. They are also concerned that it creates an unhealthy environment. The city has established a committee to consider solutions. As members of the committee, recommend solutions to this problem.

The world's oceans are being "overfished." People from throughout the world are concerned that thousands of species will become extinct. Those who fish for a living are concerned that they will no longer be able to earn an adequate living. You are members of an international committee that is charged with recommending solutions to this problem.

Many members of your community are concerned about the number of teenage drivers who are involved in automobile accidents and the number of teenage drivers who receive two or more citations for driving violations, such as speeding, running red lights, failing to yield, and so on. The state has formed a committee to study this problem and recommend solutions. You are members of this committee.

LESSON SEVEN
PUBLIC GOODS AND EXTERNALITIES

LESSON DESCRIPTION

This lesson gives students an opportunity to identify the nature of public and private goods, classify them according to the characteristics of rivalry and excludability, experience the impact of free riders and other external benefits and costs, and demonstrate that market-based solutions to externalities are often superior to inflexible government regulations.

INTRODUCTION

Even in perfectly competitive market economies, some goods and services must be provided by the government because special characteristics of those products make it impossible or inefficient for private firms to sell those goods profitably in the marketplace. These characteristics of a pure public good are nonrivalry and nonexcludability. In contrast, most goods and services can be provided in private markets because they are rival and excludable.

A product is considered rival when consumption by one person reduces the amount available to others. A nonrival good can be simultaneously or jointly consumed by people without reducing the amount available to others. A good is excludable if its use is easily limited to those who pay to use it. Conversely, a nonexcludable good or service can be used even by people who do not pay for it.

A related kind of market failure occurs when goods or services have some, but not all, of the characteristics of pure public goods – specifically, a good might be excludable but nonrival, or nonexcludable but rival. In many of these cases private firms will produce some amount of these products, but not the amount

that reflects all of the benefits or costs of the production and/or consumption of these goods and services. That happens because some of the benefits or costs fall on "third parties" – people or firms other than the producers and paying consumers of the products. Pollution is an example of such an "external cost." Homeowners whose property values increase when neighbors paint and landscape their homes benefit from an "external benefit," and gain from this "free riding" on someone else's spending and work. In these cases the government can use regulations, taxes, or tax reductions as incentives so that all of the benefits and costs associated with the production and consumption of a product are recognized.

CONCEPTS

Nonrival products
Nonexcludable products
Pure private goods and services
Pure public goods and services
External benefits and costs
Free riding

CONTENT STANDARD

There is an economic role for government to play in a market economy whenever the benefits of a government policy outweigh its costs. Governments often provide for national defense, address environmental concerns, define and protect property rights, and attempt to make markets more competitive. Most government policies also redistribute income.

BENCHMARKS

Public goods and services provide benefits to more than one person at the same time, and their use cannot be restricted only to those people who have paid to use them.

If a good or service cannot be withheld from those who do not pay for it, providers expect to be unable to sell it and therefore will not produce it. In market economies, governments provide some of these goods and services.

Markets do not allocate resources effectively if (1) property rights are not clearly defined or enforced, (2) externalities (spillover effects) affecting large numbers of people are associated with the production or consumption of a product, or (3) markets are not competitive.

Externalities exist when some of the costs and benefits associated with production and consumption fall on someone other than the producers or consumers of the product.

When a price fails to reflect all the benefits of a product, too little of the product is produced and consumed. When a price fails to reflect all the costs of a product, too much of it is produced and consumed. Government can use subsidies to help correct for insufficient output; it can use taxes to help correct for excessive output; or it can regulate output directly to correct for over- or under-production or consumption of a product.

OBJECTIVES

Students will:

♦ Explain how public goods differ from private goods and why private markets fail to provide public goods.

♦ Classify goods and services on the basis of rivalry and excludability.

♦ Demonstrate that external benefits result in too little of a good or service being produced, and external costs result in too much being produced.

♦ Demonstrate that in correcting for external benefits and costs, market-compatible public policies are often preferred to "one-size-fits-all" government regulations and policies.

TIME REQUIRED

Two class periods

MATERIALS

- Visual 1: Classifying Public and Private Goods and Services, one copy for each group of five students
- Visual 2: Finding the Efficient Level of Production
- Activity 1: Public Goods – Giving Government the Green Light, one copy per student. Part II – Cards with Characteristics of Public and Private Goods, one sheet of 20 description cards, cut up, for each group of five students; five cards each with the headings, NONRIVAL, NONEXCLUDABLE, RIVAL, and EXCLUDABLE. Part III – Product Cards, cut up, one card per student
- Activity 2: The Case of the Vanishing Streetlights, one copy per student
- Activity 3: Markets Rule at Cleaning Up, one copy per student
- Paper clips, one box

PROCEDURES

1. Introduce the concepts of **rivalry** and **excludability** to the students. Explain to students that when consumption is **nonrival**, the good or service is jointly consumed by people without reducing the amount available to others. For example, something you eat is a rival good, but a painting in an art museum is nonrival. An **excludable** good or service is only provided to someone who pays for it; **nonexcludable** goods or services, once produced, can be used even by people who do not pay for them. This characteristic does not depend on whether it is theoretically possible to exclude people from using a product. Instead, if it is prohibitively expensive to exclude people who do not pay for a product, relative to benefits of providing the good and making it available to everyone, the product is considered nonexcludable even though exclusion might be technically possible. For example, limited access highways with only a few off/on ramps are sometimes operated as excludable toll roads, whereas local road and street systems with numerous side streets feeding into main arteries are nonexcludable,

even though it might be theoretically possible to have a toll booth on every corner.

2. Explain that products that are both rival and excludable are known as **pure private goods**. These goods can be profitably sold by private firms that will provide the product only to those who pay for it.

3. Explain that **pure public goods**, on the other hand, are nonrival and nonexcludable. It is usually impossible for the market to work effectively under conditions where additional consumers can be satisfied without additional sales of the good and individuals can refuse to pay even if they consume the product.

4. Explain that some goods and services are **mixed goods,** neither pure private nor pure public goods, because they have one characteristic of each type of good. Some of these goods can be provided by private firms, but others are partly or entirely provided by government. One group of mixed goods is nonrival but excludable. A pay-for-view TV program is such an example. Other mixed goods are nonexcludable but rival, such as a city beautification project planting trees and flowers along some city streets. The existence of even one of the traits of public goods creates problems for firms attempting to provide mixed goods in market settings. In many cases, private firms will produce some of these products, but not the amount that reflects all the benefits and costs to consumers and producers.

5. Explain that the class will now do an activity to see how the characteristics of rivalry and excludability can be found, in various combinations, in various goods and services people use every day.

6. Divide the class into groups of five. Distribute copies of the first part of Activity 1, Public Goods – Giving Government the Green Light, and allow time for the students to read the Definitions and Directions. Answer any questions they have about these instructions.

7. Distribute one copy of Visual 1, Classifying Public and Private Goods, and one set of 20 description cards and five product cards from Parts II and III of Activity 1 to each group. Allow enough time for all students to present their product card in their group, identifying the rival/nonrival and exclusion/nonexclusion characteristics, and for the group to agree or disagree with the presenters' presentations. When all groups are finished, have the groups report their products and classifications to the class as a whole. Allow discussion and possible adjustments to the classifications reported.

Answers for Part II "product cards"
- *compact discs (pure private good, rival and excludable)*
- *flood control project (pure public good, nonrival and nonexcludable)*
- *haircuts (pure private service, rival and excludable)*
- *national defense (pure public good, nonrival and nonexcludable)*
- *elementary education (mixed service, nonexcludable but rival) Some aspects of education are individually consumed (rival, such as one-on-one instruction, grading) but other aspects are jointly consumed. There are benefits (nonexcludable) to others in society who interact with educated citizens*
- *bridge (mixed good, nonrival but excludable) rival during traffic jams*
- *busy city streets (mixed good, nonexcludable but rival) nonrival when not busy*
- *limited access highway (mixed good, nonrival but excludable) rival when congested*
- *pizza (pure private good, rival and excludable)*
- *fire protection (mixed service, usually nonexcludable but rival, although some private fire services only serve those who sign annual contracts for service)*

- *beaches along the ocean (sometimes a pure public good, nonrival until crowded and nonexcludable) in other cases excludable if private owners control all access to a beach*
- *lighthouse (pure public good, nonrival and nonexcludable) although in some circumstances these services were excludable using signal flags and other devices, and built by private companies or associations of merchants.*
- *flu shots (mixed good, nonexcludable but rival) nonexcludable benefits to others who interact with the protected persons*
- *pay per view television programs (mixed service, nonrival but excludable)*
- *soft drinks (pure private goods, rival and excludable)*
- *county zoo (mixed service, nonrival but excludable) nonrival until crowded*
- *open access web site (pure public service, nonrival and nonexcludable) can be made excludable through subscription fees*
- *pollution (pure public bad, nonexcludable and nonrival)*
- *fireworks (pure public service, nonrival and nonexcludable) but can charge admission for best viewing in stadiums or vast theme parks, making them rival and excludable*
- *disc jockey music at school dance (mixed service, nonrival but excludable) can sell tickets for admission*
- *math tutor (pure private service, rival and excludable)*
- *UPS delivery (pure private service, rival and excludable)*
- *live theatre performance (nonrival but excludable) rival if performances sell out*
- *hospital ER (mixed service, nonexcludable but rival) assumes service is not withheld regardless of financial circumstance*
- *police protection (pure public good, nonrival and nonexcludable)*

- *neighborhood beautification (mixed service, nonexcludable but rival) rival not in terms of one neighbor's benefits reducing others, but because flowers, trees, paint, etc., are rival*
- *Grand Canyon (pure public service, nonrival and nonexcludable) limiting access roads to certain viewing points establishes limited exclusion*
- *air conditioning (pure private service, rival and excludable) benefits are nonrival to people in the same building*
- *limited access (subscriber) web site (mixed service, nonrival but excludable)*
- *radio broadcasts (pure public service, nonrival and nonexcludable) but often provided privately by selling excludable air time for commercials*

8. Conclude Activity 1 by reviewing the traits that distinguish private goods from public goods and lead a discussion about why private firms find it difficult to produce and sell public goods.

9. Introduce the idea of **free riders** as people who are able to enjoy a good once it is provided without having to pay for it. This situation is most likely to occur when the good is jointly consumed (nonrival) and nonexcludable (it is expensive or impossible to prevent nonpayers from enjoying the good). Thus free riders are a problem associated with pure public goods, and to a lesser extent, externality goods where benefits spill over to third parties (education, inoculations).

10. Define the concept of **externalities** as positive or negative spillovers to third parties, people or firms other than the producers and paying customers of the products. Relate this to the concept of nonexcludability. Mixed goods that are rival but nonexcludable (such as a remodeling project that affects neighborhood property values) create positive externalities. These spillover benefits allow other homeowners in the neighborhood to be free-riders. Spillover costs, such as pollution, allow

polluters to free ride on others, by shifting some of the costs of their activities onto others.

11. Display Visual 2 and explain the concept of the efficient level of production and consumption for goods and services, where the benefits from the last unit produced equal the costs of producing it. Explain this idea using the numerical example in Visual 2. Then explain that the characteristics of nonrivalry and nonexcludability can prevent private markets from achieving efficiency because the costs and benefits are not reported fully by some producers or consumers, or they spill over to individuals who are neither consumers nor producers.

12. Continue the discussion by considering the effects of free riding on producing the efficient amount of a good or service. Free riders do not pay for the extra benefits they receive from consuming goods or goods that provide spillover benefits. Because they understate their demand for the products, market prices for these goods and services will be too low and too little will be produced. Tell students they will see this result in Activity 2.

13. Distribute Activity 2, The Case of the Vanishing Streetlights. Assign students to small groups and have them complete the handout together. Answers:

Harry: no; benefit of 1st light (400) is smaller than $500
Pat: no; benefit of 1st light (300) is smaller than $500
Mary: no; benefit of 1st light (250) is smaller than $500
Nonrival
1st – yes; 2nd – yes; 3rd – yes (exactly enough); 4th – no (300< 500); efficiency is achieved at 3 streetlights
Nonexcludable; free rider
If only Harry is a free rider, 1 streetlight purchased (1st brings in $550, 2nd brings in only $350, but costs $500); no (efficient amount = 3)

If only Pat is a free rider, 2 streetlights purchased (2nd brings in $500, 3rd brings in $375, but costs $500); no (efficient amount = 3)
If only Mary is a free rider, 2 streetlights purchased (2nd brings in $550, 3rd brings in $425, but costs $500); no (efficient amount = 3)

14. Summarize the results and debrief the activity. If streetlights were purchased on the basis of individual marginal benefits, no single resident would be willing to buy. When an agreement is reached among residents who jointly consume the lights, and all agree not to free ride, the efficient amount is produced because all of the residents' marginal benefits added together are equal to the costs of the last streetlight installed. If any of the residents choose to be free riders, an inefficient number of streetlights (too few) will be installed. Local government could achieve an efficient outcome by imposing a tax on those who jointly consume the public good. That way everybody who pays taxes helps to pay for the lights, and cannot free ride.

15. The final topic for the lesson is how government responds to externalities, and tries to get producers and consumers to "internalize" externalities using taxes or subsidies. Some kinds of policies are usually better than others in terms of achieving a given goal at the lowest possible cost. For example, one way to reduce pollution is for the government to establish and enforce regulations mandating pollution cleanup, and perhaps even mandating a particular method or technology that must be used to reduce certain kinds of pollutants. Essentially this forces a polluting firm to include cleanup costs in its production and profit-maximizing decisions. A problem occurs, however, if the government mandate is the same for all polluting firms, even in cases where some firms face different cleanup costs. For example, if Firm A has newer equipment than Firm B, it may well be able to reduce its pollution at much lower costs. A solution to this dilemma is to

move away from uniform regulation (sometimes referred to as command/control) and toward more price-sensitive and market-based solutions. Activity 3 will help students compare these options.

16. With stronger students, distribute Activity 3 and let students work in small groups of three or four. With weaker students, a teacher-led discussion for the entire class can be used instead.

17. Debrief the activity by comparing and contrasting the various ways in which a similar outcome (4 fewer tons of pollution) can be achieved by the government. Market-based solutions (such as the tax method) are preferred to uniform regulations, especially when the parties involved face different circumstances.

Answers: Retro - $450 (150 + 300); Novo - $240 (100 + 140); both combined - $690. With the tax, Retro would not clean up all 5 tons; it is cheaper to pay the tax ($200 each ton) than clean up the 2nd, 3rd, 4th, and 5th tons. Retro will pollute 4 tons, clean up 1 ton; Novo would not clean up all 5 tons; it is cheaper to pay the tax ($200 each ton) than clean up the 4th and 5th tons. Novo will pollute 2 tons and clean up 3 tons. Yes, this tax achieves the same 4-ton reduction as the uniform mandate, but it only costs $589. Yes, the tax is a better way to reduce this amount of pollution because the uniform mandate costs more ($690).

CLOSURE

1. On an overhead projector or blackboard, make a list with the following terms: rival, nonrival, excludable, nonexcludable

Display the following:

MIXED GOODS
trait_____
trait_____
example_____

MIXED GOODS
trait_____
trait_____
example_____

PURE PUBLIC GOODS
trait_____
trait_____
example_____

PURE PRIVATE GOODS
trait_____
trait_____
example_____

Tell students to use all possible combinations of the rival/nonrival and excludable/nonexcludable characteristics to identify the four different types goods, and to provide an example that is different from any discussed earlier by the class. Mixed goods are listed twice because there are two types.

ASSESSMENT

(Correct answers are in **bold**)

1. A pure public good is any good that is:
   a. produced by government
   b. financed by government
   c. **nonrival and nonexcludable**
   d. nonrival and excludable

2. When a good is rival in consumption, this means:
   a. **it cannot be used by others when someone else consumes it**
   b. it is jointly consumed by many individuals at the same time
   c. the government competes with private industry to produce it
   d. it generates externalities to others

3. A good that is both rival and nonexcludable is a:
   a. pure public good
   b. pure private good
   c. **mixed good**
   d. free good

4. A service that is both nonrival and excludable is a:
   a. pure public service
   b. pure private service
   c. mixed service
   d. free service

5. The problem of free-riders is most strongly associated with the goods that are:
   a. rival
   b. nonrival
   c. excludable
   d. nonexcludable

6. When free-riders exist, the amount of a public good produced is likely to be:
   a. higher than the efficient amount
   b. lower than the efficient amount
   c. equal to the efficient amount
   d. unaffected

EXTENSION ACTIVITIES

1. Ask students to check out the Stephen King experience with free riders in cyberspace. See www.stephenking.com/pages/ News/ 2000/2000-12-04a.html.

Teacher's note: In the year 2000, noted author Stephen King was the first to experiment with electronic novels. He wrote a new serial e-novel, *The Plant*, and made it available only on the internet (not in bookstores). He provided early chapters on a website, asking payment of $1 per chapter. He promised that additional chapters would be posted ONLY if payments were received from at least 75% of those who downloaded the early chapters. What does economic theory predict? (massive freeloading) What was Stephen King's experience? By the time he posted five or six chapters, only 46% paid the $1 per chapter fee, meaning that more than half of downloaders were also free riders.

2. Have students research the public goods issues associated with the Napster case, in which, for the time the website was functioning, copyrighted music of all types were available for "free" downloading on the internet. See www.thestandard.com or www.itworld.com, and Activity 4 in Lesson 2 in this volume.

3. Have capable students who are interested in public policy and the environment answer this challenge question related to Activity 3:

CHALLENGE Q: Suppose that instead of the uniform mandate or tax method of reducing pollution by 4 tons, the government sets up a permit or market-based solution to the problem. It hands out free pollution permits (six permits in all – three to each firm) and announces that every ton of pollution generated requires a permit. Firms are free to trade permits as they see fit. Note that this scheme also accomplishes a 4-ton reduction in pollution. Would any trading of permits occur between Novo and Retro? If so, who would buy and who would sell? How many? In what range of prices would you expect to see the permit(s) traded?

Answers: Because Retro faces higher pollution control costs, it is likely to be the buyer of permits from Novo. With 3 permits in hand (initial distribution from government) Novo sees that there is an opportunity cost of selling a permit to Retro. If Novo sells a permit, it would then be required to clean up an additional (3rd) ton of pollution, because it can only pollute 2 tons with 2 permits. Novo's extra cost of cleanup = $199 (see schedule). In selling a permit, Novo would ask a price at least as high as $199. If Retro buys a permit, it would have 4 permits and thus be allowed to forego the costs of cleaning up the 2nd ton. That saves Retro $300 (see schedule). Therefore, permit prices in the range of $199 to $300 allow both Novo and Retro to be better off. Trading another permit would not occur. This would leave Novo with only 1 permit, making it mandatory to incur $325 extra costs to clean up a 4th ton. The value of the additional permit to Retro, however, is no greater than $150 (the extra costs foregone with the 1st ton of cleanup). Novo *would demand a higher price than Retro is willing to pay. Thus voluntary exchange at an agreeable price for both parties is not possible.*

Conclusion: Retro buys 1 permit, sold by Novo, at a price between $199 and $300. The outcome of 4 tons reduction in pollution is achieved. Retro reduces pollution by 1 ton, holding 4 permits. Novo reduces pollution by 3 tons, holding 2 permits. Total resource cost of achieving outcome (not counting permit prices) = 150 + 100 + 140 + 199 = $589. There is no lower cost method of achieving this outcome.

Visual 1
Classifying Public and Private Goods and Services

The chart with different cells (or spaces) below is used to sort goods and services into various categories: pure private goods and services, pure public goods and services, and mixed goods and services that are either rival but nonexcludable or nonrival but excludable. Traits for the products are to be indicated using the following visual codes:

Vertical lines = RIVAL   Horizontal lines = EXCLUDABLE
No vertical lines = NONRIVAL   No horizontal lines = NONEXCLUDABLE

Cell 1 – no lines (NONRIVAL + NONEXCLUDABLE) = pure public good or service
Cell 2 – horizontal lines only (NONRIVAL + EXCLUDABLE) = mixed
Cell 3 – vertical lincs only (RIVAL + NONEXCLUDABLE) = mixed
Cell 4 – vertical + horizontal lines (RIVAL + EXCLUDABLE) = pure private good or service

Use the definitions in the handout and work with your teammates to determine which of the goods belong in cells 1, 2, 3, and 4 of the chart.

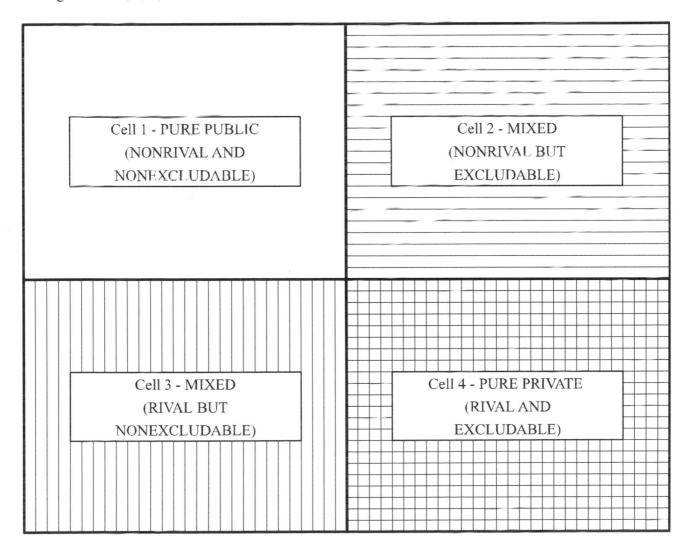

Cell 1 - PURE PUBLIC
(NONRIVAL AND NONEXCLUDABLE)

Cell 2 - MIXED
(NONRIVAL BUT EXCLUDABLE)

Cell 3 - MIXED
(RIVAL BUT NONEXCLUDABLE)

Cell 4 - PURE PRIVATE
(RIVAL AND EXCLUDABLE)

Visual 2
Finding the Efficient Level of Production

How do economists determine the best amount of a good or service to produce? As long as the dollar value of additional benefits from one more unit are greater than the additional costs, more should be produced. If the additional costs of producing the last unit are higher than the additional benefits, less should be produced. The efficient amount of output occurs when the additional benefits just equal the extra costs for the last unit produced.

Number of Units Produced	Additional Benefits of Last Unit	Additional Costs of Last Unit	Compare Additional Benefits and Costs	Produce More Output?
1	12	2	12 > 2	yes
2	9	3	9 > 3	yes
3	5	5	5 = 5	efficient
4	4	7	4 < 7	no
5	3	10	3 < 10	no

The efficient amount of output for this good or service is 3 units.

From *Focus: Institutions and Markets,* © National Council on Economic Education, New York, NY

Activity 1
Public Goods – Giving Government the Green Light

DEFINITIONS

1. **Pure Private Goods and Services**: A pure private good or service is rival and excludable. Rival means that when the good or service is consumed by one person, it cannot be used by others. Excludable means that it is relatively easy to prevent those who do not pay from consuming the good or service. It is easy to produce and sell these types of products in a free market.

2. **Pure Public Goods and Services:** A pure public good or service is nonrival and nonexcludable. Nonrival means that the good or service can be consumed jointly by any number of people at the same time without reducing the amount available to others. Nonexcludable means that it is difficult or expensive to prevent those who do not pay from consuming the good or service.

3. **Mixed Goods and Services**: A mixed good or service might be nonrival and excludable. An example is a bus with empty seats. Until capacity is reached, the bus is nonrival and the driver can control who rides, excluding those who refuse to pay. A different type of mixed good or service is nonexcludable but rival. These situations often involve externalities. Externalities are positive benefits or negative costs that spill over to individuals who are neither producers nor consumers. Because the impact is on outsiders, externalities are sometimes referred to as "third party" costs or benefits. Chicken pox vaccinations are an example of this type of mixed good. The vaccine is rival, but it also has positive externalities. There are benefits to others who come in contact with the vaccinated person, and these third parties cannot be excluded from the benefits. Air, water, and noise pollution are examples of negative externalities that spill over to others not involved directly in the market transaction.

DIRECTIONS

Your group will be given a team chart, Classifying Public and Private Goods and Services, for classifying goods, a supply of description cards to share, and one "product card" for each team member. Begin your turn by announcing the good or service listed on your "product card" and then describe its characteristics (either rival or nonrival, and excludable or nonexcludable). Other members of the group will then respond, and together you will agree which characteristics apply to each good or service. Use a paper clip to attach the description cards beneath the "products card" and place the clipped bundle in the correct location on the chart. Use the definitions above to determine what type of good you have. Announce your findings: "My good is _____ and it is (rival/nonrival and excludable/nonexcludable) and therefore belongs in (cell 1 – pure public, nonrival and nonexcludable; or cell 2 – mixed, nonrival but excludable; or cell 3 – mixed, rival but nonexcludable; or cell 4, pure private, rival and excludable.)

For example, Zoe has a "product card" that reads "athletic shoes." She and her group decide that athletic shoes are rival and excludable. Zoe selects those cards, clips them behind the product card, and places the bundle in the pure private products cell on the chart. She announces: "My good is athletic shoes and it is rival and excludable and belongs in the pure private cell." After all students have presented their product, all of the groups will report their findings to the rest of class. Further adjustments are made to the cards and locations of the "product cards" if the class determines that the good or service was not correctly classified by the small groups.

Activity 1
Part II – Cards with Characteristics of Public and Private Goods

RIVAL	NONRIVAL	EXCLUDABLE	NONEXCLUDABLE
RIVAL	NONRIVAL	EXCLUDABLE	NONEXCLUDABLE
RIVAL	NONRIVAL	EXCLUDABLE	NONEXCLUDABLE
RIVAL	NONRIVAL	EXCLUDABLE	NONEXCLUDABLE
RIVAL	NONRIVAL	EXCLUDABLE	NONEXCLUDABLE

Activity 1
PART III – PRODUCT CARDS

COMPACT DISCS	FLOOD CONTROL PROJECTS	HAIRCUTS
NATIONAL DEFENSE	ELEMENTARY EDUCATION	BRIDGE
BUSY CITY STREETS	LIMITED ACCESS HIGHWAY	PIZZA
FIRE PROTECTION	BEACH ALONG THE OCEAN	LIGHTHOUSE
FLU SHOTS	PAY-PER-VIEW TV PROGRAMS	SOFT DRINKS
COUNTY ZOO	OPEN ACCESS WEBSITE	POLLUTION
FIREWORKS	DISC JOCKEY MUSIC AT DANCE	MATH TUTOR
UPS DELIVERY	LIVE THEATRE PERFORMANCE	HOSPITAL ER
POLICE PROTECTION	NEIGHBORHOOD BEAUTIFICATION	GRAND CANYON
AIR CONDITIONING	LIMITED ACCESS (SUBSCRIBER)WEB SITE	RADIO BROADCAST

Activity 2
The Case of the Vanishing Streetlights:
A Free Rider Mystery

Harry, Pat, and Mary live on Plumb Street in an unincorporated village. Their little neighborhood is safe by day, but there are starting to be some problems after dark. There are currently no streetlights on Plumb Street, but the county engineer says there is room for up to four lights, and that the lights could be installed and maintained for $500 per year for each light. The catch is that if they want the lights, they have to pay for them. The streetlights provide different levels of benefits to Harry, Pat, and Mary, based on individual differences in their preferences for lighted streets, how much risk they feel at night, and the amount of money they make. The table below shows the dollar value of benefits each person has for each additional light.

| | Additional benefits (in $ for each additional streetlight) | | | |
	1st light	2nd light	3rd light	4th light
Harry	400	350	300	200
Pat	300	200	125	75
Mary	250	150	75	25

At a cost of $500 for each light, and assuming that each would never pay more for a light than the extra benefits they personally receive, answer the following questions:

Would Harry buy any lights *on his own*? _____ Why or why not?
Would Pat? _____ Why or why not?
Would Mary? _____ Why or why not?

Although the streetlight price is high relative to the residents' individual extra benefits, Mary thinks about the problem a little further. She remembers that streetlights can be jointly consumed. Each streetlight, once purchased, can provide benefits to all the residents simultaneously. What is the economic term for this characteristic of streetlights? _____

Mary arranges a meeting with her neighbors. They all agree to contribute to the streetlight fund as long as their payment is no more than their marginal benefits listed above. Will there be enough funds to buy the first streetlight if all residents contribute enough? _____ the 2nd? _____ the 3rd? _____ the 4th? _____

Now suppose Harry decides not to contribute to the streetlight fund. He figures out that if the streetlights are bought and installed on Plumb Street, he cannot be prevented from enjoying them even if he doesn't contribute to their purchase. What is the economic term for this characteristic associated with streetlights? _____ What is the economic term for Harry's behavior? _____

If only Harry refuses to contribute, how many streetlights will be bought? _____
If only Pat refuses to contribute, how many streetlights will be bought? _____
If only Mary refuses to contribute, how many streetlights will be bought? _____

Based on the personal benefit schedules in the table above, and the cost of each light, what is the efficient number of streetlights to purchase? _____

Activity 3
Markets Rule at Cleaning Up

Retro and Novo are the major manufacturers in a small town. Retro was founded more than a century ago and its physical plant is fairly old. Novo is the newcomer to town, and much of its equipment is state-of-the-art. They both produce the same good, and both companies release pollution into the environment. If allowed to pollute without any cleanup, each firm generates 5 tons of effluent, for a total of 10 tons per year. Recently, the local government passed a law requiring that their total pollution be reduced to 6 tons per year. To be fair to both firms, it was decided that each would bear the cost of cleaning up 2 tons. Pollution cleanup costs for the two firms, measured as the $ cost of cleaning up one additional unit of effluent, are shown below.

	Retro Company $ extra cost	Novo Company $ extra cost
1st ton reduced	150	100
2nd ton reduced	300	140
3rd ton reduced	500	199
4th ton reduced	750	325
5th ton reduced	1,100	500

Novo has lower costs of cleanup because of its newer machines and technology and both firms face rising costs as they reduce emissions by additional units. As in many production situations, reducing pollution is initially easier and less expensive, but as there is less and less pollution left to remove the cost of reducing pollution by one more unit rises.

Given this information, if the two companies obey the government order to reduce pollution by 2 tons each, what is the cost of doing this? For Retro _____ For Novo _____ For both firms combined _____

Suppose that instead of mandating an exact amount of pollution reduction, the government uses a tax (disincentive) method to generate the 4-ton reduction. Here are the details: each firm pays $200 for each ton of effluent they emit per year. Each firm decides how many tons to emit, but each ton released incurs a tax of $200.

Under this system, will Retro be willing to clean up all 5 tons of pollution? ___ Why or why not? How many tons will it pollute? _____ How many tons will it clean up? _____

Will Novo be willing to clean up all 5 tons of pollution? ___ Why or why not? How many tons will it pollute? _____ How many tons will it clean up? _____

At this tax rate ($200 per ton), does the government achieve the same outcome (4 tons of pollutions reduced) as in the earlier example, the uniform mandate? _____ What amount of resources (sum of marginal costs for both firms) were used by the firms to accomplish this cleanup? _____ (Note: do not count the tax payments, just the resource costs from the chart.)
Is this a better way to clean up? _____ Why or why not?

decisions made by all households, firms, government agencies, and others in the economy.

BENCHMARKS

Most federal tax revenue comes from personal income and payroll taxes. Payments to social security recipients, the costs of national defense, medical expenditures, and interest payments on the national debt constitute the bulk of federal government spending.

Governments provide an alternative method to markets for supplying goods and services when it appears that the benefits to society of doing so outweigh the costs to society. Not all individuals will bear the same costs or share the same benefits of those policies.

OBJECTIVES

Students will

- ◆ Identify major expenditures of the U.S. federal government and how they have changed over time

- ◆ Calculate income and consumption taxes using different rates and bases

- ◆ Compare the size and scope of government for countries around the world using fiscal burden indexes

- ◆ Use economic freedom indexes to suggest which market institutions are missing or not well developed in some countries

TIME REQUIRED

Two class periods

MATERIALS

- Visual 1: How Does the Federal Government Spend Our Money?

- Visual 2: U.S. Government Spending During War Years
- Visual 3: Progressive, Regressive, and Proportional Taxes
- Visual 4: Part I – What the Citizens of Taxville Pay; Part II – Answer Key
- Visual 5: Calculating Fiscal Burdens: An Example
- Visual 6: Fiscal Burdens for Different Countries
- Visual 7: Factor Scores for Freedom Indexes
- Visual 8: Freedom Indexes: Answer Key
- Activity 1: How Does the Federal Government Spend Our Money?, one copy per student
- Activity 2: Taxes, Taxes, Who Pays the Taxes?, one copy per student
- Activity 3: Measuring the Fiscal Burden of Government Tax and Expenditure Programs – Part A: A Grading System for Taxes and Government Expenditures, one copy per student; Part B: Calculating a Measure of Fiscal Burden, one copy per student; Part C: Student Score Cards, cut apart to provide one per student; Part D: Country Data Cards (30), cut apart to provide one per student
- Activity 4: Building Institutions for Markets, one copy per student
- Calculators

PROCEDURES

1. Briefly review the economic roles of government in a market economy. This lesson assumes that students have knowledge of defining and enforcing property rights, providing public goods and adjusting for externalities, and the economic role of government. Note that all of these ideas suggest that there is an important, but limited, economic role for government in market economies. To perform that role, the government must collect taxes and fees to shift resources away from households and businesses, so that the government can hire people and purchase or rent the other

resources required for it to operate. The basic question raised in this lesson is: How large a part of the economy is government today? After presenting evidence on the level and major categories of federal government spending, the lesson provides additional information to encourage a reasoned discussion about how large a part of the economy government at all levels (federal, state, and local) should be – recognizing that not everyone will agree about the answer to that question.

2. Explain that the size of government is measured by its revenues, expenditures, deficits, and debt. Adjustments for population (per capita), inflation, and the size of the economy (relative to GDP) are required to make meaningful comparisons across countries and over time.

3. Ask students to write down what percent of a nation's annual income or gross domestic product (GDP) they believe should be spent for goods and services provided by federal, state, and local governments combined and what percent of their income people should pay as taxes. Tabulate the results and announce the classroom averages. (Have a student ready to do this with a calculator as students announce their individual estimates.) There will probably be a considerable range in the estimates provided by individual students, but tell students you will compare these figures to actual data before discussing the students' responses.

4. Introduce the concept of **government expenditures**. Federal, state, and local governments buy goods and services and pay for those with money collected from taxes, fees, and borrowing. Military and civilian salaries, computers, office supplies, and helicopters are just a few examples of government spending on goods and services. Governments also use taxes and borrowed funds to redirect income from some individuals to others. This type of spending is

referred to as **transfer payments**. Unemployment benefits, cash subsidies to low income families, and social security benefits are examples.

5. Announce the results of the student survey, reporting the class average responses for government expenditures divided by gross domestic product (G/GDP) and taxes as a percentage of income. Discuss the range of individual student responses by reporting several of the lower-end and higher-end answers. Compare the class responses with actual data for G/GDP for the United States, which has remained relatively stable in recent years, around 30 percent. The federal government is responsible for roughly two-thirds of those expenditures, spending primarily on national defense, Social Security, Medicare, income assistance, and interest on the national debt. State and local government expenditures typically provide education, income assistance, public safety, and other municipal services.

6. Distribute Activity 1 to students, and explain that the federal government expenditure data are reported in millions of U.S. dollars. Tell students to compute the percentages of federal government spending in each category for each year. Computations for 1965 use $118,228 for the denominator, and for 2004 use $2,229,425. Display Visual 1 and have students check their work. *(Answers: **1965**: national defense, 42.8%; education/training, 1.8%; health/Medicare, 1.5%; income assistance, 8.0%; social security, 14.8%; environment, 2.1%; interest on debt, 7.3%; agriculture, 3.3%; other, 18.3%. [fed outlays]/GDP = 17.2% **2004**: national defense, 17.5%; education/training, 3.8%; health/Medicare, 22.7%; income assistance, 14.6%; social security, 22.3%; environment, 1.4%; interest on debt, 7.9%; agriculture, 0.9%; other, 8.8%. [fed outlays]/GDP = 19.7%.*

7. Guide students in discussing changes in the relative shares of federal outlays between 1965 and 2004. Note that national defense spending is a smaller share of outlays in 2004 than in 1965, but spending on social security, income assistance, and health/Medicare are up significantly. Social Security legislation was first passed in 1935 and benefits started in 1937; the Medicare program for senior citizens began in 1965. Deficit spending (outlays higher than revenues) throughout the 1970s, 1980s, and early1990s significantly raised the amount of debt owed by the federal government and the amount of interest owed on the debt. Also note that although direct government expenditures on the environment are fairly small as a percentage of the budget, many government laws and regulations have required businesses and consumers to spend more on environmental controls and products during this time period.

8. Based on the patterns observed for the federal government, ask students to draw conclusions about the trend in the overall size of government (as a percent of GDP), and to offer possible reasons for that trend. If necessary, help the students suggest possible factors, such as demographic trends (people living longer), technology changes in health care and national defense, construction of infrastructure, and so forth. Tell students that per capita disposable income rose by 124% in the United States from 1965 to 2003, (from $10,965 in 1965 to $24,562 at end of 2002, with both figures in 1996 prices to control for inflation). Ask whether the pattern in government expenditures over this period suggests an increase in demand for public services as income levels rise. *(Yes, the pattern is most evident in payments to individuals for social security, income assistance, and health/Medicare.)*

9. Display Visual 2, which shows expenditure data for various war years (WWII, Korean Conflict, Vietnam War), and discuss the opportunity costs of spending on national defense (fewer resources available for spending on other goods and services – the guns vs. butter argument).

10. Introduce **government revenues**, the money federal, state, and local governments collect to pay for their expenditures. In the United States, most of this revenue is collected through **taxes**, compulsory payments imposed on individuals or firms, or specific kinds of transactions. Some revenues are also collected as direct fees, for example for automobile registration and tags; licenses for driving, hunting, and fishing; entrance fees to state or national parks; building and inspection permits, etc.

11. Explain the connection between taxes and government spending. Increased government expenditures require higher levels of revenues, through taxes, fees, or borrowing. When people demand more goods and services from the public sector, the consequence is that they will have fewer resources to spend as individuals. Some government expenditures can promote future economic growth – such as building and maintaining highways and bridges – but all government spending and taxing limits individual choices. Thus, the size of government affects both economic growth and economic freedom, and the overall quality of life in a nation.

12. Explain that there are many different ways to structure taxes. For example, taxes can be collected using a single rate of tax, which is often referred to as a flat rate tax. Provide a simple example of this tax structure for students: suppose tax liability in a nation is 10% of all income received. Someone earning $10,000 pays $1,000 in tax and someone earning $100,000 pays $10,000 in tax. Explain that a tax that levies the same percentage of tax liability on all taxpayers is known as a **proportional tax**.

13. Introduce the concepts of progressive and regressive taxes. A **regressive tax** is one in which lower income individuals pay a greater percentage of their income in taxes than higher income individuals. A **progressive tax** is one in which higher income individuals pay a greater percentage of their income in taxes than lower income individuals. Display Visual 3, Progressive, Regressive, and Proportional Taxes, to demonstrate these concepts numerically. Tax X is a progressive tax, because tax payments as a fraction of income rise as income rises. Tax Y is a regressive tax, because taxes as a fraction of income fall as income rises. Tax Z is proportional because taxes are always the same fraction of income.

14. Distribute one copy of Activity 2 to each student. Tell them that they should complete ONLY the top half of Activity 2 during the initial phase of this activity. Divide students evenly into taxpayer groups A or B, and have them mark which group on their papers, but do not divide them into groups at this time. Students in the A group have incomes = $4,000, and students in the B group have incomes = $8,000. Instruct students to work independently and compute their own tax liability under the four separate tax policies.

15. When students are finished, pair each A group student with a partner from the B group, so that each A taxpayer sits next to a B taxpayer. Display Part I of Visual 4, What the Citizens of Taxville Pay, and ask students to provide answers for the four cases. Enter responses on Visual 4 as students provide them, using Part II of Visual 4, the Answer Key, to display correct computations, as needed. After completing all of the blanks in Part I, continue to display this visual.

16. Instruct students to transfer the answers from the overhead to the lower portion of the worksheet on Activity 2. Allow five minutes for the student pairs to review

these answers and to compare the taxes as a percentage of gross income for taxpayers A and B. Discuss whether people who earn low, middle, or high incomes would be more likely to support progressive, proportional, or regressive taxes.

17. Explain that virtually all economic decisions, whether monetary (including spending, earning, producing) or nonmonetary (such as choosing how to spend our free time) are made at the margin. In other words, we decide whether to buy a little more or a little less of various products in deciding how to spend our next dollar, and how to use our next "day off" or even our next hour of "free time." Individual decisions to earn or spend money are especially influenced by the **marginal tax rate**, the rate affecting their last (or next) dollar of taxable economic activity. In other words, what really matters is the tax rate that applies to the next dollar a person will earn, spend, save, or invest. Point out that in Case 2 on the lower half of Activity 2, taxpayer "A" faces a marginal tax rate of 10% (the next dollar is subject to a 10% tax), so the taxpayer would keep 90 cents of that dollar after taxes. Taxpayer "B" faces a marginal tax rate of 20% because the higher level of earnings put that next dollar earned in a higher rate. Therefore, this taxpayer would keep $.80 of the next dollar earned, after taxes. Note that under a progressive tax system, someone who earns a high level of income will be charged a higher marginal tax rate than the average tax rate paid by all taxpayers.

18. Distribute Activity 3, Measuring the Fiscal Burden of Government Tax and Expenditure Programs, and give each student one country data card and one student score card for Activity 3. Explain that various organizations have proposed ways in which to measure and compare fiscal burdens across countries. To demonstrate how these measurements are calculated, Activity 3 uses scales and criteria developed by the Heritage

Foundation, a conservative think tank in Washington, D.C.

19. Allow students time to read the handouts. Note that the government expenditure grading scale has different criteria for developed and developing countries. In this context, developed countries are those with high incomes per capita. Developing countries are those with low through upper middle incomes per capita.

20. Make sure students understand the criteria listed in the grading scales. Help them distinguish between the highest marginal rate in a nation's tax code and the marginal rate faced by the "average" taxpayer. The latter is defined as the marginal tax rate that applies to the mean level of income in that country. For example, the top tax rate in a nation may be very high (e.g., 70%) but a taxpayer whose income is at the average level for the country faces a much lower marginal rate.

21. Review instructions for completing the fiscal burden worksheet. Answer any questions students have regarding the example for Hungary, shown in Part A. Then display Visual 5, Calculating Fiscal Burdens: An Example, and work through each score for Slovak Republic with the class as a group. When students volunteer an answer for scores #2, 3, and 5, ask them to read the corresponding criterion from the Grading Scales that fits the situation.

22. To use countries other than those provided in this lesson or more current data on the countries that are listed, see the Heritage Foundation website: www.heritage.org.

23. Instruct students to complete their student score card individually, using their country data card, instructions, and grading scales. Then display Visual 6, Fiscal Burdens for Different Countries, and have students check their computations. Reinforce the interpretation of high and low scores: higher

scores are associated with higher government fiscal burdens and less economic freedom; lower scores are associated with lower government fiscal burdens and more economic freedom.

24. Discuss the following questions with the class:
- Which countries have low fiscal burdens because both taxes and expenditures are relatively low? (*Hong Kong, Indonesia, Singapore, Vietnam*)
- Which countries have high fiscal burdens because both taxes and expenditures are relatively high? (*Congo, Denmark, Iraq, Israel, Poland, South Africa, Ukraine*)
- Which countries have low tax burdens but high expenditure burdens? (*Albania, Estonia, Namibia, Qatar, Russia*)
- How does the United States compare with other countries regarding government expenditures as a percentage of GDP? (*G/GDP = 30 percent for the U.S. and has been relatively stable for years. Compared with other developed industrial nations the United States is at the lower end, with smaller government shares.*) Compared to other nations, the United States relies more heavily on taxes on income and wealth rather than taxes on sales, consumption, or imports. Whether the size and scope of government is too small in the United States or too large in other developed countries is a matter of longstanding debate, based largely on social and normative beliefs held by individuals in the different nations; but over the past 20 years many of the other developed countries have been moving closer to the U.S. levels.

25. Explain that fiscal burden is just one of 10 factors used by the Heritage Foundation to

determine the Index of Economic Freedom. The other factors are: trade policy, government intervention in the economy, monetary policy, capital flows and foreign investment, banking and finance, wages and prices, property rights, regulation, and black market activity. If market-supporting institutions are well established and functioning properly, the scores for those 10 areas should also be relatively low, indicating more freedom for markets to operate.

26. Explain that government and other institutions are important to a country's growth and development. Point out that Australia and Argentina are two similarly endowed countries. Both are multicultural southern hemisphere nations with abundant natural resources and similar climates. Yet Australia surpasses Argentina in almost every measure of economic well-being. Ask students why one country is experiencing growth while the other struggles. Suggest that a major difference is the institutional framework in the two nations. Australia ranked ninth on the 2002 Heritage Foundation Index of Economic Freedom Rankings, with a score of 1.85, and has more highly developed institutions supporting markets. Argentina ranked 38th with a score of 2.50. (See www.heritage.org.)

27. Explain that students will now participate in an activity in which they will consider 10 factors affecting economic freedom and identify which market institutions might be missing or underdeveloped in a country. Assign a different country and distribute a copy of Activity 4 to each student in the class. Display or distribute Visual 7, Factor Scores for Freedom Indexes, and tell students to copy the ten scores for their country onto their worksheets. (If students have already completed Activity 3 and are working with the same country, explain that the fiscal burden score they copy may be slightly different from the one they computed in Activity 3 because of different rounding procedures used by the

Heritage Foundation.) Tell students to complete the Freedom Index calculation by adding up all ten scores for their country and dividing by 10.

28. Display Visual 8, Freedom Indexes: Answer Key, and have students check their answers.

29. Explain that the Heritage Foundation groups countries by their composite Freedom Index Values using the following labels: 1.0 -1.9 free; 2.0 – 2.9 mostly free; 3.0-3.9 mostly unfree; and 4.0 and above, repressed. Have students report to the class the name of their country, its Freedom Index, and whether the Heritage Foundation would consider it to be free, mostly free, mostly unfree, or repressed.

30. Ask students to identify which aspects of their assigned country (trade, fiscal burden, government intervention, etc) might benefit from institution building or reform, based on the relative freedom scores for each of the ten categories.

CLOSURE

Instruct students to use the findings from the four cases in Activity 2 to answer the following questions:

- Adam earns half as much income as Eve and pays half as much in taxes. What type of income tax system is in place? *(Proportional – see case 1)*

- Mike earns more income than Ike and also pays more in taxes than Ike does. Is this income tax system necessarily progressive? *(No – see case 1. It is possible that the tax is progressive, but more information is needed to be certain. Because Mike earns more income, a proportional tax would create a higher tax liability for him compared with Ike. The key to determining progressivity is the tax liability as a percent of income.)*

- Why do most general consumption taxes, such as state sales taxes, tend to be regressive in impact even though they are flat rate? *(See case 3. Higher income families do not spend as much of their income on consumer goods, so less of their earned income is subject to the flat rate of the tax)*

- The State of Wisconsin exempts most food and beverage grocery items from its sales tax while the State of Illinois does tax these items. Which state is reducing the regressive impact of its sales tax? *(Wisconsin. See case 4. For lower income families, expenditures for food are a larger part of their budget than for wealthier households. By eliminating the tax on these purchases, the sales tax is made less regressive.)*

ASSESSMENT

(Correct answers are in **bold**)

1. Choose the correct statement:
   a. national defense has always been the largest category of federal government expenditures
   b. by law, social security expenditures are a constant percentage of government outlays
   c. **net interest on the debt rose as a percentage of government expenditures over time from the 1960s to 2003**
   d. expenditures on income assistance are a smaller portion of federal expenditures in the early 21st century than during the mid-20th century

2. Flat-rate taxes on income are what kind of tax?
   a. progressive
   b. **proportional**
   c. regressive
   d. uneven

3. General sales taxes tend to be _____ in impact because low income taxpayers tend to spend a _____ % of their income than high income taxpayers.
   a. progressive   higher
   b. proportional lower
   c. **regressive**   **higher**
   d. regressive   lower

4. Which of the following policies could be used to make a tax on consumption somewhat progressive?
   a. impose higher rates on low income taxpayers
   b. allow exemptions for high income taxpayers
   c. allow luxury goods such as SUVs and vacations to be exempt from the consumption tax
   d. **allow all taxpayers an exemption for the first few thousand dollars of consumption**

EXTENSION ACTIVITIES

1. Have students compare government expenditures for three years: the year one of their grandparents was born, the year one of their parents was born, and the year they were born. Have students write two or three paragraphs about the advantages and disadvantages associated with those different levels of government expenditures.

2. Assign groups of students to report on federal, state and local tax history, tax codes, tax collections, and related subjects, starting with the following websites: www.taxsites.com, www.irs.gov, http://taxhistory.tax.org, www.taxadmin.org/fta/rate/tax_stru.html, www.ustreas.gov/education/fact, and www.taxpolicycenter.org. Assign another group to report on the current federal budget at www.whitehouse.gov.

Visual 1
How Does the Federal Government Spend Our Money?

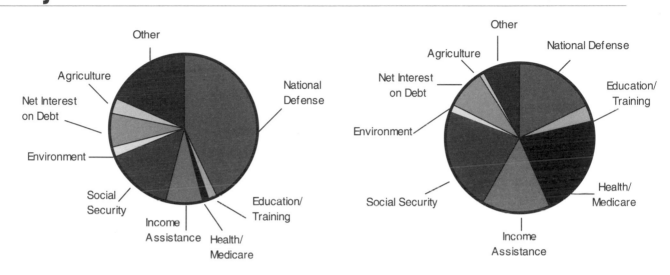

	1965		2004 (est)	
	amount ($millions)	% of outlays	amount ($millions)	% of outlays
National defense	50,620	42.8	390,419	17.5
Education/training	2,140	1.8	85,336	3.8
Health/Medicare	1,791	1.5	505,457	22.7
Income assistance	9,469	8.0	324,962	14.6
Social Security	17,460	14.8	497,299	22.3
Environment	2,531	2.1	31,586	1.4
Net interest on debt	8,591	7.3	176,395	7.9
Agriculture	3,955	3.3	20,799	0.9
Other	21,671	18.3	197,172	8.8
Total Federal Outlays	**118,228**	**100**	**2,229,425**	**100**
GDP	**687,900**		**11,303,100**	
[fed outlays]/GDP	**17.2%**		**19.7%**	

Source: *The Budget for Fiscal Year 2004*, **Historical Tables: Federal Government Outlays, by Function, Table 3.1, accessed at www.whitehouse.gov/omb/budget**

Visual 2
U.S. Government Expenditures During War Years

	1943		1951		1970	
	Amount ($millions)	% of outlays	Amount ($millions)	% of outlays	Amount ($millions)	% of outlays
National defense	66,699	84.9	23,566	51.8	81,692	41.8
Education/training	375	0.5	235	0.5	8,634	4.4
Health/Medicare	92	0.1	323	0.7	12,120	6.2
Income Assistance	1,739	2.2	3,352	7.4	15,655	8.0
Social Security	177	0.2	1,565	3.4	30,270	15.5
Environment	726	0.9	1,310	2.9	3,065	1.6
Net interest on debt	1,529	1.9	4,665	10.2	14,380	7.3
Agriculture	343	0.4	NA		5,166	2.6
Other	6,875	8.8	10,498	23.1	24,667	12.6
Total Federal Outlays	**78,555**	**100**	**45,514**	**100**	**195,649**	**100**
GDP	**180,100**		**321,000**		**1,013,200**	
[fed outlays]/GDP	**43.6%**		**14.2%**		**19.3%**	

From *Focus: Institutions and Markets,* © National Council on Economic Education, New York, NY

Visual 3
Progressive, Regressive, and Proportional Taxes

	Tax X Progressive		Tax Y Regressive		Tax Z Proportional	
Income	Tax	Tax/Income	Tax	Tax/Income	Tax	Tax/Income
200	10	5%	20	10%	20	10%
400	40	10%	30	7.5%	40	10%
600	90	15%	40	6.7%	60	10%

Tax X is a **progressive** tax, because tax payments as a fraction of income rise as income rises.

Tax Y is a **regressive** tax, because tax payments as a fraction of income fall as income rises.

Tax Z is a **proportional** tax, because tax payments are always the same fraction of income.

Visual 4
Part I – What the Citizens of Taxville Pay

	Gross Income	Tax	Tax/Gross Income (percent)

Case 1: FLAT TAX ON INCOME

A   _____   _____   _____
B   _____   _____   _____

Case 2: PROGRESSIVE TAX ON INCOME

A   _____   _____   _____
B   _____   _____   _____

Case 3: FLAT TAX ON CONSUMPTION

A   _____   _____   _____
B   _____   _____   _____

Case 4: CONSUMPTION TAX WITH EXEMPTIONS

A   _____   _____   _____
B   _____   _____   _____

Visual 4 (continued)
Part II – What the Citizens of Taxville Pay
Answer Key

Case 1: flat tax on income (rate = 15%)

A: 4,000; 4000; .15 × 4,000 = 600; 600/4,000 = 15%.

B: 8,000; 8,000; .15 × 8,000 =1,200; 1,200/8,000 = 15%

**Case 2: progressive tax on income tax (10% on first $5,000
and 20% above $5,000)**

A: 4,000; 4,000; .10(4,000) + .20(0) = 400; 400/4,000 = 10%

B: 8,000; 8,000; .10(5,000) + .20(8,000 − 5,0000 = 3,000) = 1,100;
1,100/8,000 = 13.75%

**Case 3: flat tax on consumption (rate = 10%)
Note: A consumes 95% of gross income, and B consumes 75%
of gross income**

A: 4,000; .95 × 4,000 = 3,800; .10 × 3,800 = 380; 380/4,000 =
9.5%

B: 8,000; .75 × 8,000 = 6,000; .10 × 6,000 = 600; 600/8,000 =
7.5%

**Case 4: consumption tax with an exemption on first $2,500 consumed
(rate = 10%)**

A: 4,000; 3,800 − 2,500; .10 × 1,300 = 130; 130/4,000 = 3.25%

B: 8,000; 6,000 − 2,500; .10 × 3,500 = 350; 350/8,000 = 4.38%

Visual 5
Calculating Fiscal Burdens: An Example

Country Data card:

Country: SLOVAK REPUBLIC

Top marginal income tax rate: 42%

Avg. taxpayer marginal rate: 25%

Other comments:

Developed? NO

Top marginal corporate income tax rate: 29%

G/GDP: 40.1%

Student Score Card:

1. Country: _____

2. personal income tax score _____

3. corporate income tax score _____

4. tax score _____
   (avg. of personal +
   corporation)

5. expenditure score _____

6. fiscal burden score _____

Answers:

1. Slovak Republic

2. score = 4 (top tax rate greater than 35% but less than 50%, or average tax level between 15-20% and tax structure not fully developed by government or in a state of disarray)

3. score = 3 (progressive corporate tax system with a top rate between 25-35%, or a flat system with tax levels above 25%)

4. tax score = (3 + 4)/2 = 3.5

5. score = 5 (G/GDP > 30%) note: using scale for developing countries

6. fiscal burden score = (3.5 + 5)/2 = 4.25

Visual 6
Fiscal Burdens for Different Countries

	Personal tax score	Corporate tax score	Tax score (avg.)	Expend. score	Fiscal Burden
Albania	2	3	2.5	5	3.75
Australia	5	3	4.0	3	3.50
Belarus	5	2	3.5	5	4.25
Canada	3	3	3.0	4	3.50
China, People's Rep	4	3	3.5	2	2.75
Congo, Republic of	4	4	4.0	5	4.50
Czech Republic	3	3	3.0	5	4.00
Denmark	5	3	4.0	5	4.50
Estonia	3	0	1.5	5	3.25
Hong Kong	2	2	2.0	2	2.00
India	2	3	2.5	4	3.25
Indonesia	2	3	2.5	2	2.25
Iraq	5	5	5.0	5	5.00
Ireland	5	2	3.5	3	3.25
Israel	5	4	4.5	5	4.75
Kenya	2	3	2.5	4	3.25
Lithuania	3	2	2.5	4	3.25
Mexico	5	3	4.0	3	3.50
Namibia	2	3	2.5	5	3.75
New Zealand	4	3	3.5	4	3.75
Nigeria	2	3	2.5	3	2.75
Poland	4	3	3.5	5	4.25
Qatar	1	3	2.0	5	3.50
Russia	2	2	2.0	5	3.50
Singapore	3	3	3.0	2	2.50
South Africa	4	3	3.5	5	4.25
South Korea	4	3	3.5	4	3.75
Ukraine	4	3	3.5	5	4.25
United States	5	3	4.0	3	3.50
Vietnam	3	3	3.0	2	2.50

From *Focus: Institutions and Markets*, © National Council on Economic Education, New York, NY

Visual 7
Factor Scores for Freedom Indexes

Country	Category									
	1	**2**	**3**	**4**	**5**	**6**	**7**	**8**	**9**	**10**
Albania	4	4	3	2	2	3	2	4	4	5
Australia	2	3.5	2	2	2	1	2	1	2	1
Belarus	3	4.5	4	5	4	4	5	4	5	5
Canada	2	4	2	1	3	2	2	1	2	1
China	5	3	4	1	4	4	3	4	4	3.5
Congo, Rep	5	4.5	3	1	4	4	3	4	4	5
Czech Rep	2	4.5	2	2	2	1	2	2	3	3.5
Denmark	2	4.5	3.5	1	2	1	1	1	2	1
Estonia	1	3.5	2	2	1	1	1	2	2	2.5
Hong Kong	1	2	2	1	1	1	2	1	1	1.5
India	5	3.5	3	2	3	4	4	3	4	4
Indonesia	3	2.5	2.5	4	3	4	2	4	4	4.5
Iraq	5	5	5	5	5	5	5	5	5	5
Ireland	2	2.5	2	2	1	1	2	1	2	1.5
Israel	2	5	3.5	1	1	3	2	2	3	4
Kenya	4	3.5	3	2	3	3	2	3	4	4.5
Lithuania	1	3.5	2	1	2	3	2	3	3	3
Mexico	2	3.5	2	4	3	2	2	3	4	3.5
Namibia	4	4	3.5	3	2	3	2	2	3	2.5
New Zealand	2	4	2	1	1	1	2	1	2	1
Nigeria	5	3	3	3	3	4	2	4	4	5
Poland	2	4.5	2	3	2	2	3	2	3	3.5
Qatar	2	3.5	4	1	3	4	3	3	4	2
Russia	4	3.5	2.5	5	3	4	3	4	4	4
Singapore	1	2.5	3	1	1	2	2	1	1	1
South Africa	4	4.5	2.5	2	2	3	2	3	3	3
South Korea	3	3.5	3.5	1	2	3	2	1	3	3
Ukraine	3	4.5	4	5	3	4	3	4	4	4
United States	2	3.5	2	1	2	1	2	1	2	1.5
Vietnam	5	2.5	4	1	4	4	4	5	5	4

Categories: 1–trade policy; 2–fiscal burden; 3–government intervention; 4–monetary policy; 5–foreign investment; 6–banking and finance; 7–wages and prices; 8–property rights; 9–regulation; 10–black market

Visual 8
Freedom Indexes: Answer Key

Albania	3.30	India	3.55	Nigeria	3.60
Australia	1.85	Indonesia	3.35	Poland	2.70
Belarus	4.35	Iraq	5.00	Qatar	2.95
Canada	2.00	Ireland	1.80	Russia	3.70
China	3.55	Israel	2.65	Singapore	1.55
Congo, Rep.	3.75	Kenya	3.20	South Africa	2.90
Czech Rep.	2.40	Lithuania	2.35	South Korea	2.50
Denmark	1.90	Mexico	2.90	Ukraine	3.85
Estonia	1.80	Namibia	2.90	United States	1.80
Hong Kong	1.35	New Zealand	1.70	Vietnam	3.85

Activity 1
How Does the Federal Government Spend Our Money?

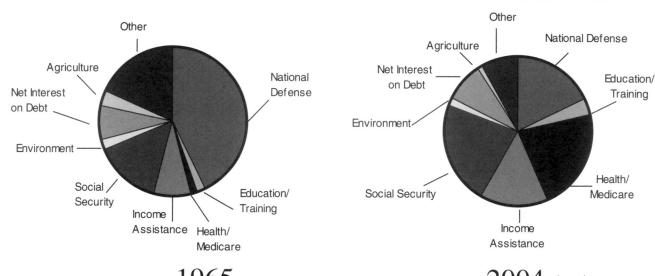

	1965		2004 (est)	
	amount ($millions)	% of outlays	amount ($millions)	% of outlays
National defense	50,620	_____	390,419	_____
Education/training	2,140	_____	85,336	_____
Health/Medicare	1,791	_____	505,457	_____
Income assistance	9,469	_____	324,962	_____
Social Security	17,460	_____	497,299	_____
Environment	2,531	_____	31,586	_____
Net interest on debt	8,591	_____	176,395	_____
Agriculture	3,955	_____	20,799	_____
Other	21,671	_____	197,172	_____
Total Federal Outlays	**118,228**	**100**	**2,229,425**	**100**
GDP	**687,900**		**11,303,100**	
[fed outlays]/GDP	**17.2%**		**19.7%**	

Source: *The Budget for Fiscal Year 2004,* Historical Tables: Federal Government Outlays, by Function, Table 3.1, accessed at www.whitehouse.gov/omb/budget

Activity 2
Taxes, Taxes, Who Pays the Taxes?

Name _____   Member of Taxpayer Group   A   B
                                                                (circle one)

Four different tax policies are being considered by the citizens of Taxville, who fall into two income groups: A and B. Members of taxpayer group A have incomes = $4,000 and consume 95% of their gross income. Members of group B have incomes = $8,000 and consume 75% of their gross income. Circle your assigned group above, and determine your tax liability and taxes as a percentage of gross income for each tax being considered.

Case 1: FLAT TAX ON INCOME, RATE = 15%

Gross income _____ Amt subject to tax _____ tax _____ tax/gross income ___%

Case 2: PROGRESSIVE TAX ON INCOME, RATE = 10% ON FIRST $5,000;
                                                    20% ON INCOME ABOVE $5,000

Gross income _____ Amt subject to tax _____ tax _____ tax/gross income ___%

Case 3: FLAT CONSUMPTION TAX, RATE = 10%

Gross income _____ Amt subject to tax _____ tax _____ tax/gross income ___%

Case 4: CONSUMPTION TAX WITH AN EXEMPTION ON FIRST $2,500 CONSUMED,
RATE = 10%

Gross income _____ Amt subject to tax _____ tax _____ tax/gross income ___%

SUMMARY OF FINDINGS FOR CITIZENS OF TAXVILLE

	Gross income	tax liability	tax/gross income (percent)
Case 1: FLAT TAX ON INCOME			
A	_____	_____	_____
B	_____	_____	_____
Case 2: PROGRESSIVE TAX ON INCOME			
A	_____	_____	_____
B	_____	_____	_____
Case 3: FLAT TAX ON CONSUMPTION			
A	_____	_____	_____
B	_____	_____	_____
Case 4: CONSUMPTION TAX WITH EXEMPTION			
A	_____	_____	_____
B	_____	_____	_____

Activity 3
Measuring the Fiscal Burden of Government Tax and Expenditure Programs

PART A: A GRADING SYSTEM FOR TAXES AND GOVERNMENT EXPENDITURES

(These scores and tax rate criteria were used by The Heritage Foundation in determining values for the fiscal burden component of its 2002 Index of Economic Freedom.)

Income Tax Grading Scale

Score	Tax Rates	Criteria
1	very low	no taxes on income, or flat rate of 10% or less
2	low	top tax rate of 25% or less, or flat rate between 10-20%, or top rate of 40% or below and marginal rate faced by average taxpayer equal to 10% or less
3	moderate	top tax rate of 35% or less, or marginal rate faced by average taxpayer of 15% or less
4	high	top tax rate greater than 35% but less than 50%, or average tax level between 15-20% and tax structure not fully developed by government or in a state or disarray
5	very high	top rate above 50% and marginal rate faced by average taxpayer greater than 20% but less than 25%, or a tax rate on average taxpayer income of 25% regardless of the top rate, or a tax system through which government confiscates most economic output resulting from government ownership of most economic activity

Corporate Tax Grading Scale

Score	Tax Rates	Criteria
1	very low	limited or no taxes imposed on corporate profits
2	low	corporate tax rate less than or equal to 25 %
3	moderate	progressive corporate tax system with a top rate between 25-35%, or a flat system with tax levels above 25%
4	high	progressive corporate tax system with top rate between 35-45%, or a tax structure not fully developed by government or in a state of disarray
5	very high	cumbersome progressive tax system with top corporate rates of more than 45%, or tax system in which government confiscates most economic output resulting from government ownership of most economic activity

Government Expenditure Grading Scale

Score	G/GDP	Criteria Developed Countries	Criteria Developing Countries
1	very low	G/GDP < or = 15%	G/GDP < or = 15%
2	low	15% < G/GDP < or = 25%	15% < G/GDP < or = 20%
3	moderate	25% < G/GDP < or = 35%	20% < G/GDP < or = 25%
4	high	35% < G/GDP < or = 45%	25% < G/GDP < or = 30%
5	very high	G/GDP > 45%	G/GDP > 30%

Activity 3, Part B
Calculating a Measure of Fiscal Burden

Fiscal burden is one of 10 factors used by the Heritage Foundation to determine the relative freedoms enjoyed by citizens in countries around the world. The other factors are: trade policy, government intervention in the economy, monetary policy, capital flows and foreign investment, banking and finance, wages and prices, property rights, regulation, and black market activity. The score for fiscal burden is averaged with the other nine factors to determine the Index of Economic Freedom for each nation.

The score for the fiscal burden of a nation's government has two components: tax rates and government expenditures. Higher scores indicate higher fiscal burdens. The tax component is based on the country's income tax and corporate income tax. Separate tax scores are determined for each of these two taxes, and then averaged. This score is then combined with the government expenditure score to determine the final average score.

INSTRUCTIONS FOR COMPLETING FISCAL BURDEN WORKSHEETS

Step 1: Obtain a tax and expenditure data slip for the country you are assigned.
Step 2: Use the grading scale to determine the country score for personal income tax.
Step 3: Use the grading scale to determine the country score for corporate income tax.
Step 4: Average the scores by dividing by 2. This is the "tax score".
Step 5: Use the grading scale to determine the country score for government expenditures. This is the "expenditure score."
Step 6: Add the "tax score" to the "expenditure score" and divide by 2. This is the score that represents the fiscal burden of government.

Higher scores (closer to 5) indicate high fiscal burdens. Lower scores (closer to 1) indicate lower fiscal burdens.

EXAMPLE:

Hungary's top income tax rate is 40 percent. The average taxpayer faces a 40% marginal tax rate, up from 30% last year. The top corporate income tax rate is 18%. In 1999, government expenditures equaled 45.6 percent of GDP. Hungary is not developed.

1. Country: <u>HUNGARY</u>
2. personal income tax score   5
3. corporate income tax score 2
4. tax score 3.5 (avg. of personal + corporate)
5. expenditure score   5
6. fiscal burden score 4.25

Country: DENMARK   Developed? YES
Top marginal income tax rate: 63.3%   Top marginal corporate income tax rate: 30%
Avg. taxpayer marginal rate: 45%   G/GDP: 52.3%
Other comments:

Country: ESTONIA   Developed? NO
Top marginal income tax rate: 26%   Top marginal corporate income tax rate: 0
Avg. taxpayer marginal rate: 26%   G/GDP: 35.8%
Other comments: income tax is flat rate; government has eliminated the corporate tax on income that is reinvested in the domestic economy.

Country: HONG KONG   Developed? YES
Top marginal income tax rate: 15%   Top marginal corporate income tax rate: 16%
Avg. taxpayer marginal rate: 15%   G/GDP: 21.9%
Other comments: income tax is progressive (2-17% rates after deductions OR flat 15% of salary, whichever produces lower tax liability; for grading purposes, flat 15% is used. Corporate income tax is flat 16%.

Country: INDIA   Developed? NO
Top marginal income tax rate: 30%   Top marginal corporate income tax rate: 35%
Avg. taxpayer marginal rate: 0%   G/GDP: 26.8%
Other comments:

Country: INDONESIA   Developed? NO
Top marginal income tax rate: 30%   Top marginal corporate income tax rate: 30%
Avg. taxpayer marginal rate: 5%   G/GDP: 19.5%
Other comments:

Country: IRAQ (at the end of the Hussein regime)
     Developed? NO
Top marginal income tax rate: N/A   Top marginal corporate income tax rate: N/A
Avg. taxpayer marginal rate: N/A   G/GDP: N/A
Other comments: taxes are generally in the form of confiscated property. There is no meaningful taxation system in place. Government has not published a budget since the mid-1980s.

Country: IRELAND   Developed? YES
Top marginal income tax rate: 44%   Top marginal corporate income tax rate: 20%
Avg. taxpayer marginal rate: 44%   G/GDP: 30.9%
Other comments: top corporate rates scheduled to drop to 16% in 2002 and 12.5% in 2003. Use the
20% rate for purposes of forming the current index.

Country: ISRAEL   Developed? YES
Top marginal income tax rate: 50%   Top marginal corporate income tax rate: 36%
Avg. taxpayer marginal rate: 30%   G/GDP: 47.2%
Other comments:

Country: KENYA   Developed? NO
Top marginal income tax rate: 30%   Top marginal corporate income tax rate: 30%
Avg. taxpayer marginal rate: 10%   G/GDP: 25.2%
Other comments:

Country: LITHUANIA   Developed? NO
Top marginal income tax rate: 33%   Top marginal corporate income tax rate: 24%
Avg. taxpayer marginal rate: 33%   G/GDP: 30%
Other comments: income earned from primary job is taxed at flat rate = 33%; income earned from
second job is taxed progressively from 10 35%.

Country: MEXICO   Developed? NO
Top marginal income tax rate: 40%   Top marginal corporate income tax rate: 35%
Avg. taxpayer marginal rate: 35%   G/GDP: 22%
Other comments:

Country: NAMIBIA   Developed? NO
Top marginal income tax rate: 36%   Top marginal corporate income tax rate: 35%
Avg. taxpayer marginal rate: 0%   G/GDP: 41.4%
Other comments:

Country: NEW ZEALAND   Developed? YES
Top marginal income tax rate: 39%   Top marginal corporate income tax rate: 33%
Avg. taxpayer marginal rate: 19.5%   G/GDP: 40.9%
Other comments:

Country: NIGERIA   Developed? NO
Top marginal income tax rate: 25%   Top marginal corporate income tax rate: 30%
Avg. taxpayer marginal rate: 10%   G/GDP: 23.8%
Other comments: Nigeria's G/GDP rose from 15.6% to 23.8% in one year.

Country: POLAND   Developed? NO
Top marginal income tax rate: 40%   Top marginal corporate income tax rate: 28%
Avg. taxpayer marginal rate: 19%   G/GDP: 44.7%
Other comments:

Country: QATAR   Developed? YES
Top marginal income tax rate: 0%   Top marginal corporate income tax rate: 35%
Avg. taxpayer marginal rate: 0%   G/GDP: 48.9%
Other comments: the oil industry accounts for 35% of GNP, and Qatar has the third largest natural gas reserves in the world (behind Russia and Iran); there are no income taxes imposed on individuals

Country: CONGO (REPUBLIC OF)   Developed? NO
Top marginal income tax rate: 50%   Top marginal corporate income tax rate: 45%
Avg. taxpayer marginal rate: 15%   G/GDP: 39%
Other comments: conflicts in neighboring Democratic Republic of Congo (formerly Zaire) and Angola affect the political and economic situation in the Republic of Congo.

Country: RUSSIA   Developed? NO
Top marginal income tax rate: 13%   Top marginal corporate income tax rate: 24%
Avg. taxpayer marginal rate: 13%   G/GDP: 35.3%
Other comments: newly reformed income tax is flat rate = 13%.

Country: SINGAPORE

Developed? YES

Top marginal income tax rate: 28%

Top marginal corporate income tax rate: 25.5%

Avg. taxpayer marginal rate: 12%

G/GDP: 18%

Other comments:

Country: SOUTH AFRICA

Developed? NO

Top marginal income tax rate: 45%

Top marginal corporate income tax rate: 30%

Avg. taxpayer marginal rate: 19%

G/GDP: 45.5%

Other comments:

Country: SOUTH KOREA

Developed? NO

Top marginal income tax rate: 40%

Top marginal corporate income tax rate: 28%

Avg. taxpayer marginal rate: 20%

G/GDP: 25.2%

Other comments: the average taxpayer marginal rate was 10% in the previous year; a 10% "resident surtax" increases the top corporate rate to 30.8%.

Country: UKRAINE

Developed? NO

Top marginal income tax rate: 40%

Top marginal corporate income tax rate: 30%

Avg. taxpayer marginal rate: 20%

G/GDP: 35.9%

Other comments:

Country: UNITED STATES

Developed? YES

Top marginal income tax rate: 39.6%

Top marginal corporate income tax rate: 35%

Avg. taxpayer marginal rate: 28%

G/GDP: 30%

Other comments:

Country: VIETNAM

Developed? NO

Top marginal income tax rate: 60%

Top marginal corporate income tax rate: 32%

Avg. taxpayer marginal rate: 0%

G/GDP: 19%

Other comments:

Activity 4
Building Institutions for Markets

Name _____   Country _____

	Heritage Foundation Factor Score (1 = most free)	**Suggestions for Building Institutions**
1. trade policy	___	
2. fiscal burden	___	
3. government intervention	___	
4. monetary policy	___	
5. foreign investment	___	
6. banking/finance	___	
7. wages/prices	___	
8. property rights	___	
9. regulation	___	
10. black market	___	

___ Index of Economic Freedom (add all scores for your country and divide by 10)

Categories most in need of building institutions:

Categories least in need of building institutions:

LESSON NINE
THE DISTRIBUTION OF INCOME AND INVESTMENTS IN HUMAN CAPITAL

LESSON DESCRIPTION

This lesson introduces students to some key facts about the distribution of income in the United States, and provides some information and tools for analyzing changes in the distribution of income over the last three decades. Students' intuition about who earns more or less, and why, is the basis for several activities; but in some cases their intuition will likely be challenged.

INTRODUCTION

Human capital is created through education, training, improved health, and other factors that improve the productivity and quality of labor. The World Bank *World Development Report 2002: Building Institutions for Markets* identifies human capital formation as an essential part of institutional reform in developing nations.

Over the past 30 years, human capital has played an increasingly important role in determining how much income different workers earn. While the overall share of national income going to labor has not changed markedly over this period, studies of the distribution of personal income in the United States and other industrialized market economies show that workers with higher levels of education and training are receiving a larger share of national income. Workers with little or no formal education are receiving a smaller share.

This lesson focuses on the U.S. experience and demonstrates the importance of human capital investment to these recent changes in the personal distribution of income.

CONCEPTS

Investment in human capital
Factor income
Functional distribution of income
Personal distribution of income

CONTENT STANDARD

Income for most people is determined by the market value of the productive resources they sell. What workers earn depends primarily on the market value of what they produce and how productive they are.

BENCHMARKS

People's incomes, in part, reflect choices they have made about education, training, skill development, and careers. People with few skills are likely to be poor.

Two methods for classifying how income is distributed in a nation – the personal distribution of income and the functional distribution – reflect respectively the distribution of income among different groups of households and the distribution of income among different businesses and occupations in the economy.

OBJECTIVES

Students will:

♦ Identify the four different kinds of factor incomes (wages and salaries, rent, interest, and profits) and describe the functional distribution of income in the U.S. economy.

♦ Describe the personal distribution of income in the U.S. economy, which shows the percentages of national income received by different quintiles of families, from the 20% of families that earn the highest levels of income to the 20% that earn the lowest levels of income.

♦ Explain the relationship between people's choices about investments in human capital and the distribution of personal income.

♦ Analyze recent changes in the distribution of personal income, and especially the role of higher returns to investments in human capital.

TIME REQUIRED

Two class periods. Day one – procedures 1-6. Day two – procedures 7-11 and Assessment.

MATERIALS

- Visual 1: U.S. Functional Distribution of Income, 2001
- Visual 2: U.S. Functional Distribution of Income, 1981
- Visual 3: Distribution of U.S. Household Income by Quintiles, 2001
- Visual 4: Distribution of U.S. Household Income by Quintiles, 1981 and 2001
- Visual 5: Characteristics of High and Low-Income Quintiles
- Visual 6: Income Distribution by Quintile and Educational Attainment
- Visual 7: Distribution of Earners in the Lowest and Highest Income Quintiles
- Four signs, one each labeled: Land, Labor, Capital, Entrepreneurship
- Four calculators
- Activity 1: The Functional Distribution of Income, one copy per student
- Activity 2: Testing Your Intuition About Who Earns Higher Incomes, one copy per student
- Activity 3: Comparing Income Differentials Over Time, one copy per student

PROCEDURES

1. Explain that this lesson is about the distribution of income in the United States. This is a very controversial issue in many political elections, and for that matter in discussions and arguments between friends and family members. Some of those debates come down to normative questions in which different people disagree about what is fair or unfair. But many of the debates are never resolved simply because people don't know the basic facts about what the distribution of income is, how it has changed over time, or how people can make choices that affect their future earnings.

2. Explain that economists actually look at the distribution of income in two different ways, which deal with very different kinds of issues. The first way is called the **functional distribution of income**, which shows the four basic kinds of income that people can earn: wages and salaries, rent, interest, and profits. These are **factor incomes,** resource payments made to the four different kinds of factors of production: labor, land, capital and entrepreneurship.

3. Distribute Activity 1 and tell students this activity may require them to exercise their intuition as well some basic knowledge. Let students work in pairs and discuss the questions, but all students should produce their own estimates and pie chart. You may want to demonstrate one or two possible pie chart answers to help them answer question 3, but if you do, try to choose some obviously wrong and unlikely examples. Once they have answered the questions, ask them to redraw and enlarge the pie chart so that it covers the back of their paper. Then designate one corner of the room for each of the factors of production: land, labor, capital, and entrepreneurship. Have students take their activity sheets to the corner of the room that corresponds to their choice of the factor of production that receives the largest share of income. Ask at least one person from each corner why they chose this factor of production and what percentage of national income they estimated was paid each year to the factor they chose.

4. Appoint a recorder for each corner and ask him or her to calculate the average estimates

From *Focus: Institutions and Markets,* © National Council on Economic Education, New York, NY

for the percentage of income received by that factor, using the calculators you supply. Write the percentages on the chalkboard or an overhead, and have students return to their seats.

5. Display Visual 1 with the actual data on the functional distribution of income for the U.S. economy in 2001. Discuss the following questions:

A. How many students picked wages and salaries as the most important source of factor income in the U.S.? *(Answers will vary.)* Labor is by far the largest factor of production, accounting for well over 70% of factor incomes.

B. How close did your class percentages come to the actual data? Were there any factors that were consistently over or underestimated? *(Answers will vary.)*

C. Note that the official data include "proprietors' income" as a separate category. This category includes income earned by sole proprietors (single-owner businesses). These are generally small business owners and farmers. Payments/income for this category are a mix of profits and wages/salaries, because these owners are often working long hours in their own enterprises.

D. Ask the students to exercise their economics intuition again. If you were to go back 20 years, would this distribution be significantly different, or substantially the same? Take a variety of answers and then conduct a straw poll. Display Visual 2 and note that the share to labor has remained fairly stable. Profits, and interest declined slightly, but overall the returns to the factors were fairly stable.

6. Tell students that over this same period, another measure of the **personal distribution** of income showed something very different.

Display the first two columns of Visual 3, which shows the distribution of U.S. Household Income in 2001. Income here refers to pretax income, and does not include government transfer payments or in-kind assistance such as food stamps. Explain that each quintile represents one-fifth, or 20%, of all U.S. households. (As will be shown in a later activity, that is not one-fifth of the population, however, because all households are not the same size.) The first row of numbers shows the percentage of total U.S. income that the lowest (poorest) quintile receives. Therefore, in 2001 the 20% of U.S. households that earned the lowest incomes received about 3.5% of all income, while the highest quintile earned 50.1%, or slightly more than all four other quintiles combined. Briefly display Visual 4, to show that the distribution of household income became less equal from 1981 to 2001, with higher-income families receiving a larger share of the total, and lower-income families receiving a smaller share. (Note: In the assessment activity for this lesson students are asked to discuss and investigate why that has happened over the past few decades, so try to hold any extended discussion of that topic until then.)

7. Ask students if this distribution seems fair. Accept a variety of answers without comment, then remind students that we have a mixed-market economy in which the rewards for effort and special talents or even luck in the marketplace is reflected in individual incomes. Then provide some additional information that many students find surprising: The minimum income needed to get into the top quintile in 2001 was only $83,500, $53,000 for the fourth quintile, $33,314 for the third quintile, and $17,970 to reach the second quintile. The minimum level of income needed to be in the 5 percent of households with the highest income was $150,499.

8. Ask students to discuss how much the choices people make can affect where they end up in these quintiles. Allow the discussion to

continue for several minutes, then distribute Activity 2, Testing Your Intuition About Who Earns Higher Incomes. Allow a few minutes for students to review the activity on their own and make some quick judgments about which group – the lowest or the highest quintile – would be more likely to have a higher percentage of people with the given characteristics. They are to place an X sign in the appropriate column.

9. After allowing about five minutes for individual work, put the students in small groups and ask them to discuss their answers in the groups. Have each group appoint a spokesperson to present the group's answer to the questions on the activity.

10. Ask each group to report and give a reason for each answer. After all of the groups have reported, review the following results from economic research on these questions: The general point to be made here is that decisions made by individuals lead to real economic consequences. Higher income households have more income earners and more education. Households with only one adult wage earner are smaller and less often able to reach the highest income range. The average household size is 3.0 for lowest income group and 3.4 for the highest quintile largely because more high income households are married couples with at least two adults in the labor force. Display Visual 5 to summarize these results, then discuss each of the individual items shown in the table:

A. There should be little surprise about putting the X in the lowest quintile for high school dropouts. Ask students to describe the general relationship between education and income, and if necessary explain the idea of people **investing in their human capital**. Stress that this is a clear case where individuals' decisions have significant economic consequences for many years or even decades. To show that point

more dramatically, display and review Visual 6.

B. Family status is another case in which choices have predictable economic consequences. Display Visual 7. Single-parent families are much less likely to be in the top quintile, and in fact in over three-fourths of the top-quintile families both spouses work fulltime. In the families in the lowest quintile more than one-third report "zero earners," which means that no one in that household had a job or reported any self-employment for the past year. This would include, for example, families where all adults are retired, disabled, or unemployed.

C. The age of the household head is not a matter of personal household choice, but it is still a subject of economic analysis. Households that are either very young or old are less likely to be in the top quintile. Workers in the prime working ages have both the experience and the education to earn higher wages.

D. The persons per family answer usually surprises students because they think higher income families are smaller families. But remember that a single parent is very unlikely to be in the top quintile, so the additional adult in the top quintile families helps tip the scale in favor of a larger household. There are also more small households of retired workers with no children and in some cases only one adult in the lowest quintile.

11. Point out that students should now realize that their place in the income distribution is not just a matter of chance or powers beyond their control, but will be affected by important choices they make in areas as diverse as education and family formation.

CLOSURE

Review the major points of the lesson by asking the following questions:

1. What are the four types of factor incomes? (*wages and salaries, rent, interest, and profits*)

2. In the U.S. economy, which resource receives the largest share of factor incomes? (*labor, which receives wages and salaries*)

3. Has the functional distribution of income changed much in the U.S. over the last 20 years? (*No. Payments to labor continue to account for about 75 percent of all national income.*)

4. How has the personal income distribution changed in the U.S. over the last 20 years? (*Personal income has become more concentrated in the top quintile.*)

5. What personal choices do people make that affect their place in the distribution of income? (*Choices about lifestyle, education, and other forms of investment in human capital play a significant role in determining one's place in the income distribution.*)

ASSESSMENT

To develop the idea of interactions between individual decisions and changes in the economy, display Visual 4 again, which compares the U.S. distribution of personal income in 1981 and 2001. Ask students for some general comments. They should see that income has become more concentrated in the top quintile and the top 5% of families who earn the highest incomes. But why? Activity 3 presents important data that help us to understand. Assign Activity 3 as homework or an in-class essay assignment. Students should understand that education is highly correlated with income, as demonstrated in Activity 2 and Visual 6. Workers who choose to invest in higher education are generally rewarded with higher incomes. But in the 1980s and 1990s the college premium rose as the level of skills required by workers increased all around the world, and in the United States the rate of growth in college graduates slowed down. Therefore, the payoff to college education and advanced training became even greater, and the penalty for dropping out of school also increased. As the premium to those at the upper end of the income distribution became higher, their incomes rose faster than the non-college educated population.

While the link between education and income has become even stronger in recent decades, the general relationship has been well established and known for a long time, as shown in the following table linking education and the poverty rate:

Poverty Rate for Full-Time Workers, Classified by Educational Attainment in 1979 and 1990

Education	1990 Poverty Rate	1979 Poverty Rate
HS Dropout	15.7%	11.1%
HS Graduate	6.3%	4.5%
Some College	4.1%	3.8%
College Graduate	1.9%	2.2%

Source: Sar Levitan et al., *Working but Poor*, Baltimore: Johns Hopkins, 1993, p. 65.

EXTENSION

Teach "Rich Man, Poor Man…" from the National Council on Economic Education publication *Focus: High School Economics.* Then have students compare the current U.S. income distribution with income distributions from other nations. Data for income per capita and income distribution for many developed and less developed nations can be found in Tables 1 and 2 of the World Bank *World Development Report, 2002.* Can students discern any pattern of distribution based on the level of development? In most cases developed countries exhibit greater equality of distribution than less developed economies, but this should be another good test of students' economic intuition.

Visual 1
U.S. Functional Distribution of Income, 2001

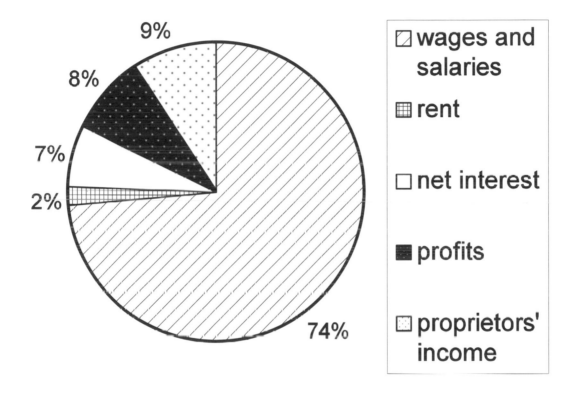

Source: *Economic Report of the President: 2002.* Website: www.access.gpo.gov/eop/

Visual 2
U.S. Functional Distribution of Income, 1981

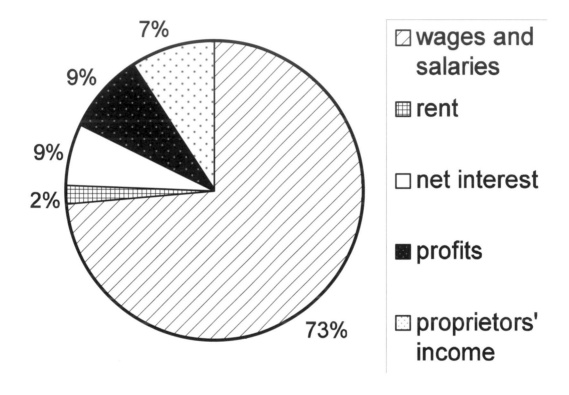

Source: *Economic Report of the President: 2002.* Website: www.access.gpo.gov/eop/

Visual 3
Distribution of U.S. Household Income by Quintiles, 2001

QUINTILE	% of Income in quintile	Cumulative Percentage
LOWEST	3.5	3.5
SECOND	8.7	12.2
THIRD	14.7	26.9
FOURTH	23.0	49.9
HIGHEST	50.1	100.0
Top 5%	22.4	

Source: *Current Population Reports, Series P-60,* U.S. Bureau of the Census, March 2002. Data are compiled from the 2002 Survey and refer to income in 2001. Website: http://www.census.gov/prod/2002pubs/p60-218.pdf

Visual 4
Distribution of U.S. Household Income by Quintiles, 1981 and 2001

QUINTILE	PERCENT OF INCOME	
	1981	2001
LOWEST	4.2	3.5
SECOND	10.2	8.7
THIRD	16.8	14.7
FOURTH	25.0	23.0
HIGHEST	43.8	50.1
Top 5%	15.6	22.4

Source: *Current Population Reports, Series P-60*, U.S. Bureau of the Census, March 2002.
http://www.census.gov/prod/2002pubs/p60-218.pdf

Visual 5
Characteristics of High and Low Income Quintiles

	Lowest 20%	Highest 20%
Education		
% H.S. dropout	_X_ 35	4
% College Grads	6	_X_ 54
Family Status		
Married couple	48	_X_ 94
Both spouses work	4	_X_ 51
Single parent	_X_ 52	6
Age of Household Head		
Under 35	_X_ 34	12
35-64	44	_X_ 79
65+	_X_ 22	9
Persons per family	3.0	_X_ 3.4
Earners per family	0.8	_X_ 2.2

Source: *Money Income in the United States: 1997,* U.S. Department of Commerce (Washington, D.C. Government Printing Office 1998).

Visual 6
Income Distribution by Quintile and Educational Attainment

	Lowest Quintile	2nd Quintile	3rd Quintile	4th Quintile	Highest Quintile
Less than High School Education	34.4%	20.1%	12.5%	6.4%	2.6%
College Graduate	8.2%	13.0%	21.3%	32.6%	58.1%

From *Focus: Institutions and Markets*, © National Council on Economic Education, New York, NY

Visual 7

Distribution of Earners in the Lowest and Highest Income Quintiles

Earners per Family	Lowest Quintile	Highest Quintile
Zero earners	35.5%	1.0%
One earner	47.9%	20.7%
Two earners or more	16.6%	78.3%
Total	100%	100%

Source: U.S. Census Bureau, March 2002 http://ferret.bls.census.gov/macro/032001/faminc/new06_000.htm

Activity 1
The Functional Distribution of Income:
Who Gets the Largest Share of the Pie?

1. Economists traditionally classify all factors of production into one of four categories. Given the word list below, match the four factors of production with the type of payment that is made to each type of productive resource, which also represents the kind of income that each factor of production earns.

    Word List: Profit, Rent, Capital, Entrepreneurship, Labor, Land, Wages, Interest

    <u>Factor of Production</u>   <u>Payments/Income for this Factor</u>

    _____   _____

    _____   _____

    _____   _____

    _____   _____

2. Which factor do you believe accounts for the largest share of the money earned in the U.S. economy, and what percentage of national income do you believe it receives?

    I believe the factor that received the largest share of income in the U.S. economy is _____, and I believe its return, known as _____, receives _____% of all income in the U.S.

3. In the pie chart shown below, shade in the amount of national income that you believe is received by the factor that receives the largest percentage of income. For example if you believe land (also called natural resources) receives 50% of national income, shade half of the pie and label the shaded part with the name of the income payment made to land.

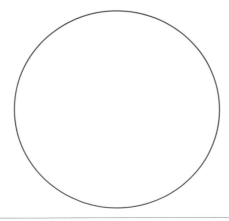

From *Focus: Institutions and Markets*, © National Council on Economic Education, New York, NY

Activity 2
Testing Your Intuition About Who Earns Higher Incomes

In the space below, put an X in the blank under the quintile column that you believe has a higher percentage of households with the characteristic mentioned in the first column. (The lowest quintile refers to the 20% of U.S. families who receive the lowest levels of income in a given year; the highest quintile refers to the 20% of families that receive the highest levels of income.)

	Lowest Quintile	Highest Quintile
Education		
% High School Dropouts	_____	_____
% College Graduates	_____	_____
Family Status		
Married Couples	_____	_____
Single Parents	_____	_____
Percentage of married-couple families where both spouses work	_____	_____
Age of Household Head		
Under 35	_____	_____
35 to 64	_____	_____
65 and over	_____	_____
More persons in family	_____	_____
More earners in family	_____	_____

Activity 3
Comparing Income Differentials Over Time

Name _____

The table below shows, in percentage terms, the difference between annual median incomes for male and female college graduates compared to high school graduates who never attended college. For example, in 1974 the median income of male college graduates was 27% greater than the income of male high school graduates, but by 1999 that difference had grown to 60%. (Median income for a group is the mid-point of income, with half of the members making more than that amount and half making less.)

What do these trends suggest would have happened to the level of income inequality in the United States from 1974 to 1999? Explain your answer below.

Percentage that Income of College Graduates Exceeds Income of H.S. Graduates

YEAR	MALES	FEMALES
1974	27	54
1984	49	74
1999	60	65

Source: U.S. Commerce Department, *Current Population Reports*, Series P-60, No. 167, Table 50; and *Money Income of Households, Families, and Persons in the United States: 1992*, No. 184, Table 24 and P-60-209, *Money Income in the United States: 1999*, Tables 7 and 8.

LESSON TEN
MACROECONOMIC STABILIZATION POLICIES AND INSTITUTIONS

LESSON DESCRIPTION

This lesson begins by reviewing the discovery and adoption of Keynesian fiscal policies in the United States and other nations following World War II. Students then participate in several exercises to ascertain their understanding of appropriate demand-side tools of fiscal policy, which is conducted by national legislative and executive branches of government, and tools of monetary policy, which is conducted by a nation's central bank (in the United States, the Federal Reserve System).

INTRODUCTION

The World Bank *World Development Report 2002: Building Institutions for Markets* emphasizes the role of political institutions and governance in promoting a sound economy capable of sustaining significant annual increases in the standard of living. This includes "the provision of sound macroeconomic policies that create a stable environment for market activity." (p. 99) Different government institutions establish fiscal policies and monetary policies that can promote macroeconomic stabilization.

CONCEPTS

Unemployment
Inflation
Fiscal policy
Automatic stabilizers
Monetary policy

Central banks (e.g., the U.S. Federal Reserve Bank)
Discount rate
Reserve requirement
Open market operations

CONTENT STANDARD

Federal government budgetary policy and the Federal Reserve System's monetary policy influence the overall levels of employment, output, and prices.

BENCHMARKS

Fiscal policies are decisions to change spending and tax levels by the federal government. These decisions are adopted to influence national levels of output, employment, and prices.

Monetary policies are decisions by the Federal Reserve System that lead to changes in the supply of money and the availability of credit. Changes in the money supply can influence overall levels of spending, employment and prices in the economy by inducing changes in interest rates charged for credit and by affecting the levels of personal and business investment spending.

OBJECTIVES

Students will:

♦ Define fiscal policy.

♦ Distinguish between discretionary and automatic fiscal policies.

♦ Define monetary policy.

♦ Analyze economic data and recommend appropriate expansionary or contractionary fiscal and monetary policies to counteract high unemployment or high inflation.

TIME REQUIRED

Three class periods. Day one – procedures 1-7. Day two – procedures 8-14. Day three – procedures 15-20 and Assessment.

MATERIALS

- Visual 1: The Employment Act of 1946
- Visual 2: Fiscal Policy
- Visual 3: Timing Problems
- Visual 4: Automatic Stabilizers
- Visual 5: The Tools of Monetary Policy
- Activity 1: U.S. Unemployment Rates and the Federal Budget: 1928-1946
- Activity 2: Expansionary or Contractionary Fiscal Policies? That Is the Question.
- Activity 3: Automatic Stabilizers
- Activity 4: Memorandum from the President of the United States
- Activity 5: Monetary Policy Prescription
- Activity 6: Memorandum from the Chairman of the Federal Reserve System

PROCEDURES

1. Show Visual 1 and read the quotation from the Employment Act of 1946. Tell students this is considered to be a landmark piece of legislation because it put Congress on record as taking responsibility for providing maximum employment and stable prices, working with the President and other government agencies (including the Federal Reserve System, which will be discussed later in the lesson). This Act also established the Council of Economic Advisers (CEA), a three-member panel of economists appointed by the president and confirmed by the Senate. The chief responsibility of the CEA is to advise the President on economic issues and legislation, and to explain the President's economic policies to Congress and the public.

2. Break the class into small groups and distribute copies of Activity 1. Have students discuss the questions in small groups and prepare an answer to share with the class.

3. In reviewing Activity 1, students should see that although the **unemployment** rate (defined as the percentage of the labor force that is unemployed, which means adults who are not working but are actively seeking work) had fallen from its 1933 peak of 25% to about 10% when the United States entered World War II in December of 1941, it remained at historically very high levels – "double-digit unemployment" – until massive federal expenditures began in World War II.

4. Display Visual 2 and define fiscal policy. Since the Great Depression and World War II, most economists have accepted the idea that changes in the federal budget (spending, taxes, or both) can have a significant effect on the national economy. In periods of high unemployment and low inflation – such as the Great Depression of the 1930s, although fortunately never again on that scale – expansionary fiscal policies designed to stimulate the overall level of spending and demand in the economy are appropriate. That can be done by having the government spend more, or by lowering taxes on consumers and businesses. Lowering taxes leaves more money for consumers to spend on goods and services, and for businesses to spend on production or new investments, or to distribute to owners as profits. All of this will help to stimulate the economy and lower the unemployment rate.

5. Contractionary fiscal policy is appropriate in situations where total spending in the economy is increasing so rapidly that it creates **inflation**, a persistent rise in the

general level of prices. To reduce total spending, the federal government can raise taxes or reduce government spending. Raising taxes means that consumers and businesses will have less money to spend, reducing the overall level of demand for goods and services and thus the upward pressure on the price level for those products.

6. Distribute Activity 2 to assess students' understanding of the appropriate fiscal policy response to different situations. Expansionary policy is called for when the economy is significantly below full employment and there is no indication of severe inflationary problems; contractionary policy is appropriate when inflation is a major problem, but unemployment is not. No change in fiscal policies is called for when there are no serious unemployment or inflationary problems. The answers to the questions in Activity 2 are: 1. E, 2. NC, 3. C, 4. E, 5. C.

7. Tell students to look at the Table in Activity 1 again. Explain that while the New Deal offered some trial of fiscal policy, compared to spending levels in World War II the level of expansionary fiscal policy used by the federal government in the 1930s was very small, and to some extent was undercut by contractionary polices being run by many state and local governments. The much greater level of spending during World War II was not done as an attempt to stimulate the economy. Rather, spending was increased because of the military threat from other nations; but the lower unemployment rates that resulted supported the idea of using fiscal policy to fight unemployment or inflation. Those ideas were first formalized in an important book written by the leading economist of the first half of the 20th century, John Maynard Keynes (1883-1946). Keynes' book was *The General Theory of Employment, Interest and Money* (1936).

8. Ask if there are any future politicians in your class. If none volunteer, select some likely candidates and ask if they thought they could win a national election by supporting Keynesian discretionary policies. Have students refer back to Activity 2 and let them help the candidates formulate their answers to this question. If the students do not come up with these points on their own, ask specifically: 1) Would using expansionary fiscal policy to fight high unemployment be politically popular? (*Generally yes, because consumers and businesses gain directly from tax cuts, and at least some of them also benefit from government spending programs.*) 2) Would using contractionary fiscal policies to fight high inflation be politically popular? (*The answer here should be a clear "No". Raising taxes takes money away from consumers and businesses, and although some people support cutting government spending, often the people who will be hurt by cutting the spending programs are much more upset and likely to vote against candidates proposing such cuts than the "average" taxpayer whose taxes will be reduced by a relatively small amount.*) 3) Does the political response to actions taken by Congress and the President to raise or lower government spending or taxes mean that fiscal policy might be more effective in fighting unemployment than in fighting inflation? (*Yes.*)

9. This political problem with discretionary fiscal policy is not its only drawback. In addition to having the political courage to "do the right thing" even when it is unpopular with voters, the Congress and President also have to "know when to do it." That raises the issue of different kinds of systematic "time lags." Begin a discussion of time lags with the following example: Anyone who has waited in their car while the traffic light turns from red to green has

experienced the problem of time lags. The light changes but no one moves instantly. The first driver in the line must see the light change, step on the car's accelerator, and only then will the car move forward. The driver of the second car in the line must see the light change and wait for the first car to move before accelerating his or her car. Each driver in the line must wait for every preceding driver. This process takes time. Similar kinds of time lags affect fiscal policies as well as the other stabilization policies discussed later in the lesson.

10.   Display Visual 3 and discuss each type of time lag:

A. Recognition lag – this is the time between the start of a serious macroeconomic problem (such as inflation or a recession) and recognition of the problem by decision-makers. In the traffic example it is the time between the light turning green and each driver recognizing that they can legally move forward. But in the economy things are seldom that simple, in part because data are often contradictory when a period of high unemployment or inflation is just beginning.

A recession is defined as six consecutive months of falling national output and income (GDP). Because macroeconomic data on a particular month or quarter can not be collected, tabulated, and released until some period after that, different economists and policymakers often offer significantly different predictions about what is happening in the economy at any given time. Therefore, members of Congress and other policymakers may be unsure of what action to take until a problem has been around long enough to become evident. Moreover, it is not uncommon to see both

unemployment and inflation rising or falling at the same time, which makes it much more difficult to formulate fiscal policy because policies that address one of these problems will typically make the other problem worse.

B. Administrative lag - once policymakers have defined the problem, they still have to decide what action to take, first individually and then as a group, or at least a majority of the group. To implement new changes in taxes or spending, both the Congress and the President must act. This means that hearings must be scheduled and a bill must be written and passed by Congress, which must then be signed by the President before any policy can be put in place. All of that takes time, and a degree of political consensus that is often difficult to develop.

C. Operational lag – even after a fiscal policy is put in place, it will still be some time before the policy has an effect on the economy in terms of changing output, employment, and price levels.

11.   Explain that because of the time lag problems and the effects of other forces in the economy, many economists strongly question the practical or even theoretical effectiveness of fiscal policies that have to be passed and implemented in response to a macroeconomic problem. These economists sometimes use the "idiot in the shower" analogy. Explain the analogy by drawing a stick figure on the overhead transparency, showing the figure in a shower with two faucet handles for hot and cold water. The idiot wakes up in the morning and wants to take a warm shower. He steps into the shower and opens each handle half way. Ask the students what they expect to happen? (*Both the hot and the cold water will probably be cold early in the morning.*) When the idiot realizes the water is too cold

(recognition lag), he decides to turn off the cold and open the hot water all the way (administrative lag). The water heats up (operational lag), but because only the hot water is on, the idiot is scalded! The idiot turns the hot water off and opens the cold, but that leads to another disaster. The lags are giving the idiot serious shower problems. Someone who is not an idiot can no doubt do better, but even intelligent people can have problems getting their shower water adjusted, especially when they have to face a new problem (such as using a new shower, or having someone else turn on water elsewhere in the house while they are trying to use the shower). If such a simple thing as getting shower water can be so difficult because of these lags, imagine how difficult it can be to use fiscal policies to deal with problems in an economy with millions of consumers and producers. This is one of the reasons why some economists oppose the idea that fiscal policy can be used to "fine tune" the ups and downs of the national economy.

12. Display Visual 4. Explain that not all fiscal policies are "discretionary," requiring current actions by members of Congress and the President. Instead, some changes in tax collections and government spending are "automatic," based on tax or spending programs that have already been voted into law. For example, as the unemployment rate rises, spending for unemployment compensation automatically goes up, while revenues from income taxes automatically fall. Conversely, during periods of high inflation, the average level of wages and prices rise. (Actually, average wages rise in monetary terms, but not in real terms of what goods and services they will buy.) That leads to higher government revenues from income and sales taxes. These automatic fiscal stabilizers do not face the same degree of political disadvantages in fighting inflation and unemployment as discretionary fiscal

policies, although over time tax increases caused by inflationary "bracket creep" did become controversial, and during recessions there is certainly political pressure to extend or increase expenditures for unemployment compensation and other assistance programs. These stabilizers are very important in the United States. Some studies suggest that every dollar decrease in GDP decreases tax revenues and increases transfer payments by approximately 22 cents (Jan Hogendorn. *Modern Economics*. Englewood Cliffs, N.J.: Prentice Hall, 1995. pp. 563-564). That means government fiscal programs automatically help to compensate for falling demand by increasing transfers payments and reducing tax revenues. Both actions put more money in the hands of consumers.

13. Distribute Activity 3 and ask students to identify which of the policies listed there are automatic fiscal stabilization policies. (*correct answers: ✓'s for 1, 2, 4, and 7; and X's for 3, 5, and 6*) The first program brings more revenue to the federal treasury when the economy is booming because corporations are generally earning higher profits during prosperous times. In bad economic times corporate profits decline and tax revenues decrease. Both the second item, unemployment compensation, and the fourth item, welfare programs, increase government expenditures during periods of rising unemployment and low inflation, and decrease spending in times of low unemployment and rising inflation. The federal income tax, item 7, is progressive – with tax rates rising somewhat as taxpayers' income levels rise. Therefore, federal revenues from the income tax decrease in times of rising unemployment and low inflation, and increase when unemployment rates fall and inflation increases. National defense spending (item 3), higher education spending (item 5), and social security (item 6) are, for the most part, discretionary budget items that change as a

result of new legislation passed by the Congress and signed by the president. However, because social security payments are now indexed to the level of inflation, rising more when inflation rates are higher, they may actually be somewhat pro-cyclical (reinforcing), rather than stabilizing.

14. Divide the class into groups of three and have each group play the role of the Council of Economic Advisers. (Remind students that the Employment Act of 1946 set the number of presidential appointees on the council at three.) Distribute one copy of Activity 4 to each group and have them read it and prepare a report for the President (you) on appropriate fiscal policy actions, based on the economic data provided in the handout. Before you collect their papers take some sample answers verbally. (*The CEA should recommend expansionary fiscal policies such as tax cuts and/or expenditure increases.*) Ask the class what they would have recommended to the president if the problem had been rapid inflation during a period of low unemployment? (*Contractionary fiscal policies – raising taxes and cutting government spending – but those policies might be politically unpopular.*) Would their recommendation have changed if the President was serving his or her second term, rather than a first term? (*If the President's reelection is not an issue, the politically unpopular fiscal polices might be more likely to be adopted. However, those policies would have to be passed by Congress before the President could sign them into law, and at any given time most members of Congress plan to stand for re-election.*)

15. Students should now be aware of some of the difficulties and shortcomings of fiscal policy – especially when political leaders try to use discretionary fiscal policy such as higher taxes to counteract an inflationary situation. The United States and most other market economies have another institution with a major responsibility for carrying out macroeconomic stabilization policy, the central bank. The U.S. central bank is called the Federal Reserve System (often referred to as simply The Fed). The Fed was created in 1913 when President Woodrow Wilson signed The Federal Reserve Act. It is directed by a seven-member Board of Governors with headquarters in Washington, D.C., and twelve district Federal Reserve Banks located in major cities throughout the United States, many with branches in other major cities. Members of the Fed's Board of Governors are appointed to 14-year terms by the President and confirmed by the Senate, but the Fed is technically a nonprofit institution owned by its member banks, and does not depend on Congress for annual funding. (It actually gives money to the U.S. Treasury each year, after paying its expenses out of the revenues it earns by providing services to banks and from the money it earns on bonds that it buys and sells as part of its open market operations, described below.) Most important, the U.S. Federal Reserve Bank is allowed to establish and carry out monetary policies that are independent of Congress and the President. Research has shown that in countries where central banks have this level of independence from the executive and legislative branches of government, monetary policy is usually far more effective in holding down the rate of inflation. In countries where the central bank is not independent, the same kinds of political pressures that make expansionary fiscal policies more popular than contractionary policies are brought to bear on monetary policy, which makes it harder for the central bank to prevent or reduce the rate of inflation.

16. Explain that the Fed uses **monetary policy** to influence interest rates and price levels through its ability to regulate the supply of money and credit in the economy. By

increasing bank reserves in the economy the Fed can increase the money supply. A larger money supply should lead banks to lower interest rates, which in turn will lead to increased rates of borrowing. This higher level of borrowing leads to more investment and consumption, which stimulates both employment and output. If the Fed contracts the money supply by draining reserves from the system, interest rates rise and economic activity is reduced. A slowdown in economic activity will reduce inflationary pressures in the economy but an increase in economic activity may put upward pressure on the average level of prices.

17.   Display Visual 5, which lists the major tools of monetary policy available to the Federal Reserve. Briefly explain each tool:

A. The **discount rate** is the interest rate that the Fed charges banks that borrow reserves from the Fed. Raising this rate means that the Fed is trying to slow the economy by making it more expensive to borrow money. If the Fed wants to stimulate the economy, it will lower this rate.

B. The **reserve requirement** is the percentage of deposits that commercial banks are not allowed to lend out. If the central bank raises the reserve requirement it is trying to slow down the economy to fight inflation, by reducing the amount of funds banks can lend and that other businesses and consumers can borrow. That pushes up interest rates, reducing spending for "big ticket" items that are usually financed by borrowing, such as business investments in new plants and equipment, and consumer purchases of housing, automobiles, and major appliances. By lowering the reserve requirement a central bank stimulates the national economy by increasing the

available amount of loanable funds. As a practical matter, however, the Fed and most central banks rarely use this tool.

C. **Open market operations**, or purchasing and selling bonds, is the monetary policy tool used most frequently. Money is widely accepted as final payment for all kinds of goods and services, so clearly bonds are not money (just try to buy something at the grocery store with a bond!) while currency, coins, and checks are. If the Fed buys bonds it pays with a check, which increases the money supply because the people or firms that used to own the bonds now have more money in their bank accounts. If the Fed sells bonds it decreases the money supply because the money people or firms use to buy these bonds is withdrawn from their bank accounts and given to the Fed, which means that money is no longer in circulation in the economy. If the Fed wants to stimulate the economy it buys bonds, increases the money supply, and decreases interest rates; if the Fed wants to slow the economy it sells bonds, decreases the money supply, and increases interest rates.

18.   Divide the class into small groups of 3 or 4 students and distribute Activity 5. Have the groups discuss the appropriate monetary policy for maintaining a stable economy with low inflation and low unemployment. The correct answers are:

	Monetary Policy Tool		
Problem	Discount Rate	Reserve Requirement	Open Market Operations
High Unemployment	↓	↓	buy
High Inflation	↑	↑	sell

19. When you are sure that students have a basic understanding of the direction the Fed would like to move interest rates to counter inflation or unemployment, distribute Activity 6. Tell the students that they have been appointed as a Governor of the Federal Reserve System (their relatives should be very proud), and now they are being asked for their opinion on an economic policy problem. Give them some time to read over the problem and let them consult in small groups, but in this case have each student write down their own answer to the problem.

20. Conclude the lesson by noting that central banks in other nations face similar problems, but their ability to cope with those problems depends on more than just their economic expertise. The relative degree of political independence of the Federal Reserve System and other central banks has played an important role in maintaining price stability. Nations where the central bank and monetary policy are more directly controlled by current political leaders have been shown to be much less effective in avoiding inflation. Political leaders in these nations often put pressure on central banks to finance deficit spending through money creation, which can soon become inflationary.

CLOSURE

Ask the following questions:

1. When did Congress officially go on record as taking responsibility for the overall performance of the national economy? *(with the Employment Act of 1946)*

2. What are fiscal policies? *(changes in government revenues and expenditures that affect the economy)*

3. Distinguish between discretionary and automatic fiscal policy. *(Discretionary fiscal policy involves a deliberate policy change by Congress and the President in response to some problem in the economy, such as high unemployment or inflation. Automatic fiscal*

policies occur when government tax revenues or spending change in response to higher or lower unemployment or inflation without any new legislation or other policy action, in ways that help to moderate those problems.)

4. What is the appropriate fiscal policy response to high unemployment during a period of virtually no inflation? *(expansionary policies – i.e., increased government expenditures and/or decreased taxes)*

5. What is the appropriate fiscal policy response to high inflation during a period of little or no unemployment? *(contractionary policies that decrease government expenditures or increase taxes.)*

6. What is the name of the U.S. central bank? *(the Federal Reserve System, sometimes referred to as simply The Fed.)*

7. What are the major monetary policy tools of the Fed? *(the discount rate, the reserve requirement, and open market operations)*

8. What is the appropriate monetary policy to counter high inflation during a period of very low unemployment? *(contractionary monetary policies that reduce or slow the growth of the money supply and raise interest rates.)*

9. What is the appropriate monetary policy to counter very high unemployment during a period of very low inflation? *(expansionary monetary policies that increase the growth of the money supply and lower interest rates.)*

ASSESSMENT

1. Have students write a short essay on the following question: Given that automatic stabilizers work without any direct congressional or presidential action, would an amendment that required the Federal budget be balanced, no matter what, lead to the appropriate fiscal policy in the event of a recession? Make sure that you

remind students to explain the direction that government taxes and revenues would change to pursue the kind of stabilization policy advocated by Keynes during the Great Depression. Then suggest that they explain how government revenues and taxes would have to be adjusted to balance the budget annually during periods of either high unemployment or high inflation.

2. Have students write one or two paragraphs reacting to this statement: Good economic policy does not always lend itself to good politics. That is why anti-inflation stabilization policies are almost always done using monetary policy rather than fiscal policy in the United States.

EXTENSION

1. Teach "How Can Changes in the Federal Budget Stabilize the Economy?" in the National Council for Economic Education's (NCEE) *Civics and Government: Focus on Economics.*

2. Teach "Economic Ups and Downs" in the NCEE's *Focus: High School Economics.*

3. Have students locate a newspaper article that discusses some element of federal fiscal or monetary policy. Have them write a paragraph indicating what problems in the economy the policies are supposedly designed to address, and whether or not they feel the policies are appropriate steps to deal with that problem.

4. Teach "Central Banking With or Without Central Planning," in the NCEE's *Focus: Economic Systems.*

Visual 1
The Employment Act of 1946

"The Congress hereby declares that it is the continuing policy of the Federal Government to use all practicable means…to promote maximum employment, production, and purchasing power."

From *Focus: Institutions and Markets*, © National Council on Economic Education, New York, NY

Visual 2
Fiscal Policy

Changes in federal spending or tax levels that influence national levels of output, employment and prices.

A. Expansionary
1. Increase federal spending
2. Decrease federal taxes

B. Contractionary
1. Decrease federal spending
2. Increase federal taxes

Visual 3
Timing Problems

Recognition lag – the time it takes policymakers to recognize that unemployment or inflation have become a serious national problem.

Administrative lag – the time it takes to change government spending or taxes once the problem with unemployment or inflation is recognized.

Operational lag – the time between adopting the change in government spending or taxes and when the policy begins to have an effect on the economy's output, employment, or price levels.

Visual 4
Automatic Stabilizers

Fiscal policies that, without any new action by Congress or the President, decrease government expenditures or increase tax revenues during periods of rising inflation and falling unemployment, and increase expenditures or reduce tax revenues in times of rising unemployment and low or falling inflation.

Visual 5
The Tools of Monetary Policy

1. Discount rate – the interest rate charged by the central bank on loans to commercial banks.

2. Reserve requirement – the minimum level of deposit reserves commercial banks must hold.

3. Open market operations – the central bank buys and sells government bonds

From *Focus: Institutions and Markets*, © National Council on Economic Education, New York, NY

Activity 1
U.S. Unemployment Rates and the Federal Budget, 1928-1946

Year	Unemployment Rate	Federal Expenditures (billions $)	Annual Federal Surplus (+) or Deficit (-)
1928	4.4	3.103	+0.939
1929	3.2	3.298	+0.734
1930	8.7	3.440	+0.738
1931	15.9	3.577	-0.462
1932	23.6	4.659	-2.735
1933	24.9	4.623	-2.602
1934	21.7	6.694	-3.630
1935	20.1	6.521	-2.791
1936	16.9	8.493	-4.425
1937	14.3	7.756	-2.777
1938	19.0	6.792	-1.177
1939	17.2	8.858	-3.862
1940	14.6	9.062	-3.918
1941	9.9	13.262	-6.159
1942	4.7	34.046	-21.490
1943	1.9	79.407	-57.420
1944	1.2	95.059	-51.423
1945	1.9	98.416	-53.941
1946	3.9	60.448	-20.676

Source: U.S. Bureau of the Census, *Historical Statistics of the United States: Colonial Times to 1957*, Washington D.C., 1960, p. 73 and 711.

Using the data on unemployment over this period and your general knowledge of history and economics, answer the following questions:

1. Herbert Hoover was elected as President in 1928 by a landslide (444 electoral votes to 87). In 1932 he was defeated by the Democratic candidate, Franklin Roosevelt, by an even wider margin (472 to 59 electoral votes). Based on the table above, what might be one reason Hoover was defeated?

Activity 1 (continued)

2. Between 1932 and 1938 Roosevelt and the Democratically controlled Congress initiated a series of programs known as the "New Deal," which greatly expanded the size and the role of the federal government in the American economy. Based on the table above, did the New Deal programs succeed in ending the Great Depression by 1938, or even by 1940 or 1941?

3. The unemployment rate continued to fall dramatically from 1941-1945. Why do you believe that happened?

4. Do you believe that the U.S. economic experience from 1929-1946 helps to explain why the Employment Act of 1946 was passed and signed into law by President Truman? Why or why not?

Activity 2
Expansionary or Contractionary Fiscal Policies? That Is the Question.

In the situations presented below, you must decide whether the appropriate fiscal policy response is expansionary (E), contractionary (C), or no change (NC). Write E, C, or NC next to each of the following statements, to indicate the policy you believe is most appropriate.

____ 1. The economy is suffering from its worst slowdown in 30 years. Unemployment has reached 10%.

____ 2. The annual inflation rate is slowing and now stands at 2.5%.

____ 3. We have some good news and some bad news: The unemployment rate has fallen to the lowest level in a decade, 2.3%. But inflation has risen to 8%.

____ 4. The unemployment rate remains steady at 11%.

____ 5. The annual inflation rate is 8.5% and rising.

Activity 3
Automatic Stabilizers

Automatic stabilizers are fiscal policies that raise or lower government revenues and taxes in ways that generally reduce either unemployment or inflation, but without requiring Congress or the President to pass any new laws or take any other actions.

Review the list of programs below and check (✓) the blank before each of the policies that you believe are automatic stabilizers, because they change revenues or taxes in an appropriate way to reduce unemployment when inflation is low, or reduce inflation when unemployment is low. Put an (X) in the blanks for all of the policies that you believe are not automatic stabilizers.

____ 1. Federal taxes on corporate profits

____ 2. Unemployment compensation programs

____ 3. National defense spending on the military

____ 4. Welfare programs for the poor

____ 5. Education programs for colleges and universities

____ 6. Social Security payments for retired workers

____ 7. The federal personal income tax

From *Focus: Institutions and Markets*, © National Council on Economic Education, New York, NY

Activity 4
Memorandum from the President of the United States

To: Council of Economic Advisers

Re: Current Economic Problems

I appreciate your willingness to serve during my first term as President, but we have no time to waste. I have received the following economic data and would appreciate your recommendations for policy regarding tax or spending changes.

	Unemployment Rate	Inflation Rate
Last Year	6.2%	2.6%
This Year	8.5%	2.5%
Forecast for Next Year	9.6%	2.3%

1. Given the information in the table, what is the major economic problem confronting the U.S. economy?

2. Please summarize your suggested changes for fiscal policy.

Activity 5
Monetary Policy Prescription

Problem	Monetary Policy Tool		
	Discount Rate	Reserve Requirement	Open Market Operations
High Unemployment			
High Inflation			

You write the prescription: What is the correct policy direction for each tool?

For the discount rate indicate whether you would want to increase or decrease the rate by writing "↑" for an increase or "↓" for a decrease in the appropriate box.

For the reserve requirement indicate whether you would want to increase or decrease the requirement by writing "↑" for an increase or "↓" for a decrease in the appropriate box.

For open market operations indicate whether you would want to buy or sell government bonds in the open market by writing "buy" or "sell" in the appropriate box.

Activity 6
Memorandum from The Chairman of the Federal Reserve System

To: Members of the Federal Reserve Board

Re: Current Economic Problems

I have received the following economic data and would appreciate your recommendations for future monetary policy.

	Unemployment Rate	Inflation Rate
Last Year	4.2%	2.6%
This Year	3.9%	5.4%
Forecast for Next Year	3.8%	7.3%

1. What is the major economic problem confronting the U.S. economy?

2. What appropriate actions should the Federal Reserve take to promote stability?

LESSON ELEVEN "HEY, HEY! HO, HO! WHY DO WE NEED THE WTO?"

LESSON DESCRIPTION

Several activities are used to introduce students to six international institutions that play important economic roles, especially in the areas of international trade, finance, and development: the World Trade Organization (WTO), the International Monetary Fund (IMF), the Organization for Economic Cooperation and Development (OECD), the United Nations Department of Economic and Social Affairs (UNDESA), the International Bank for Reconstruction and Development (The World Bank), and the International Court of Justice (The World Court). The WTO is examined in greater depth, and students explore issues related to recent global protests of the WTO.

INTRODUCTION

In November 1999, in Seattle, Washington, protesters smashed windows at a McDonald's, a Starbucks Coffee, an FAO Schwartz toy store, a Joan and David shoe store, and a bank (see Activity 1). Were these violent demonstrations part of "traditional" anti-war protests or protests against U.S. government policy in Central America? No, the protestors were trying to disrupt the annual meeting of the World Trade Organization (WTO). Many people had never heard of the WTO, so media covering the protests had to try to explain – often very incompletely – what the organization does, and why it had suddenly sparked so much controversy.

Since the end of WWII, economic activity has become increasingly globalized, mainly through dramatic increases in the level of international trade (imports and exports), and related changes in the financial arrangements required to make that trade possible. Inevitably, those developments raised important political issues, too, and during this same period many **international economic institutions** were established or evolved to provide the necessary 'formal or informal sets of rules' for the global economy.

Such international economic institutions are not new, however. For example, in the 11th century, the Maghribi tribe of North Africa wanted to expand their trading beyond their borders. At that time, cross-border trade entailed many high risks, including robbery by thieves, legal taxes on or outright prohibitions against imports, and greater uncertainty about prices and product quality for competing goods in other countries. The Maghribi solved many of these problems by developing one of the earliest international networks of overseas trade agents: representatives who looked after Maghribi interests and communicated back to the traders.[1]

Since World War II, the global economy has faced similar, but much larger and even more complicated problems. Today, the international institutions listed above try to help nations achieve common but important economic goals. These institutions sometimes do this by providing financial aid, or in other cases by promoting sound economic policies and developing institutions in nations that help to:

- Improve economic efficiency and maintain competitive markets.
- Provide **public goods** (e.g., elementary education and inoculations against infectious diseases) and correct for other **market failures** (e.g., externalities such as pollution).

---

[1] World Bank. *World development report 2002: Building institutions for markets.* New York, NY: Oxford University Press; 2002, p. 3.

- Clearly define and enforce **property rights** (i.e., the rights of individuals to own and distribute property).
- Promote economic development in low-income nations.
- Improve the quality of life while lowering the costs of both intranational and international trade by providing better public infrastructure (e.g., transportation systems and basic health and safety services and regulations).
- Encourage sound macroeconomic stabilization policies (i.e., fiscal and **monetary policies**) that help to reduce unemployment and inflation not only in the short run, but especially over the long run.
- Reduce **tariffs** and other barriers to trade.

CONCEPTS

International economic institutions
Gains from trade
Tariffs
Public goods
Market failures
Monetary policy
Property rights
Competition

CONTENT STANDARDS

Voluntary exchange occurs only when all participating parties expect to gain. This is true for trade among individuals or organizations within a nation, and usually among individuals or organizations in different nations.

When individuals, regions, and nations specialize in what they can produce at the lowest cost and then trade with others, both production and consumption increase.

Institutions evolve in market economies to help individuals and groups accomplish their goals. Banks, labor unions, corporations, legal systems, and not-for-profit organizations are examples of important institutions. A different kind of institution, clearly defined and enforced

property rights, is essential to a market economy.

Investment in factories, machinery, new technology, and in the health, education, and training of people can raise future standards of living.

There is an economic role for government to play in a market economy whenever the benefits of a government policy outweigh its costs. Governments often provide for national defense, address environmental concerns, define and protect property rights, and attempt to make markets more competitive. Most government policies also redistribute income.

BENCHMARKS

Free trade increases worldwide material standards of living.

Despite the mutual benefits from trade among people in different countries, many nations employ trade barriers to restrict free trade for national defense reasons or because some companies and workers are hurt by free trade.

When imports are restricted by public policies, consumers pay higher prices and job opportunities and profits in exporting firms decrease.

As a result of growing international economic interdependence, economic conditions and policies in one nation increasingly affect economic conditions and policies in other nations.

Economic growth is a sustained rise in a nation's production of goods and services. It results from investments in human and physical capital, research and development, and technological change, and from improved institutional arrangements and incentives.

When a price fails to reflect all the benefits of a product, too little of the product is produced and consumed. When a price fails to reflect all the costs of a product, too much of it is produced and consumed. Government can use subsidies to help correct for insufficient output; it can use taxes to help correct for excessive output; or it can regulate output directly to correct for over- or under-production or consumption of a product.

Governments often redistribute income directly when individuals or interest groups are not satisfied with the income distribution resulting from markets; governments also redistribute income indirectly as side-effects of other government actions that affect prices or output levels for various goods and services.

A government policy to correct a market imperfection is not justified economically if its expected costs exceed its expected benefits.

OBJECTIVES
Students will:

♦ Identify six international institutions and the important roles those institutions play in the areas of international trade, finance, and economic development.

♦ Summarize the major benefits, criticisms, and misunderstandings that have been identified in recent debates about the World Trade Organization.

TIME REQUIRED
Two class periods

MATERIALS
- Visual 1: Trends in Global Trade, 1950-2001
- Visual 2: International Institutions, or Alphabet Soup
- Five or six varieties of "bite-sized" candy bars; one candy bar per student
- Activity 1: International Institutions, or Alphabet Soup, one copy per student

- Activity 2: International Institutions, Headline Bingo, one bingo card and 24 bingo markers (cut apart) for each student. There are eight different bingo cards, and each student gets one card, so for a class of up to 24 students make three copies of each card; for classes of 25-32 students make four copies of each card; etc. There are 72 markers on the master duplicating page, so three copies of this page provide enough markers for eight students.
- Activity 3: What's All the Fuss About the WTO?, one copy per student
- Internet access (preferably in a computer lab) for Activity 3 and extension activities

PROCEDURES
1. Tell students they are going to participate in a short simulation to see if they can use their skills as traders to make themselves happier. Hand out one small candy bar per student using many different types of candy (mixed bags of "bite size" versions of popular candy bars work well). After the students have each received one candy bar, before they trade and before they eat the candy, have each student rate the satisfaction that candy bar gives her or him on a one-to-five scale, where one is low and five is high.

2. Ask students to write down their satisfaction score on a piece of paper and turn it in. You (or an aid or student helper) will calculate the average level of satisfaction while the students engage in a trading round. Tell the students they will have two or three minutes to trade with anyone else in the room *if* they choose to do so, but make it clear that no one is required to trade. Conduct the trading round.

3. After the trading round, once again ask students to rate their satisfaction on a 1-5 scale, based on the item they have now. Collect the ratings from students; calculate the average level of satisfaction and display or announce the average pre- and post-trading ratings to the class. Ask students why satisfaction increased after trading. (*People traded when both valued*

the other's candy bar more than their own. After the trades people were generally more satisfied than before.) Note that while the candy bars are still the same as those originally handed out, now they are held by people who value them more highly. Voluntary trade created gains in satisfaction just by moving the items to people who valued them more highly. This increased satisfaction is an illustration of gains from trade.

4. Did everyone trade? Was everyone "better off" after the trading round? *(Some people were already more satisfied with the kind of candy they received than any other kind that was available; some may have wanted to trade for a candy bar that nobody else was willing to give up. On average, however, the group had greater satisfaction, and in most cases no one will have had a lower satisfaction level. It is possible that someone traded for a candy bar they had never tried before, only to discover that they didn't like it.)* Trade does not guarantee everyone will gain greater satisfaction; but people only trade when they expect to be better off, and the class as a whole should always show greater total and average satisfaction after the trading.

5. Display Visual 1. Ask students to discuss what is shown by the information on the visual, and why that is important. Be sure to point out that global trade has increased dramatically over the last 50 years and ask the following questions: What was the percentage increase in global trade between 1990 and 2000? *(Approximately 80%)*. In 1950 only 7% of total world production was exported; today 23% is exported. Why does the United States (or any other nation) engage in trade with other countries? Why don't we just 'buy American'? *(Explain that just as in the candy bar trading activity, one key reason is that whenever two or more people trade – whether they live in the same nation or in different nations – they all expect to gain from the trade.)*

6. Explain to students that following the end of World War II, global trade increased as a result of several factors, including lower transportation and communications costs, rising income levels in many countries, and greater cost savings from increased specialization and economies of scale with large factories and assembly-line production methods. There were also several policy initiatives shortly before and after the end of the war designed to reduce trade barriers such as tariffs and quotas on imported products. All of this sharply increased trade activity (see Visual 1), which made the international organizations and institutions dealing with trade, finance, and development even more important.

7. Ask students to discuss the various reasons for, and roles of, economic institutions in a market as outlined in the introduction to this lesson. Display Visual 2. Briefly review each of these roles with students.

8. Distribute Activity 1. Allow time for students to read the brief descriptions of each international institution. Ask students to complete the left column in the chart for Activity 1. When students have finished, display Visual 2 again and fill in the left column as shown on the next page to compile and review student responses.

Suggested answers for Activity 1:

WTO IMF OECD	Improve economic efficiency and maintain competitive markets.
World Bank UNDESA	Provide public goods (e.g., elementary education and inoculations against infectious diseases) and correct for other market failures (e.g., externalities such as pollution).
WTO World Court OECD	Clearly define and enforce property rights.
World Bank WTO UNDESA	Promote economic development in low-income nations.
World Bank IMF UNDESA	Provide public infrastructure (e.g., transportation systems and basic health and safety regulations).
IMF	Encourage sound macroeconomic stabilization policies (monetary and fiscal policies).
WTO World Court OECD	Reduce tariffs and other barriers to trade.

9. Distribute copies of the International Institutions – Headline Bingo game cards and markers, all taken from Activity 2. Give each student one bingo card (make sure to alternate the eight different forms of these cards as you pass them out) and 24 markers. Tell students that, for the first round, <u>any</u> five markers in a row wins.

10. Slowly read and repeat each headline in Activity 2, International Institutions: Headline Bingo. Instruct students to listen carefully as each headline is read and to place a bingo marker over the name of the organization they think is most likely to be associated with the action occurring in each headline. Remind students that, in order to get a bingo, they must have correctly placed five markers in a row. Offer small incentives to the winners; you may have some leftover candy bars from the trading activity.

11. Once "bingo" is called, have students read back the squares they had marked. Check these against the headlines read. Be certain the

spaces the student has covered correspond correctly to the headlines read. If not, resume play until a correct bingo is called. Award prizes. Play additional rounds using several variations of the basic bingo format to check students' comprehension. For example, require that winners' markers must form a cross (middle vertical row, middle horizontal row) on their card or that only the top or bottom row may be completed for a win.

12. Review again the major institutional roles played by international organizations, stressing the importance of international trade using Visual 1. This time put special focus on the role played by the World Trade Organization and, if Internet access is available, visit the WTO website. Ask students to summarize the role the WTO plays in international trade. *(The WTO is the only international organization dealing with the global rules of trade between nations. Its main function is to ensure that trade flows as smoothly and freely as possible.)* Ask students the following questions: What might happen if

the WTO did not exist? (*Countries might try to negotiate trade agreements individually, but the costs of those negotiations would probably be higher.*) Why is international trade easier and more efficient with an international institution like the WTO? (*Trade barriers such as tariffs or quotas are reduced, and without the WTO countries would be forced to settle disputes among themselves, leading to potential conflicts.*)

13. Ask students if they recall hearing about the WTO meetings in Seattle in 1999. Perhaps they recall seeing the protestors smashing windows of Starbucks and McDonald's restaurants and being arrested. Ask students if they recall what the protests were about. Distribute copies of Activity 3 and have students read the article, "WTO in Seattle: Protestors Smash Landmarks; Delegates Debate Trade Agreements."

14. Briefly discuss the article, and call attention to both sides of the debate, in this case represented by Mike Moore, the WTO Director-General, and Tom Hayden, a political activist. Ask students to summarize the two views. (*Moore: people are better off under a system of free trade because voluntary trade is a "win-win" situation whether trade takes place between people who live in the same city or nation, or between people in different countries; Hayden: free trade – as promoted by WTO – exploits workers and the environment and promotes the agenda of big corporations over the poor.*)

15. The next portion of the lesson requires Internet access, preferably in a computer lab. In small groups, have students use the Internet resources provided in Activity 3 to answer the guiding questions and to complete the data retrieval chart provided.

Sample responses for Activity 3, questions 3 through 5

Issue/Claim	Protestors say...	WTO says... (sample responses drawn from WTO documents)
The WTO dictates policy.	"WTO inappropriately intervenes in domestic and regional affairs in order to enforce international trade policy, undermining the democratic process and contributing to predatory multi-national corporations' strangle-hold over declining nation-states." (from oneworld.com's analysis of trade issues.)	"The WTO does not tell governments how to conduct their trade policies; it is a "member-driven" organization: ▪ the rules of the WTO system are agreements resulting from negotiations among member governments, ▪ the rules are ratified by member nations' legislatures, ▪ in the WTO, virtually all decisions are made by consensus among all members."
The WTO ignores development in low-income nations.	"If the GATT was heavily weighted in promoting the interests of the developed countries, the WTO is even more in danger of being an instrument of domination by the strong over the weaker and smaller countries."	"Sustainable development is a principal objective of the WTO: ▪ Developing countries are allowed more time to apply numerous provisions of the WTO agreements. Least-developed countries receive special treatment, including exemption from many provisions.

	(Third World Network, quoted on http:// www.oneworld.net/ campaigns/wto/)	▪ The needs of development can also be used to justify actions that might not normally be allowed under the agreements, for example governments giving certain subsidies."
The WTO is anti-environment.	"Environmentalists express concern that years of work negotiating environmental treaties could be disrupted if WTO rules of trade are used to nullify those environmental enforcement measures under the assumptions that they violate free trade principles." (from greennature.com)	"Many provisions take environmental concerns specifically into account: ▪ Beyond the broad principles, specific agreements on specific subjects also take environmental concerns into account. ▪ Subsidies are permitted for environmental protection. Environmental objectives are recognized specifically in the WTO agreements dealing with product standards, food safety, intellectual property protection, etc."
The WTO destroys jobs.	"The AFL-CIO agrees that the WTO rules encourage exploitation of labor, the degradation of our environment, and do nothing to limit the growing power of multinational corporations and capital. The WTO has undermined the legitimate national regulations protecting the environment, human rights, and public health." (AFL-CIO Executive Council Statement, 8/4/99, cited at www.disinformation.com.)	"The accusation is inaccurate and simplistic. Trade can be a powerful force for creating jobs and reducing poverty: ▪ Freer-flowing and more stable trade boosts economic growth. It has the potential to create jobs, it can help to reduce poverty, and frequently it does both. ▪ The biggest beneficiary is the country that lowers its own trade barriers. The countries exporting to it also gain, but not as much. In many cases, workers in export sectors enjoy higher pay and greater job security. ▪ However, producers and their workers who were previously protected clearly face new competition when trade barriers are lowered. Some survive by becoming more competitive. Others don't."

16. Have students use the information they uncovered during the Internet activity to compose a fictional "letter to the editor" that summarizes each side's arguments and concludes with a statement of the necessity of organizations such as the WTO that perform crucial roles in the global economy.

CLOSURE

Stress that, especially since 1945, trade and other economic activities have become increasingly international in scope. In order to facilitate this increased international activity, certain economic institutions have evolved. These institutions play important roles in developing economic policies that improve economic efficiency and maintain competitive markets, provide public goods and correct for other market failures, define and enforce property rights, promote economic development in low-income nations, encourage sound macroeconomic stabilization policies, and reduce tariffs and other barriers to trade. Although some international institutions and organizations – and the policies they have implemented – remain controversial, most economists believe that successful development for low-income nations hinges on the evolution of these key market institutions.

EVALUATION

1. Ask students to write a short essay about why economic institutions might be important to economic growth and development. For example, ask them to briefly consider what might happen in the United States if no institutions played some of the roles outlined above (e.g., well-defined property rights, lower tariffs, etc.). How might the students' lives be different if no institutions existed to fulfill these roles, in terms of what products they purchased or the prices for those products?

2. Now ask students to think about low-income, developing countries. Ask: What might be some benefits of strengthening these economic institutions in such countries? Ask students to reflect on why persistent poverty might be in some ways associated with a lack of these economic institutions.

EXTENSION ACTIVITIES

1. If the class has access to the Internet (preferably in a computer lab), take a few minutes to visit the webpages of the World Bank, the WTO, the IMF, the World Court, the OECD, and the UNDESA. Have students read the description of the organization (generally found in the 'About...” section of the webpage; e.g., 'About the IMF'). Ask students to describe how each organization's objectives contribute to institution building and/or economic development.

2. Revisit Activity 1. Have students add a third column to the data retrieval chart entitled "Comparable Institutions in the United States." Ask students to list at least one organization that fulfills the same institutional role in the United States, at the domestic (national) level rather than international issues and agreements. For example, the Antitrust Division of the Department of Justice is charged with maintaining competitive markets in the United States.

Suggested answers for Extension of Activity 1:

International Institution(s)	Institutional Role	Comparable Institution(s) in the United States
WTO IMF OECD	Improve economic efficiency and maintain competitive markets.	Securities and Exchange Commission Federal Trade Commission Antitrust Division of Dept. of Justice
World Bank UNDESA	Provide public goods (e.g., elementary education and inoculations against infectious diseases) and correct for other market failures (e.g., externalities such as pollution).	Federal, State, and Local Government Environmental Protection Agency

WTO World Court OECD	Clearly define and enforce property rights.	Civil and criminal court systems U.S. Patent and Trademark Office
World Bank WTO UNDESA	Promote economic development.	U.S. Small Business Administration U.S. Economic Development Administration U.S. Patent and Trademark Office
World Bank IMF UNDESA	Provide public infrastructure (e.g., transportation systems and basic health and safety regulation).	Centers for Disease Control Federal Interstate Highways Federal Aviation Administration Dept. of Transportation FDA OSHA
IMF	Macroeconomic stabilization (monetary and fiscal policies) and stable exchange rates.	Federal Reserve System
WTO World Court OECD	Reduce tariffs and other barriers to trade	*U.S. Constitution Interstate Commerce Commission U.S. Department of Justice

* Barriers to interstate trade are prohibited by the U.S. Constitution.

Visual 1
Trends in Global Trade, 1950-2001

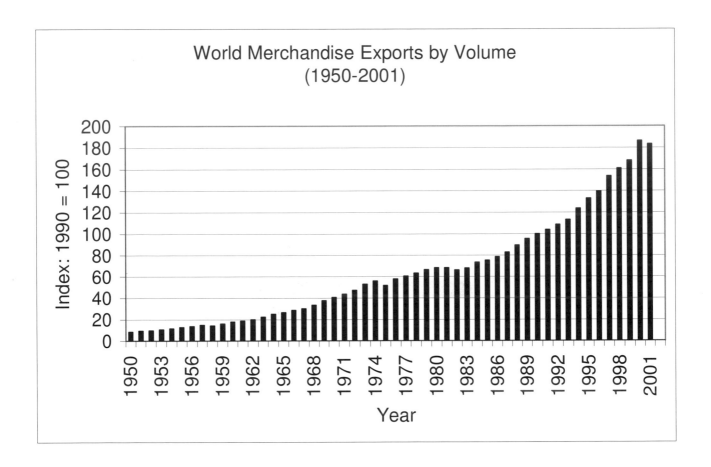

World Merchandise Exports by Volume (1950-2001)

Source: World Trade Organization: *Selected Long Term Trends.* (accessed at http://www.wto.org/english/res_e/statis_e/its2002_e/its02_longterm_e.htm)

Note: The index of world exports is based on the value of exports, first aggregated to obtain regional totals, then aggregated and adjusted to reflect world price levels.

Visual 2
International Institutions, or Alphabet Soup

International Institution(s)	Institutional Role
	Improve economic efficiency and maintain competitive markets.
	Provide public goods (e.g., elementary education and inoculation against contagious diseases) and correct for other market failures (e.g., externalities such as pollution).
	Clearly define and enforce property rights.
	Promote economic development in low-income nations.
	Provide public infrastructure (e.g., transportation systems and basic health and safety regulations).
	Encourage sound macroeconomic stabilization policies (monetary and fiscal policies) and stable exchange rates.
	Reduce tariffs and other barriers to trade.

Activity 1
International Institutions, or Alphabet Soup

Directions

Dozens of organizations deal with different aspects of the global economy – including legal, political, and cultural issues. This activity describes six key international institutions that deal with economic issues: the **International Monetary Fund** (IMF), the **World Bank** (or, more correctly, the International Bank for Reconstruction and Development), the **World Trade Organization** (WTO), the **Organization for Economic Cooperation and Development** (OECD), the **United Nations Department of Economic and Social Affairs** (UNDESA), and the **International Court of Justice** (The World Court).

Read the brief descriptions of these six institutions below. Website addresses are provided for each of these organizations; if time permits and you have Internet access, visit those sites, too. Then complete the chart below by listing in the left column the abbreviation or short name of the organizations that fulfill each of the roles described in the right column. (Some of the six institutions will be listed more than once, and more than one organization may be listed for some of the roles described in the right column.)

Brief Descriptions
The International Monetary Fund (IMF) (http://www.imf.org/)
The IMF was established in 1946 and now has 183 member countries. The primary goals of the IMF are to: (1) promote international monetary cooperation, (2) promote currency exchange stability, (3) facilitate the expansion and balanced growth of international trade, and, (4) support policies that foster economic growth and development, and high levels of employment around the world.

The IMF tries to accomplish these goals by providing temporary financial assistance (basically loans) to countries experiencing short-term economic crises such as rapid decreases in the value in their currency. The hope is that the loans will allow countries to quickly restore conditions conducive to sustained economic growth. More specifically, the assistance can enable countries to rebuild levels of international trade, stabilize their currencies, and continue paying for imports without having to impose trade restrictions or capital controls. The IMF rarely lends for specific capital investment projects designed to promote a nation's economic growth, so it is not a development bank.

The International Bank for Reconstruction and Development (The World Bank)
(http://www.worldbank.org/)
Based in Washington D.C. and established in 1945, the World Bank (WB) was originally developed to help European nations rebuild following World War II. Today the WB is the world's largest source of development assistance for less-developed nations, providing nearly $16 billion in loans each year. The projects funded by these loans target a wide range of issues, including:
 ▪ developing social institutions (e.g., the WB funded a Palestinian Authority project to staff its Ministry of Social and Labor Services)

Activity 1 (continued)

- institution-building (e.g., WB funded a project to develop capital markets by strengthening legislation, regulatory capacity, infrastructure, and insurance supervision in Romania.)
- environmental protection (e.g., WB funded a project in Tanzania to reclaim polluted water sources for drinking water)
- private business development (e.g., WB supported a project in Romania to restructure the national savings bank (CEC) in preparation for its privatization)
- macroeconomic stabilization (e.g., WB funded a project in Nepal to support renewed government efforts to improve the banking sector, promote macroeconomic stability, and encourage private-sector-led economic growth)
- poverty reduction (e.g., WB sponsored a project in Vietnam to support efforts to achieve higher growth and reduce poverty).

The World Bank provides financial support for global public goods that are critical for the well-being of poor people in all countries, and for necessary institutional reforms such as anticorruption measures. The World Bank is owned by its 182 member countries, and has 67 country offices around the world.

The World Trade Organization (WTO) (http://www.wto.org/)
The WTO was created in 1995, as a successor organization to the General Agreement on Tariffs and Trade (GATT). The goal of the WTO is to help both importing and exporting businesses conduct their business more efficiently, with fewer barriers to trade, and to improve the welfare of member countries.

The World Trade Organization (WTO) is the only global organization dealing with the rules of trade between nations, trying to reduce trade barriers such as tariffs and quotas, but also to define rules for "fair trade" that establish penalties for dumping (selling goods below production costs) or other proscribed practices. WTO agreements have been negotiated and signed by 144 of the world's trading nations and ratified in their national legislative bodies. Essentially, these agreements are contracts, guaranteeing member countries important trade rights and requiring governments to keep laws and regulations that restrict trade within agreed limits.

On October 30, 1947, the General Agreement on Tariffs and Trade (GATT) was signed by 23 nations. The Agreement contained tariff reductions agreed to during the first multilateral trade negotiations and a set of rules designed to prevent these concessions from eroding. Between 1947 and 1995, seven additional agreements were negotiated, all but the last focusing on tariff and trade-barrier reduction. Economists have estimated that GATT reduced worldwide tariffs from 40% of the value of all exports in 1947 to only 4% in 1995.[2]

Organization for Economic Cooperation and Development (OECD): (http://www.oecd.org)
This organization has 30 member countries committed to market economies and a pluralistic

---

[2] B. McDonald, *The World Trading System: The Uruguay Round and Beyond,* New York, New York: St. Martin's Press, 1998, p. 69.

Activity 1 (continued)

democracy. The OECD provides a regular forum for the governments of these nations to discuss and develop economic and social policies, and the OECD has developed formal agreements between members in such areas as banking regulations, encouraging free trade, cracking down on bribery, and on limiting government intervention in markets (e.g., ending subsidies for shipbuilding). The OECD's Secretariat in Paris forecasts economic performance and trends, and conducts research on a wide range of issues, including trade patterns, agriculture, technology, taxation, and the environment.

United Nations Department of Economic and Social Affairs (UNDESA):
(http://www.un.org/esa/desa.htm)
Established in 1945, the mission of the United Nations' Department of Economic and Social Affairs (UNDESA) is to provide administrative expertise to coordinate global efforts to solve problems that challenge humanity, including poverty. While the UNDESA rarely funds large development projects, it does provide research and advice for projects in developing countries that monitor the advancement and empowerment of women and focus on public sector development. The UNDESA often coordinates conferences on important political and social issues including sustainable development. UNDESA also compiles and disseminates analytical data and statistics and economic and social indicators used by policy makers throughout the world. The agency's work and major goals, programs, and research findings are summarized in an annual report, the World Economic and Social Survey.

The International Court of Justice (The World Court)
(http://www.icj-cij.org/icjwww/icj002.htm)
The International Court of Justice is the judicial branch of the United Nations. Located at The Hague (in The Netherlands), the Court has two major roles: 1) to settle in accordance with international law the legal disputes submitted to it by national governments, and to give advisory opinions on legal questions referred to it by duly authorized international agencies. The Court rules on economic issues including sovereignty of member states (e.g., border disputes), and property rights disputes between nations.

Use the brief descriptions above to complete the chart on the next page. Remember that more than one international institution may perform a particular role, and that the institutions may also perform more than one role.

Activity 1 (continued)

International Institution(s)	Institutional Role
	Improve economic efficiency and maintain competitive markets.
	Provide public goods (e.g., elementary education and inoculations against contagious diseases) and correct for other market failures (e.g., externalities such as pollution).
	Clearly define and enforce property rights.
	Promote economic development in low-income nations.
	Provide public infrastructure (e.g., transportation systems and basic health and safety regulations).
	Encourage sound macroeconomic stabilization policies (monetary and fiscal policies) and stable exchange rates.
	Reduce tariffs and other barriers to trade.

Activity 2
International Institutions: Headline Bingo

Use these headlines with the International Institutions Headline Bingo Game Cards and markers. Once game cards and markers have been distributed to students, read the following headlines slowly until a bingo is called. (Be careful not to read the suggested answers printed in bold.) As the student who calls bingo reads back his or her answers, check to make certain they have covered the correct squares.

1. BRAZILIAN CURRENCY CRUZADO CRASHES AMIDST ELECTION RESULTS **(IMF)**

2. POLAND ACCUSED OF UNFAIR TARIFFS ON LATVIAN LUMBER **(WTO or World Bank)**

3. NICARAGUA AND COLOMBIA IN COURT CASE DISPUTE FISHING RIGHTS IN CARRIBEAN **(World Court)**

4. JAPAN ACCUSED OF "DUMPING" CHEAP STEEL IN U.S. MARKET **(WTO)**

5. POLITICAL, ECONOMIC UNCERTAINTY REIGN FOLLOWING EARTHQUAKE IN TURKEY **(World Bank)**

6. CONFERENCE DEBATES ENDING SUBSIDIES FOR EUROPEAN AIRPLANE MANUFACTURERS **(OECD)**

7. XIANGFAN HIGHWAY PROJECT TO PROVIDE EFFECTIVE TRANSPORT INFRASTRUCTURE FOR CHINA **(World Bank)**

8. CZECH REPUBLIC CHARGED WITH FAILING TO HALT SOFTWARE PIRACY **(WTO)**

9. EL SALVADOR USES LOAN TO MODERNIZE JUDICIAL SYSTEM WITH TRAINING FOR JUDGES AND STAFF **(World Bank)**

10. 22 COUNTRIES IN AFRICA GET DEBT RELIEF SUPPORT TO PREVENT CURRENCY DEVALUATION **(IMF)**

11. DELAYS IN PRIVITIZATION OF PHONE COMPANY CAUSE ROMANIA TO SEEK POVERTY REDUCTION ASSISTANCE **(World Bank OR UNDESA)**

12. REPORT EXPECTED TO BE RELEASED TODAY ON SUSTAINABLE DEVELOPMENT AND TRENDS IN WORLD CONSUMPTION AND PRODUCTION **(UNDESA)**

Activity 2 (continued)

13. DELEGATES ARRIVE IN SAN SALVADOR FOR CONFERENCE TO DISCUSS ECONOMIC OPPORTUNITIES FOR WOMEN, POOR IN DEVELOPING COUNTRIES (**UNDESA**)

14. BULGARIA SEEKS SUPPORT TO STABILIZE ITS FINANCIAL SYSTEM (**IMF**)

15. MEXICO, U.S. REACH AGREEMENT DESIGNED TO CURB BORDER CORRUPTION (**OECD**)

16. NIGERIA'S TRADE DEFICIT RISES AND VALUE OF NIGERIAN CURRENCY NAIRA FALLS RAPIDLY (**IMF**)

17. BENIN BUILDS 79 SCHOOLS WITH DEVELOPMENT GRANT (**World Bank OR UNDESA**)

18. JAPAN ENCOURAGED TO PRESS AHEAD WITH REFORMS IN TRADE POLICY AND CORPORATE RESTRUCTURING (**WTO**)

19. U.S. TO MEET WITH CANADA OVER SOFTWOOD LUMBER IMPORT DUTIES (**WTO**)

20. NIGER AND BENIN DEBATE OWNERSHIP OF LÉTÉ ISLAND (**World Court**)

21. LIECHTENSTEIN SUES GERMANY OVER CONSFICATED PROPERTY (**World Court**)

Activity 2 (continued)

Bingo Marker	Bingo Marker	Bingo Marker	Bingo Marker	Bingo Marker	Bingo Marker	Bingo Marker	Bingo Marker
Bingo Marker	Bingo Marker	Bingo Marker	Bingo Marker	Bingo Marker	Bingo Marker	Bingo Marker	Bingo Marker
Bingo Marker	Bingo Marker	Bingo Marker	Bingo Marker	Bingo Marker	Bingo Marker	Bingo Marker	Bingo Marker
Bingo Marker	Bingo Marker	Bingo Marker	Bingo Marker	Bingo Marker	Bingo Marker	Bingo Marker	Bingo Marker
Bingo Marker	Bingo Marker	Bingo Marker	Bingo Marker	Bingo Marker	Bingo Marker	Bingo Marker	Bingo Marker
Bingo Marker	Bingo Marker	Bingo Marker	Bingo Marker	Bingo Marker	Bingo Marker	Bingo Marker	Bingo Marker
Bingo Marker	Bingo Marker	Bingo Marker	Bingo Marker	Bingo Marker	Bingo Marker	Bingo Marker	Bingo Marker
Bingo Marker	Bingo Marker	Bingo Marker	Bingo Marker	Bingo Marker	Bingo Marker	Bingo Marker	Bingo Marker
Bingo Marker	Bingo Marker	Bingo Marker	Bingo Marker	Bingo Marker	Bingo Marker	Bingo Marker	Bingo Marker

Activity 2 (continued)

Card #2

UNDESA	WTO	OECD	IMF	World Bank
OECD	WTO	IMF	World Bank	WTO
IMF	World Court	FREE	IMF	UNDESA
WTO	IMF	OECD	World Court	WTO
World Court	OECD	WTO	UNDESA	IMF

Card #1

WTO	UNDESA	OECD	IMF	World Bank
OECD	WTO	World Bank	World Bank	World Court
IMF	World Court	FREE	IMF	UNDESA
World Bank	WTO	OECD	World Court	IMF
IMF	OECD	WTO	UNDESA	WTO

Activity 2 (continued)

Card #4

WTO	IMF	UNDESA	WTO	World Bank
WTO	OECD	IMF	World Bank	IMF
UNDESA	WTO	FREE	WTO	OECD
OECD	World Bank	World Court	OECD	WTO
IMF	World Bank	IMF	World Court	UNDESA

Card #3

UNDESA	WTO	World Court	WTO	OECD
OECD	World Bank	IMF	OECD	WTO
IMF	World Bank	FREE	World Court	UNDESA
World Bank	World Court	UNDESA	IMF	WTO
WTO	OECD	World Bank	UNDESA	IMF

Activity 2 (continued)

Card #6

WTO	WTO	UNDESA	OECD	UNDESA
IMF	OECD	WTO	World Bank	IMF
UNDESA	IMF	FREE	World Court	IMF
WTO	World Court	WTO	OECD	World Court
World Bank	IMF	OECD	WTO	UNDESA

Card #5

UNDESA	OECD	IMF	World Bank	WTO
OECD	World Bank	World Bank	World Court	OECD
World Court	IMF	FREE	UNDESA	World Bank
WTO	OECD	World Court	IMF	UNDESA
OECD	WTO	World Court	WTO	IMF

Activity 2 (continued)

Card #8

World Court	IMF	OECD	World Bank	WTO
UNDESA	WTO	WTO	IMF	OECD
IMF	World Court	FREE	OECD	UNDESA
IMF	World Bank	OECD	WTO	UNDESA
World Bank	World Court	World Bank	OECD	WTO

Card #7

IMF	World Bank	OECD	WTO	UNDESA
World Bank	World Court	World Bank	OECD	WTO
IMF	UNDESA	FREE	OECD	World Court
World Court	IMF	OECD	World Bank	WTO
UNDESA	WTO	WTO	IMF	OECD

Activity 3
What's All the Fuss About the WTO?

Article
WTO IN SEATTLE: PROTESTORS SMASH LANDMARKS; DELEGATES DEBATE TRADE AGREEMENTS[3]

SEATTLE, WA (Nov. 30-Dec. 2, 1999) – The demonstrations and police crackdowns were reminiscent of the violent protests that struck the United States during the Vietnam War. For those involved in the Seattle disturbances, however, it was all new – to these young people, the social unrest of 30 years ago is history, and not part of their personal past.

Although free trade may not be the subject of shouting at the family dinner-table as the Vietnam War was four decades ago, it has aroused genuine passions that led to an unusual alliance in Seattle. Anarchists, union laborers, animal rights activists, environmentalists and senior citizens all protested against globalization and international trade, and the World Trade Organization (WTO) meeting that took place in Seattle over a three-day period.

During the WTO conference, riot police fired tear gas and pepper spray in an attempt to clear the streets. Seattle's police chief was quoted as saying, "those who were arguing that they were going to shut the WTO down were in fact successful today."

The WTO "reflects an enormously narrow ideology," one protestor was quoted as saying. "People who favor trade, who would really like the world to become closely integrated, have been frustrated in their efforts to have that done in a way that is environmentally responsible and that will raise the standard of living around the world."

"Trade is the ally of working people, not their enemy," WTO Director-General Mike Moore was quoted as saying prior to the conference, which opened November 30, 1999. "As living standards improve, so too does education, health, the environment and labor standards, and when living standards rise, human rights rise, and people demand better environmental outcomes."

A WTO American liaison officer who lives in the Seattle area, one of many who couldn't make it inside for the conference because of the demonstrations, was quoted as stating, "I believe in free expression and I believe they have a right to protest. But not like this. We have a job to do. It seems tolerance only goes one way with them. The fact of the matter is, where there's greater prosperity, there's greater freedom. So I don't know what they're thinking."

Former 60s activist Tom Hayden was quoted as saying, "I haven't seen anything like it in a very long time. I saw Teamsters and Machinists who were concerned about losing jobs to sweat shops. I saw environmentalists. I saw women. I saw people in the street doing the most phenomenal acts and courageous acts, I might say, of civil disobedience who actually managed to stop this organization of 135 countries in its tracks. What were they so upset about?" What indeed, were all the protests over?

---

[3] Sources for this article include on-line reports from CNN, ABC News and Online News Hour.

Activity 3 (continued)

Internet Hunt
You will use the on-line resources outlined in this activity to research the debate surrounding the 1999 World Trade Organization protests in Seattle and to develop a fictitious letter to the editor of your local newspaper (presenting your own view of the debate) that answers Tom Hayden's question, "What were they so upset about?"

Resources:

University of Washington digital history of the Seattle protests	http://depts.washington.edu/wtohist/
U. of Washington general information site about the protests	http://content.lib.washington.edu/WTOweb/more-info.html
disinformation.com analysis of the WTO	http://www.disinfo.com/pages/dossier/id216/pg1/
oneworld.com's views of the WTO	http://www.oneworld.net/campaigns/wto/
greennature.com analysis of global trade and the environment	http://greennature.com/article447.html
Tom Hayden *Washington Post* column about the Seattle protests	http://www.globalpolicy.org/globaliz/cultural/seattle.htm
WTO "10 Common Misunderstandings About the WTO"	http://www.wto.org/english/thewto_e/whatis_e/10mis_e/10m00_e.htm
WTO "10 Benefits to the WTO Trading System."	http://www.wto.org/english/thewto_e/whatis_e/10ben_e/10b00_e.htm

Guiding Questions:
1. First visit the two University of Washington sites. What organizations were involved in the protests? What were these groups protesting?

2. Next visit the *disinformation.com, oneworld.com,* and *greennature.com* sites, and the *Washington Post* article by Tom Hayden. What are four key issues the various protest groups agree on? In other words, what do they say is so bad about the WTO?

3. Now visit the WTO sites. What is the WTO's response to the protestors claims?

4. Use your research to summarize the Seattle protestors' claims on the four issues in one column of the chart, and WTO reaction to these claims in another column.

5. When you have completed the chart, write a letter that you might send to the editor of your local newspaper if the WTO decided to hold its annual meetings in your community next year. In this letter: (1) summarize the events that took place in Seattle, (2) describe the WTO, (3) summarize the major charges made by the protestors, (4) summarize the WTO responses to those charges, and (5) conclude by describing why you believe an international institution/organization responsible for encouraging free trade and managing trade disputes (such as the WTO) is or is not essential in the modern global economy.

LESSON TWELVE
SOCIAL CAPITAL: NORMS AND NETWORKS THAT SUPPORT MARKETS

LESSON DESCRIPTION

Students are introduced to the idea of "social capital," and learn how to distinguish it from physical capital. The importance of social capital in promoting economic growth and allowing a market economy to operate more efficiently is considered in several activities, including a "rigged" card game (BLOOG) and short surveys of the students and their parents or guardians. Finally, students investigate several kinds of voluntary consumer and civic associations and discuss how they can also represent examples of social capital.

INTRODUCTION

Social capital is sometimes described as the aspects of social, political, and economic life that allow people in communities and nations to interact and work together to achieve common objectives, which benefit everyone in the society, or at least a wide range of people and organizations. That definition obviously covers many different kinds of things, including such general ideas as widely held social norms and moral and religious codes of behavior (e.g., what is often referred to as the "Protestant work ethic"). Social capital can also refer to the basic trust individuals have in their society and its political and economic institutions including many kinds of local or regional associations – formal or informal – such as neighborhood associations.

Why is social capital important in market economies? Market transactions rely on many different social norms, including a basic degree of trust between buyers and sellers. In most market transactions, both parties generally assume that what they accept from another party really belongs to them in the first place, and that there is generally no intent by the other party to commit fraud in the transactions. A growing body of evidence shows that social capital, and the social cohesion it brings, helps societies develop and prosper. Conversely, the lack of social capital makes it much harder, if not impossible, for a nation to sustain economic growth and development.

Social capital is especially important in less developed nations, because in these nations there tend to be fewer effective formal institutions in place (such as contract enforcement through an effective police and legal system). For example, consider a rural farm cooperative in Botswana where farmers agree to exchange a limited supply of tools. Because the farmers can get more work done using less physical capital, productivity increases. (See C. Siriani and L. Friedland, (n.d.). "Social capital." Retrieved March 3, 2003 from http://www.cpn.org/sections/tolls/models/social_capital.html.) Similar efficiencies can be provided by employment associations that facilitate job searches by making information about jobs and job seekers available to a larger group of prospective employers and employees, or by credit associations that encourage economic growth by providing financial capital to small-scale entrepreneurs.

Perhaps the most important aspect of social capital, however, is a broad degree of trust and acceptance of the political and economic system and institutions. In the economic arena, this trust implies that people accept the "rules of the game" for buying and selling products and factors of production (including labor) as clear and relatively predictable. In particular, consumers must believe that producers will regularly "deliver the goods" in all (or at least almost all) routine market transactions. Otherwise, the costs of market transactions become substantially higher – similar to the extensive credit and title searches people in countries like the United States usually experience only when purchasing very expensive items that will take years to pay for, such as real estate or automobiles.

Tax-compliance is another important example of social capital. In deciding whether to fully comply with tax laws, taxpayers consider at least three factors. First, there is their own internalized norm of honesty, often developed as part of a shared belief system in families, schools, and local communities. Second, there may be important social or religious sanctions for noncompliance (e.g., if a society shuns a tax cheat, rather than condoning tax evasion as something that "everyone does," like modern day Robin Hoods). Finally, there are legal penalties, including fines or prison terms, which a person must pay *if* they are caught and convicted.

In countries where the social capital factors supporting tax compliance are weak, and the only effective means of enforcement are legal penalties, the costs of collecting taxes are likely to be considerably higher and the levels of compliance are likely to be lower, leading to low levels of government revenues. This has proven to be a major problem in most of the transition economies over the past decade or two, making it far more difficult for these governments – which are sometimes viewed as corrupt in the first place, further compounding the problem – to provide public goods, including basic infrastructure such as roads and bridges, which are key to economic growth.

CONCEPTS

Social capital
Incentives

CONTENT STANDARDS

People respond predictably to positive and negative incentives.

Institutions evolve in market economies to help individuals and groups accomplish their goals. Banks, labor unions, corporations, legal systems, and not-for-profit organizations are examples of important institutions. A different kind of institution, clearly defined and well-enforced property rights, is essential to a market economy.

BENCHMARKS

Responses to incentives are predictable because people usually pursue their self-interest.

Changes in incentives cause people to change their behavior in predictable ways.

Incentives can be monetary or non-monetary.

Property rights, contract enforcement, standards for weights and measures, and liability rules affect incentives for people to produce and exchange goods and services.

OBJECTIVES

Students will:

♦ Define social capital and distinguish examples of social capital from examples of physical capital.

♦ Explain the importance of various aspects of social capital (e.g., social trust, well-defined and widely accepted rules) in maintaining economic and social stability.

♦ Investigate several consumer associations/networks and describe how those groups provide information and other services that help people make better purchasing decisions as consumers, or achieve other objectives.

TIME REQUIRED

Two to three class periods, with a short homework assignment (Activity 1) to be completed before the first class

LESSON TWELVE

MATERIALS

- Visual 1: Social capital defined
- Visual 2: The Degree of Trust Survey and Results of the Degree of Trust Survey
- Activity 1: The Degree of Trust Survey
- Activity 2, Part I: BLOOG Role Play and Rule Cards (one per student); Part II: 3 BLOOG Dollars per student (NOTE: each page provides enough dollars for 13 students)
- One half-deck of playing cards for every group of four students in Activity 2
- Internet access (preferably in a computer lab) for Activity 3
- Activity 3: Consumer Associations/ Networks (one copy per student)
- Assessment: Social vs. Physical Capital; Social Capital True/False (one copy per student)

PROCEDURES

1. The day before this lesson distribute Activity 1: The Degree of Trust Survey. Tell students to complete the survey and have at least one parent (or guardian) complete the survey. Explain that the information will be summarized in class and that this will be an important part of a lesson on the concept of social capital. You may wish to offer a small incentive to insure that the surveys are completed. For example, if at least 90 percent of class returns the surveys, you might reward those students with 10 minutes free time on Friday, while the other 10 percent sweep the floor.

2. On the day of the lesson, begin by arranging students in small groups (usually four students per group, but several groups of three are acceptable). Try to assign at least one vocal and outgoing student to each group. Tell students that they are going to play an exciting card game called BLOOG. Distribute one half-deck of cards and the role-play cards from Activity 2 to each group. Give an outgoing student in each group the "BLOOG Dealer" card. Also distribute three (3) BLOOG dollars

to each player, including the dealer. Make sure the BLOOG dealers all understand how the game will be played (see the BLOOG Role Cards in Activity 2), and tell them NOT to explain the rules on their cards to the other students. You may want to meet with the dealers for a few minutes privately to explain this, before starting the activity.

3. Have the BLOOG dealers follow the rules and play until all players have lost all BLOOG dollars to the dealers. Ask who won the most BLOOG dollars and why? (*The dealer always wins.*) Ask students if they are ready to play BLOOG for real dollars? Why not? (*Most students lost all their fake money and are likely to lose any real money as well; they don't trust the dealer; they don't know the rules.*) What would it take to get them to play for real money? (*Learning the rules, getting a different dealer, getting different rules or a different game that gives everyone a fair chance of winning, etc.*)

4. Explain that the key topic in class today will be what economists refer to as **social capital.** Explain that one important aspect of social capital is knowing, understanding, and generally accepting the "rules of the game" in our society and our market economy. Why might having rules and knowing what they are be important? Ask students to describe how they felt playing BLOOG. (*frustrated, upset, cheated*) Ask students if knowing the rules for BLOOG would have made a difference. (*They might well have chosen not to play.*) Ask students to imagine what driving on roads and highways would be like if there were no rules? (*chaos, more fatalities, perhaps fewer people would drive out of fear of being killed*).

5. Ask students to list the three most important driving rules on the board. Ask students to describe how these rules help provide a safer and more efficient driving experience. Ask students to explain how these rules help drivers of cars, buses, and trucks arrive at their destinations. Explain that market

economies also have rules, and that well-defined and widely accepted rules for buyers and sellers in markets are one example of what economists refer to as **social capital**. Display Visual 1 and discuss the different types and examples of social capital.

6. Ask students to list three school rules on the board. Ask, "How do these rules help the school run more smoothly and provide a better atmosphere for learning and getting along together at school?" Explain that market economies also have rules, and that well-defined and widely accepted rules for buyers and sellers in markets are one example of what economists refer to as **social capital**. Display Visual 1 and discuss the different types and examples of social capital.

7. Explain that one important aspect of social capital is often referred to as *social trust*. Economists believe social trust is important because, among other things, a high degree of social trust in market transactions, usually based on earlier experiences in other markets, makes it easier to start markets for new goods and services, and to expand markets for existing products. In this setting, high levels of trust indicate that buyers and sellers have developed high levels of expected reciprocity, or in other words a social norm or convention is established in markets, so that people expect "If I do this for you, you'll do this for me..." as a matter of course. Competitive markets are highly efficient ways to organize the production, distribution, and exchange of most goods and services, so anything that makes it easier to establish and expand markets – such as social capital – promotes higher levels of economic efficiency and cooperation.

8. Ask students to recall a decision they made based on trust. (For example, a student may have agreed to trade a shift at the fast-food restaurant with a co-worker, provided the other employee agrees to a similar trade at some later date.) How would these decisions have been different if the other people involved could not be trusted?

9. Have students turn in their Degree of Trust questionnaires. Compile results for both students and parents or guardians on the board. Summarize these results on Visual 2, and ask the following questions: "What conclusions can you draw from these results?" "What can you say about general level of 'social trust' in our class?" "Was there a difference between parents and students?" "Which group was more trusting?" *(Answers will vary.)* To stress the broader, social implications of these results, ask the following two questions: "What are potential problems for a person, community, or nation, when there is a low degree of social trust?" (*The lack of trust will require more use of formal institutions to regulate social and economic activity; that implies higher transactions costs for a wide range of activities, and less willingness to rely on others or to count on cooperation from strangers, and perhaps even from friends and some family members.*) "In a market economy such as the United States, what are potential benefits of having a high degree of social trust?" (*less reliance on formal institutions such as legislation and the court system to regulate social and economic activities; lower transactions costs for daily exchanges and interactions with others; higher levels of cooperation*)

10. Social networks or associations are also important aspects of social capital. A network or association is defined as a group of individuals organized to facilitate a goal or objective. For example, booster clubs and Parent Teacher Organizations (PTOs) are networks of parents concerned about their children's education. These networks share information, muster resources, and accomplish tasks that could not be accomplished by individuals acting alone. People with serious diseases or other problems, or family members of those who have such diseases and problems, often join or simply participate in networks of

people facing similar problems (for example, the American Heart Association or the Juvenile Diabetes Foundation).

11. Ask students to think of several social networks or associations they belong to. (NOTE: Be very careful to focus on 'legitimate' associations. That is, focus the discussion away from school cliques or gangs and onto groups such as the chess club, science clubs, booster clubs, Parent Student Teacher Organizations, etc.) List some of these on the board. What is the purpose of some of these networks or associations? How does the presence of these associations or networks improve the educational experience for students? How do these associations contribute to social cohesion in the school? (*Building 'school spirit' can help a school establish or maintain its identity; students may be less likely to damage school property; cohesion may contribute to stronger community support for the school, etc.*)

12. Some networks or associations provide access to information that consumers can use to make decisions in the marketplace. For example, Underwriters Laboratories Inc. (UL) is an independent, not-for-profit product testing and certification organization that has tested products (especially electrical devices) for safety for more than a century. The UL stamp-of-approval provides important information for consumers.

13. The next portion of the lesson requires Internet access, preferably in a computer lab. In small groups, have students use the Internet resources listed in Activity 3 to complete the data retrieval chart provided. Once completed, begin a discussion of how these consumer associations/networks provide access to social capital by asking students what benefits these associations/networks provide. (*access to safety information and product quality information that reduces the risk associated with purchasing and consuming a particular product; provide additional incentives to firms to improve*

product quality) Ask students to think about what would happen if consumers did not have access to this type of information network. (*Imperfect information about reliability and safety of products might lead to poor consumption decisions; firms might be slower to improve quality.*)

14. Before closing the lesson, distinguish social capital from physical capital. Explain that physical capital is the stock of equipment, tools, inventories, and structures used to produce finished goods and services. Examples include factories, machines, vehicles, and computers owned by businesses (including sole proprietorships). Physical capital is obviously easier to see and to count than social capital, but both are important. And while physical capital depreciates with use, some economists believe that social capital appreciates with use. In other words, the more people in a nation make use of its stock of social capital, the more valuable it becomes.

CLOSURE

Review the definition of social capital as the trust, norms, and networks and associations in a society that help people achieve economic, political, and social objectives more easily and efficiently. Having a high level of social capital can contribute to economic efficiency, stability, and growth. When social capital is low, countries must devote more resources to providing formal institutions to address these concerns. Poorer nations often lack these formal institutions, which makes developing higher levels of social capital especially important in these countries, to support and sustain the growth of markets

ASSESSMENT

Have students complete the following quiz. Answers are provided on the page following the quiz.

Social vs. Physical Capital

For the following examples, indicate whether each of the listed items is an example of social capital (S), physical capital (P), or if you are uncertain circle (U).

S	P	U	1. A youth baseball team sponsored by a local business.
S	P	U	2. A factory where automobiles are produced.
S	P	U	3. A neighborhood crime watch.
S	P	U	4. A telemarketing firm's calling list
S	P	U	5. A church-sponsored program to provide assistance to the unemployed.

Social Capital True/False (circle T or F)

T	F	1. Unlike physical capital, social capital almost always depreciates over time.
T	F	2. Well-defined and enforced rules or laws can be social capital.
T	F	3. A high degree of social capital helps developing nations grow and prosper.
T	F	4. A high degree of social capital is usually associated with greater stability in a society or an economy.
T	F	5. A low degree of social trust can lead to lower transactions costs when people buy and sell in the marketplace.
T	F	6. Social capital can be developed through active participation in church or school programs.

Answers:

S	P	U	1. A youth baseball team sponsored by a local business. *(S – this is an example of a network or association.)*
S	P	U	2. A factory where automobiles are produced. *(P – this is a classic example of physical capital.)*
S	P	U	3. A neighborhood crime watch. *(S – this is an example of an information-sharing network or association.)*
S	P	U	4. A telemarketing firm's calling list. *(P or U – while this may seem like an information network, in fact the list is developed as part of someone's job and is used to maximize the firm's profits. The list may be considered physical capital; it is not social capital.)*
S	P	U	5. A church-sponsored program to provide assistance to the unemployed. *(S – this is an example of an informal information-sharing network or association.)*

Social Capital True/False

T	F	1. Unlike physical capital, social capital often depreciates over time. *(F – physical capital depreciates over time; social capital may appreciate.)*
T	F	2. Well-defined and enforced rules or laws can be social capital. *(T – rules or laws can contribute to market stability.)*
T	F	3. A high degree of social capital helps developing nations grow and prosper. *(T – that's the main reason it is considered a different kind of capital.)*
T	F	4. A high degree of social capital is usually associated with greater stability in a society or an economy. *(T – especially where social trust is concerned.)*
T	F	5. A low degree of social trust can lead to lower transactions costs when people buy and sell in the marketplace. *(F – low social trust implies that more formal enforcement mechanisms and information-seeking are required, increasing transactions costs.)*
T	F	6. Social capital can be developed through active participation in church or school programs. *(T – through church membership and volunteer programs at schools people can "tap into" informal networks and associations.)*

Visual 1
Social Capital Defined

Social Capital

Arrangements and personal beliefs and norms in social, political, and economic life that allow people in a nation to interact and work together to achieve common objectives, which benefit everyone, or at least a wide range of people and organizations.

Types of Social Capital

Networks of civic engagement:
   o Neighborhood associations (e.g., "block watches")
   o Service organizations (e.g., The Rotary Club)
 	
Social networks
   o Sports clubs/organizations (e.g., YMCA, soccer leagues)
   o Religious organizations
 	
Informal institutions
   o Information sharing-networks (e.g., newsletters issued by clubs and volunteer groups)
   o Food banks

 From *Focus: Institutions and Markets*, © National Council on Economic Education, New York, NY

Visual 2
The Degree of Trust Survey

STUDENT

1. Generally speaking….		
Most people can be trusted.	You can't be too careful with people.	It depends.

2. I am _____ to buy a used CD from a friend.		
Very likely	Somewhat likely	Unlikely

3. I am _____ to buy a used CD from a friend of a friend.		
Very likely	Somewhat likcly	Unlikely

4. I am _____ to buy a used CD from a stranger.		
Vcry likely	Somewhat likely	Unlikely

5. I would be willing to lend a friend (but not a closc friend) $10.00 if he or she promised to pay me back in two weeks.		
I would be very willing.	I would be hesitant.	I would never agree to this.

PARENT

1. Generally speaking….		
Most people can be trusted.	You can't be too careful with people.	It depends.

2. I am _____ to buy a used CD from a friend.		
Very likely	Somewhat likely	Unlikely

3. I am _____ to buy a used CD from a friend of a friend.		
Very likely	Somewhat likely	Unlikely

4. I am _____ to buy a used CD from a stranger.		
Very likely	Somewhat likely	Unlikely

5. I would be willing to loan a friend (but not a close friend) $50.00 if he or she promised to pay me back in two weeks.		
I would be very willing.	I would be hesitant.	I would never agree to this.

Visual 2 (continued)
Results of the 'Degree of Trust Survey'

Item	Percentage responding:		
1. Generally speaking...	*Most people can be trusted.*	*You can't be too careful with people.*	*It depends.*
Students			
Parents			
2. I am _____ to buy a used CD from a friend.	*Very likely*	*Somewhat likely*	*Unlikely*
Students			
Parents			
3. I am _____ to buy a used CD from a friend of a friend.	*Very likely*	*Somewhat likely*	*Unlikely*
Students			
Parents			
4. I am _____ to buy a used CD from a stranger.	*Very likely*	*Somewhat likely*	*Unlikely*
Students			
Parents			
5. I would be willing to lend a friend (but not a close friend) $10.00/$50.00 if he or she promised to pay me back in two weeks.	*I would be very willing.*	*I would be hesitant.*	*I would never agree to this.*
Students			
Parents			

From *Focus: Institutions and Markets,* © National Council on Economic Education, New York, NY

Activity 1
The Degree of Trust Survey

One aspect of social capital is the degree of trust for individuals in society. Complete the short "student" questionnaire below by circling your response to each question, or by putting an X in one of the three boxes for each item. Have a parent or guardian complete the "parent" questionnaire.

STUDENT

1. Generally speaking….		
Most people can be trusted.	You can't be too careful with people.	It depends.

2. I am _____ to buy a used CD from a friend.		
Very likely	Somewhat likely	Unlikely

3. I am _____ to buy a used CD from a friend of a friend.		
Very likely	Somewhat likely	Unlikely

4. I am _____ to buy a used CD from a stranger.		
Very likely	Somewhat likely	Unlikely

5. I would be willing to lend a friend (but not a close friend) $10.00 if he or she promised to pay me back in two weeks.		
I would be very willing.	I would be hesitant.	I would never agree to this.

PARENT

1. Generally speaking….		
Most people can be trusted.	You can't be too careful with people.	It depends.

2. I am _____ to buy a used CD from a friend.		
Very likely	Somewhat likely	Unlikely

3. I am _____ to buy a used CD from a friend of a friend.		
Very likely	Somewhat likely	Unlikely

4. I am _____ to buy a used CD from a stranger.		
Very likely	Somewhat likely	Unlikely

5. I would be willing to loan a friend (but not a close friend) $50.00 if he or she promised to pay me back in two weeks.		
I would be very willing.	I would be hesitant.	I would never agree to this.

Activity 2, Part I
BLOOG Role Play and Rule Cards

BLOOG Dealer

Shuffle the cards. Tell each player to place one BLOOG dollar on the desk in front of them. Tell all players that if they beat your hand, you will pay them one BLOOG dollar, but if they lose, you win the BLOOG dollar. Deal three cards to each player, including yourself. Have the other players place their cards face up in front of them. Quickly add up your total (K, Q, J=10; A=1). If your total is less than 15, declare a "BLOOG" and collect all other players' money. If your total is more than 15 declare a "GLOOB" and collect all other players' money. Play until all players are out of BLOOG Dollars.

Player

You are going to play BLOOG, a fun and exciting card game. The goal is to win as many BLOOG dollars as you can. Start by placing one BLOOG dollar on the desk in front of you. The dealer will give you three cards. Look at them and then turn them over and show them to the dealer. The dealer's ruling is always final. Please do not argue with the dealer or you will be fined one BLOOG dollar. Continue play until told to stop.

Player

You are going to play BLOOG, a fun and exciting card game. The goal is to win as many BLOOG dollars as you can. Start by placing one BLOOG dollar on the desk in front of you. The dealer will give you three cards. Look at them and then turn them over and show them to the dealer. The dealer's ruling is always final. Please do not argue with the dealer or you will be fined one BLOOG dollar. Continue play until told to stop.

Player

You are going to play BLOOG, a fun and exciting card game. The goal is to win as many BLOOG dollars as you can. Start by placing one BLOOG dollar on the desk in front of you. The dealer will give you three cards. Look at them and then turn them over and show them to the dealer. The dealer's ruling is always final. Please do not argue with the dealer or you will be fined one BLOOG dollar. Continue play until told to stop.

Activity 2, Part II
BLOOG Dollars

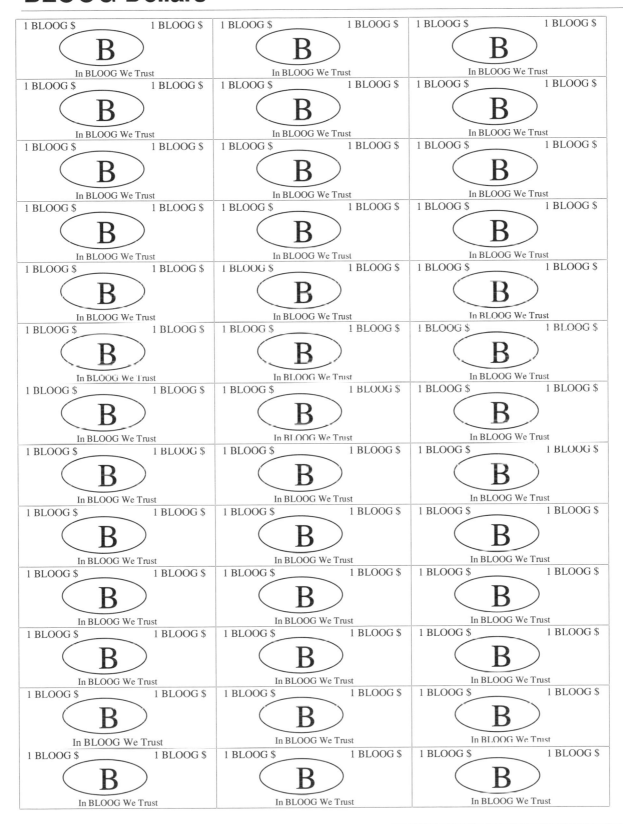

Activity 3
Consumer Associations/Networks

Economists define social capital as arrangements and personal beliefs and norms in social, political, and economic life that allow people in a nation to interact and work together to achieve common objectives, which benefit everyone, or at least a wide range of people and organizations. One increasingly common type of arrangement is an information network, which uses a variety of methods and technologies to provide information that helps consumers make more informed decisions in the marketplace. These information networks or associations can be very informal, such as neighbors sharing, by word-of-mouth, a particularly good experience with a car dealer. Or they can have a much more formal membership structure, such as the publication *Consumer Reports*. The table below lists six consumer information networks or associations. Using the URLs provided, briefly research each of these and provide a summary of the mission (or goal) of each. After completing the data chart, answer the questions in Part II.

Association/Network	URL	Mission
PIRG	http://www.pirg.org/	
Juvenile Diabetes Research Foundation	http://www.jdrf.org/	
Habitat for Humanity	http://www.habitat.org	
Better Business Bureau	http://www.bbb.org/	
Underwriters Laboratory	http://www.ul.com/consumers/	
Insurance Institute for Highway Safety	http://www.hwysafety.org/	

Activity 3
Part II – Discussion Questions on Internet Search

1. What do these networks/associations have in common?
2. How are these examples of social capital?
3. How does the information these networks/associations provide help consumers make better decisions?
4. If consumer networks/associations such as these did not exist, what might the consequences? How would consumers gather the same information these networks/associations provide?

Answers

Association/Network	URL	Mission
PIRG	http://www.pirg.org/	"The state Public Interest Research Groups are an alliance of state-based, citizen-funded organizations that advocate for the public interest. We uncover threats to public health and well-being and fight to end them, using the time-tested tools of investigative research, media exposés, grassroots organizing, advocacy and litigation. The state PIRGs' mission is to deliver persistent, result-oriented activism that protects the environment, encourages a fair marketplace for consumers and fosters responsive, democratic government." (PIRG Homepage)
Juvenile Diabetes Research Foundation	http://www.jdrf.org/	"JDRF was founded in 1970 by the parents of children with juvenile diabetes. Volunteers help define research priorities, select research grant recipients, lead advocacy efforts, and provide guidance to overall operations. JDRF is the world's leading nonprofit, nongovernmental funder of diabetes research. JDRF is the only major diabetes organization focused exclusively on research." (JDRF Homepage)
Habitat for Humanity	http://www.habitat.org	"Habitat for Humanity International seeks to eliminate poverty and homelessness from the world, and to make decent shelter a matter of conscience and action. Habitat invites people of all backgrounds, races and religions to build houses together in partnership with families in need. Habitat has built more than 125,000 houses around the world, providing more than 625,000 people in more than 3,000 communities with safe, decent, affordable shelter. HFHI was founded in 1976 by Millard Fuller along with his wife Linda." (Habitat International Homepage)
Better Business Bureau	http://www.bbb.org/	"Since the founding of the first BBB in 1912, the BBB system has proven that the majority of marketplace problems can be solved fairly through the use of voluntary self-regulation and consumer education. The BBB's Core Services include: Business Reliability Reports; Dispute Resolution; Truth-in-Advertising; and Consumer and Business Education." (Better Business Bureau Homepage)
Underwriters Laboratory	http://www.ul.com/consumers/	"Underwriters Laboratories Inc. (UL) is an independent, not-for-profit product-safety testing and certification organization. We have tested products for public safety for more than a century. Since our founding in 1894, we have held the undisputed reputation as a leader in product-safety testing and certification within the United States." (Underwriters Laboratory Homepage)
Insurance Institute for Highway Safety	http://www.hwysafety.org/	"For over 30 years the Insurance Institute for Highway Safety has been a leader in finding out what works and doesn't work to prevent motor vehicle crashes in the first place and reduce injuries in the crashes that still occur." (Insurance Institute Homepage)